P9-CBI-660

Bowling

FOR

DUMMIES®

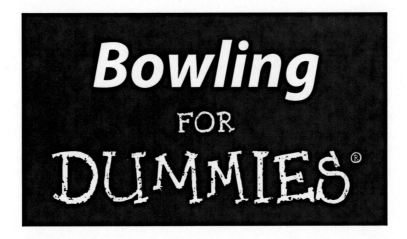

by A.J. Forrest and Lisa Iannucci

Wiley Publishing, Inc.

Bowling For Dummies®

Published by
Wiley Publishing, Inc.
111 River St.
Hoboken, NJ 07030-5774
www.wiley.com

WILEY

About the Authors

Over his 15-year amateur bowling career, **A.J. Forrest** has racked up a host of accomplishments, including a total of twelve 300 games, eight 800 series, multiple 299 and 298 games, and 20 games where he bowled 11 strikes in a row. In 1996, he was a member of the Region 15 College Team, and in 1997, he was on the National Junior College Athletic Association All-American Bowling Team. He qualified for and participated in the Empire State Games, New York's Olympic-style amateur athletic program, and has been a coach for the Empire State Games bowling team since 2006. In 2006, A.J. was the Dutchess County/Putnam County All-Events Bowling Champion, the Dutchess/Putnam Singles Bowling Champion, and the Dutchess/Putnam Doubles Champion. In 2008, the Hudson Valley chapter of the United States Bowling Congress presented A.J. with its Award of Distinction, and in 2010, he was a recipient of the Shaker Award, given by the Greater Southern Dutchess Chamber of Commerce.

A.J. has coached college bowling for four years, leading the Dutchess Community College bowling team to its first regional championship in 2007. He was named the Region 15 Coach of the Year and is a level one and level two certified bronze medal coach. Previously, A.J. owned his own pro bowling shop in Dover Plains, New York. Currently, he is general manager of all five HoeBowl Family Fun Centers in upstate New York (hoebowlfamilyfun. blogspot.com). You can reach A.J. at hoebowlfamilyfun@yahoo.com.

Lisa Iannucci is an award-winning veteran of magazine and book publishing who has been in the business for more than 20 years. She has written articles for *USA WEEKEND, SHAPE, Parenting, Frequent Flyer,* the Travel section of the *Los Angeles Times, The COOPERATOR,* BobVila.com, and many more publications and Web sites. She writes on many topics, including health, travel, celebrities, and real estate. Lisa is also the founder of a celebrity-do-gooders blog (celebrity-do-gooders.blogspot.com) and the author of young adult biographies of Ellen DeGeneres and Will Smith. She has been bowling since she was a kid and now has two children in the USBC Youth League program, where they have won multiple awards in league and tournament play as well as a scholarship. You can reach Lisa at lisawriter@msn.com.

Dedication

From A.J.: I dedicate this book to my boys — 2-year-old Tyler and 6-year-old Baylee. They're young and yet already bowlers. Helping them has been so much fun and has shown me how much fun it would be to help others, so they're my inspiration for writing this book. I'd also like to dedicate this book to my mom, Barbara Forrest. She has always been a positive influence and inspiration.

From Lisa: When I wrote my first book, my kids — Nicole, Travis, and Samantha Brinkley — were 6, 4, and 2. Today, 11 years and many books later, they're slowly making their way out into the world, yet they still inspire me every day. Thanks to my mom, Patricia Quaglieri, who not only modeled for this book but is also my hero. The family that bowls together stays together, and we're a bowling family.

Authors' Acknowledgments

This book wouldn't be what it is without these people who helped us along the way: our acquisitions editor, Mike Lewis; our fantabulous, amazing project editor, Vicki Adang; our Dummifier, Sharon Perkins; our amazing copy editor, Jen Tebbe; and our technical editor, Joan Taylor.

Special thanks to our agent, Marilyn Allen, who was behind this project since the beginning, and our models, Chrissy Gallagher, Travis Brinkley, Heidi Hoffman Kane, Patricia Stein, Patricia Quaglieri, Venus Worthy, and Walter Sankar II. Thanks to Diane Hoe, owner of HoeBowl Centers in New York's Hudson Valley, for the use of her center for our photo shoot and to photographer Mark Engelman. Thanks also to the entire staff at Holiday Bowl in Wappingers Falls, especially Eric Brought and Marshall Smith; to Gene Pedicone, owner of GT's Behind The Line bowling pro shop; to the USBC's and the PBA's press departments; and to physicians Dr. Jeannette Anderson and Dr. Dolly Garnecki.

Lisa thanks A.J. for all of his hard work and sacrifice during the writing of this book. A.J. would also like to thank Lisa for asking him to write a fun book on a fun topic.

Publisher's Acknowledgments

We're proud of this book; please send us your comments at http://dummies.custhelp.com. For other comments, please contact our Customer Care Department within the U.S. at 877-762-2974, outside the U.S. at 317-572-3993, or fax 317-572-4002.

Some of the people who helped bring this book to market include the following:

Acquisitions, Editorial, and Media Development

Project Editor: Victoria M. Adang

Acquisitions Editor: Michael Lewis

Copy Editor: Jennifer Tebbe

Assistant Editor: Erin Calligan Mooney

Senior Editorial Assistant: David Lutton

Technical Editor: Joan Taylor

Editorial Manager: Michelle Hacker

Editorial Assistants: Rachelle S. Amick, Jennette ElNaggar

Art Coordinator: Alicia B. South

Cover Photo: © iStock / James Steidl

Cartoons: Rich Tennant (www.the5thwave.com)

Composition Services

Project Coordinator: Patrick Redmond

Layout and Graphics: Brooke C. Graczyk, Brent Savage, Erin Zeltner

Proofreaders: Betty Kish, Jessica Kramer

Indexer: Rebecca Salerno

Special Help

Sharon Perkins; photographs by Mark Engelman

Publishing and Editorial for Consumer Dummies

    Diane Graves Steele, Vice President and Publisher, Consumer Dummies

    Kristin Ferguson-Wagstaffe, Product Development Director, Consumer Dummies

    Ensley Eikenburg, Associate Publisher, Travel

    Kelly Regan, Editorial Director, Travel

Publishing for Technology Dummies

    Andy Cummings, Vice President and Publisher, Dummies Technology/General User

Composition Services

    Debbie Stailey, Director of Composition Services

Contents at a Glance

Table of Contents

⬩ ⬩

Part III: Time to Get Rolling: Making Your Shot.......... 121

Introduction

※ ※

Anyone can bowl — whether you're 2 or 102, a league bowler or someone who has never picked up a bowling ball before — and we want you to have just as much fun with bowling as we do. And at a time when many folks are looking for an affordable activity that's closer to home, bowling is an outing an entire family can enjoy for less than the cost of heading to the movies and springing for overpriced popcorn, soda, and candy.

If you've never bowled before, you'll wonder why you waited so long to have so much fun, and we guarantee you'll come back again. If you've been away from bowling for a while and need a refresher course, welcome back, we've missed you. And if you've been bowling for a few years and want to raise your game to the next level, then get ready to bowl better and achieve higher scores with the information we present in this book.

About This Book

Bowling isn't a complicated sport. All you need to know to start knocking down some pins are the basic rules of the game, a few tidbits about scoring, and some simple tips on how to throw the ball. Getting started bowling really is that easy, and this book is just as easy to understand. *Bowling For Dummies* takes you through every aspect of the game with simple terminology, as well as illustrations and photographs to help you understand more complex points.

Bowling For Dummies starts with an overview of bowling and then moves into the specifics, including how to move your body, how to throw a hook shot, and how to throw strikes and pick up spares. We go on to share how you can get kids excited about bowling and what you can do to keep yourself in tiptop condition (and what to do when an injury slows you down or age catches up with you).

The great thing about *Bowling For Dummies* is that it includes something for every skill level. If you're new to bowling, you find out about the proper shoes and equipment to start with. If you're more advanced, we give you tips for picking up difficult shots and fill you in on what you can do to improve your score. Regardless of your bowling expertise (or lack thereof), we're certain you'll discover something helpful in the following pages.

Conventions Used in This Book

We use the following conventions throughout the book to make things consistent:

- All Web addresses appear in `monofont`. (Note that we haven't inserted any extra punctuation if an address breaks across a page. Just type it in exactly as you see it.)

- New terms appear in *italics* and are closely followed by an easy-to-understand definition.

- **Boldface** is used to highlight the action parts of numbered steps and keywords in bulleted lists.

You'll also find that we refer consistently to bowling centers rather than bowling alleys. Years ago, bowling alleys were called alleys because they were just for bowling and bore a resemblance to a back alley. Bowlers smoked, ate, drank, and bowled; they didn't have any other activities available to them. Today's bowling facilities are now smoke free, and many have even been expanded to include additional fun activities such as rock climbing, paintball, and arcades, as well as fancy restaurants. Some state-of-the-art centers even resemble night clubs with catering services and big-screen televisions. So now that bowling alleys offer more than just bowling, people refer to them as bowling centers.

Additionally, in some of the photos throughout this book, it may look like the bowlers are standing at the foul line as they're preparing to make their shot. Rest assured, they're not; they're standing in the right place to begin their approach. The photos were taken at a bowling center that has two different shades of flooring, which makes it look like the pictured bowler is already at the foul line.

As a final note on the convention front, we recognize that every bowler is different, so we kept that in mind when writing this book. Even though it may seem that what we tell a right-handed bowler to do is pretty much just the reverse of what we tell a lefty, we often provide the instructions for both right-handed and left-handed folks.

What You're Not to Read

Whenever you come across sidebars (the information in gray-shaded boxes), trust that the material in them is interesting but not essential to your understanding of bowling basics. Feel free to skip over sidebars for now (or forever!).

Foolish Assumptions

We know the old saying that you shouldn't assume anything about anyone because you make an . . . well, we'll assume you know that saying. However, we did have to make some assumptions about you while we were writing. Here's what we came up with:

✔ You've either never been inside a bowling center and bowled a game or you've bowled years ago and are just now thinking about returning to the sport.

✔ You want to take your bowling skills to the next level, improve your average score, and pick up perplexing spares.

✔ You've seen advanced bowlers throw amazing hook shots, and you want to know how to throw one just like 'em.

✔ You understand that practice is the only way to get better in any sport, so you're ready to practice on your own, with friends, or both.

How This Book Is Organized

Bowling For Dummies is divided into six parts that group together important information so you can easily find what you're looking for. Following is a short rundown of what the different parts cover.

Part I: The Opening Frame

Here's where you discover what bowling is all about, from why it's so popular and how it's played to how it's scored and what equipment you need to get started. Not only do we walk you through an actual bowling center so you know what to expect when you arrive but we also give you some insight into the many health and social benefits bowling offers and fill you in on how to buy your own bowling ball, bag, shoes, and other equipment. By the time you're done with this part, you'll be ready to bowl.

Part II: Body Basics: Throwing Yourself into the Game

The secret to bowling well lies in your form, which is why this part gives you step-by-step instructions on holding the ball, starting your approach to the lane, and throwing the ball. We show you where to aim and explain how to get your ball to go to the sweet spot that makes a strike a sure thing. Whether you're a lefty, a righty, a hook bowler, or a straight bowler, we cover it all right here. We also help you troubleshoot any problems you may be having, such as too much of a hook, too little of a hook, and not hitting your target.

Part III: Time to Get Rolling: Making Your Shot

Bowlers love high scores, and strikes are what make those high scores possible. This part shows you how to knock 'em all down and helps you understand how the angle of your throw affects the number of pins you knock down. And because most people can't bowl a strike every single frame, we also show you how to pick up spares (which is when you knock down all the pins with your second throw) and splits (which are what you have when the pins left standing after your first throw have a varying amount of distance between them). This part is a great guide to refer to over and over again during your game so you can ace every throw, especially if you want to score strikes, pick up spares, and convert splits.

Part IV: Staying on Your Game

Lots of factors can affect your game, from the oil on the lanes to your own mental state. In this part, we show you how each lane is different, explain how the oil that's used to condition the lanes affects how your ball travels toward the pins, and give you tips on adapting to potential game-changing factors. This is also the part where we get into your head and show you how to keep a positive attitude and stay injury free, both of which will improve your game. And if you think you need some extra help to better your game, this part even tells you all you need to know about finding and working with a bowling coach. We also review cautions for those bowlers who are pregnant or have other special considerations that may cause them to adjust how they normally bowl.

Part V: Joining Others at the Center

Bowling is a social sport, and this part helps you find others to play with. First, we reveal everything you need to know to take the kids bowling, including the type of equipment they need and how to sign them up for a youth league. Of course, adults deserve a little playtime too, so this part also addresses adult bowling leagues, including league rules and costs as well as how the scoring differs from traditional scoring. It also covers bowling tournaments and how to sign up for one.

Part VI: The Part of Tens

This part is short and sweet but filled with a great deal of helpful information. It contains three chapters that are chock-full of ways to improve your score, throw a better hook, and make bowling even more fun. Refer to these chapters often for quick tips on improving your game or making bowling a bigger and better part of your life.

We also include a glossary containing some familiar and some not-so-familiar bowling terms. You can turn to these pages when you need a refresher about a word's meaning.

Icons Used in This Book

Even though all the information in this book is useful, we mark especially important text with an icon. Here's a key to what each icon represents.

If you take nothing else away from your read of *Bowling For Dummies* but the information marked by this icon, then you'll have a solid foundation for years of bowling fun.

Text marked with this icon includes suggestions for different things you can do to improve your game. You don't have to follow them, but if you do, you may wind up having an easier time with bowling.

When you see a paragraph marked with a Warning icon, pay attention because you're about to absorb something you need to know to avoid harming your game and stay safe (or keep others around you safe) while you're bowling.

Where to Go from Here

Excited about throwing a hook? Then jump to Chapter 9. Interested in signing up for a league but want the inside scoop before the first week? Jump ahead to Chapter 18. Where you decide to start reading is up to you. However, if you're not sure where to start, especially if you've never bowled before, we recommend that you start right at the beginning. That way you can progress with your bowling as you go through each chapter.

Part I
The Opening Frame

"Oh, quit looking so uncomfortable! It's a bowling party! You can't wear a cape and formal wear to a bowling center!"

In this part . . .

This part is your opportunity to take a closer look at the sport of bowling, including how and where it's played. We get you familiar with the rules and scoring and reveal that those little marks on the lane aren't just there for decoration — they're actually there to help you become a better bowler. We also run through the equipment you need to get started, from your very own bowling ball (should you want one) to bowling shoes (they're not all ugly, we promise).

Chapter 1

Welcome to the Wonderful World of Bowling

In This Chapter

▶ Reviewing the finer points of bowling

▶ Enjoying the social benefits of the sport

▶ Looking at bowling as a form of cardiovascular and strength-training exercise

*E*very year, millions of people go bowling and have a great time with their family and friends. Bowling is a sport that just about anyone can play, you can enjoy it year-round, it's easy to learn (not to mention affordable), and you can get started right away without having to buy any special equipment. All you have to do is walk into your local center, rent some shoes, borrow a ball, and you're ready to go.

Consider this chapter your introduction to the sport of bowling. In it we give you an overview of the various aspects of the game and highlight its mental and physical benefits.

Figuring Out How the Game Works

Several types of bowling exist, including duckpin, five pin, and candlepin. In this book, however, we focus on ten-pin bowling because that's the most popular version of the sport in the United States.

Ten-pin bowling involves knocking down bowling pins with a bowling ball. The pins are set up in a triangle at the end of a lane that's 60 feet long. Your task is to stand behind what's called the foul line (if you cross it, you don't get any points), throw the ball down the lane, and try to knock down all the pins. You earn points for each pin you knock down, plus bonus points if you throw well enough to knock down all the pins with one shot. At the end of the game, the person with the highest score wins.

In the following sections, we cover the basics of bowling so you can be ready to head to the lanes tonight.

Seeing what equipment you need

One of the best things about bowling is that you don't have to invest hundreds of dollars in equipment in order to start playing. In fact, you don't have to buy any equipment at all. The center has bowling shoes that you can rent and bowling balls that you can borrow (flip to Chapter 3 to read all about bowling shoes and house balls). All you have to do is pay for your shoe rental, the number of games that you bowl, and any snacks or drinks that you consume.

Exploring the different types of bowling

This book focuses on traditional ten-pin bowling, but if you travel around North America, you'll find bowlers who participate in other forms of bowling, such as the following:

✔ **Candlepin bowling:** Candlepin bowling is popular in the northeast portion of the United States and in parts of Canada. The major difference between candlepin and ten-pin bowling is the size of the pins and the bowling ball. Candlepins are much thinner and a bit taller than traditional bowling pins, and the ball is smaller and lacks finger holes. In fact, a candlepin ball weighs slightly less than a single pin, making candlepin bowling more difficult than other forms of bowling. You get three tries per frame as opposed to two, but after each throw, the fallen pins aren't cleared away from the lane, increasing the game's difficulty. Because of these differences, strikes are rare in candlepin bowling.

Another difference between candlepin and ten-pin bowling is the *lob line,* a heavy black line located 10 feet down the lane from the foul line. The ball must be in contact with the lane prior to reaching this line, or else the pins struck by that throw don't count toward your score.

✔ **Duckpin bowling:** You can think of duckpin bowling almost like a miniature version of ten-pin bowling. Duckpin bowling balls weigh only 2 to 4 pounds, and the pins are shorter and fatter than the pins used in ten-pin bowling. Another difference between duckpin and ten-pin bowling is that you get three chances per frame to knock down all ten pins. If you knock down all ten pins with your three shots, that's called "getting a ten."

✔ **Five-pin bowling:** Popular in Canada, five-pin bowling is actually the result of complaints. According to the Canadian 5 Pin Bowlers' Association, ten-pin bowling came to Canada in the 1880s, but customers complained about the size and weight of the bowling balls and thought that the game was too strenuous. A bowling center owner had his father reduce the size of five of the standard pins down to approximately three-quarters of their original size. The owner then took the five smaller pins, spaced them out equally on the 36-inch ten-pin triangle, and rolled a hand-sized hard rubber ball (approximately 5 inches in diameter and 3½ pounds in weight) down the ten-pin lane at the five pins, inventing the new game of five-pin bowling. In this version of bowling, you get three chances to knock down all five pins.

Street shoes and bare feet are a no-no on the lanes, so you must wear bowling shoes. These shoes are designed to protect the lanes and allow you to slide properly when you're releasing the ball. If you try to get away with wearing anything but bowling shoes while bowling, you may wind up damaging the lanes and injuring yourself or other bowlers.

Of course, just because you don't *have* to buy equipment to bowl doesn't mean you can't decide to buy your own bowling ball if you really like the sport. When you're ready to invest in your own equipment, head to Chapter 4; it contains everything you need to know about buying a bowling ball, shoes, and other accessories.

Bowling in a nutshell

Bowling is probably one of the easiest sports to learn how to play because you don't need to memorize a bunch of complicated rules (although if you want to know the basic rules of the game, you can refer to Chapter 2). You just need to become familiar with the main concepts of the sport. Here they are:

- ✔ A game of bowling consists of ten frames. In each frame, you get two chances to knock down all ten pins.
- ✔ You throw a specially weighted ball, which ranges in weight from 4 to 16 pounds, down the lane to try and knock down the pins.
- ✔ As you bowl, you move your arms, legs, hands, and wrist in certain ways to make the ball go where you want it to. (When you're ready to tackle the specifics of form and throw, take a look at the chapters in Part II.)
- ✔ If you knock down all the pins with your first throw, your turn ends and the other bowlers, if there are any, take their turn until that frame is over.
- ✔ If you don't knock down all the pins with your first throw, you get a second try. After you throw the ball a maximum of twice in one frame, your turn is complete.
- ✔ The tenth frame works like a bonus frame. If you knock down all ten pins on your first try, you get two bonus throws. If you knock down all ten pins with two throws, you get one bonus throw.

Looking at scoring

Scoring a game of bowling is pretty easy because each pin you knock down is worth 1 point. However, it becomes slightly more complex when you start throwing *strikes* (when you knock down all ten pins on your first throw) and *spares* (when you knock down all ten pins with two throws). Strikes are automatically worth 10 points, plus whatever you get on your next two throws. Spares count for 10 points plus the number of points you get on your next throw. (We show you how to throw strikes in Chapter 10 and spares in Chapter 11.)

Nowadays, most bowling centers have automated scoring machines, so you don't need to fuss with all the adding when you just want to bowl. Yet even with automatic scoring, it's good to know how to keep score in case the computer messes up. We delve into the details of scoring in Chapter 2.

Surveying the Main Benefits of Bowling

Bowling provides two main kinds of benefits: the mental ones and the physical ones. On the mental front, bowling is a great way to socialize with other bowlers and have fun with family and friends. On the physical side of things, bowling is an activity that gets you up off the couch and moving your body, which can lead to improved health in the long run. We delve deeper into the details of these benefits in the sections that follow.

Providing a social outlet

Sure, you can bowl alone, but bowling is even more fun when you do it with others. It can even be a way to meet new people if you've moved to a new area. Whether you're just bowling casually with friends or you have a competitive game going, bowling is a social sport. When you play it, you have the opportunity to share laughs, conversation, and good times with family, friends, co-workers . . . the list goes on and on.

Bowling centers offer many opportunities for you to expand your social circle, either as an individual or with a group of friends or family. Here are just a few of them:

✔ **Leagues:** Leagues are a great way to socialize and compete with other bowlers. You can find all kinds of leagues, including ones for beginners, advanced bowlers, and children, that fit into just about any schedule. You can even choose a league based on how long it lasts. For instance, if you're looking for a long-term commitment, sign up for a league that runs from September through April. Want a shorter-term commitment? Join a summer or short-season league that lasts anywhere from 12 to 16 weeks. Turn to Chapter 18 for more information about leagues and ask your local center for a list of its leagues to find one that's right for you.

✔ **Tournaments:** Tournaments offer another opportunity to engage in friendly bowling competition with others. Some tournaments raise funds for charities; others are just about competing for fun and prizes, including cash. Whatever the purpose, you can find a tournament that sounds fun to you by checking with your center. (For insight into how to sign up for a tournament, see Chapter 18.)

✔ **Charity bowling events:** You can meet other bowling do-gooders through charity bowling events, such as bowl-a-thons. Sign up to help out the charity and meet others while having fun for a good cause.

✔ **Other social groups:** Bowling centers host bowl-and-mingle events for singles and other groups all the time. Coauthor A.J.'s centers have worked with local online dating sites to host their speed-dating events. Ask the folks at your center what events are coming up.

Have an idea for a group that doesn't exist at your local center yet? Let the managers at the center know about it. They're always looking for great ideas to get bowlers in the door, and some of the best ideas come from bowlers like you.

If you want to bowl by yourself during *open bowling* (when the lanes are open to the public and aren't being used for tournaments and leagues) but you still want to enjoy some camaraderie, ask the staff person at the front desk whether he can put you on the lane next to a solo bowler or a group of people so you can strike up a conversation.

Improving your health

Contrary to what some people may believe, bowling is a good form of exercise because it moves your entire body. It's a great low-impact sport that combines fun with an activity that keeps your joints and muscles in action, making it great for people who've had minor joint surgery and other operations where mild activity is recommended during healing. (*Low-impact sports* cause minimal wear and tear to your weight-bearing joints, which include your feet, knees, and hips.)

When you bowl, your muscles and joints flex, turn, and swing. This movement helps keep your muscles and joints moving and flexible. As a result, it also helps your body burn calories. If you're the type of person who likes the couch more than the treadmill yet you're looking to get out and be a little more active, then bowling is a perfect activity for you.

Bowling also improves your hand-eye coordination, flexibility, and balance. When you bowl, you need to be able to hold the ball, focus on your target, swing the ball back, walk to the foul line, bend down, and release the ball. (We show you how to do all of this in one quick, graceful motion in Chapters 6 and 7.) These actions require you to maintain your coordination, stay limber, and keep from falling down. The more you practice bowling with the proper form, the more your coordination, flexibility, and balance will improve.

The next sections explain how bowling can be both a cardiovascular and strength-training activity.

Bowling as cardiovascular activity

From a heart-healthy standpoint, bowling isn't going to give you the same cardiac workout as, say, skiing or aerobics would because you typically don't build up a consistent cardiac-intense workout while bowling. The sport does, however, keep you moving, and any kind of movement and activity helps your heart.

Want to burn more calories or get your heart beating faster for a better cardio-vascular workout? Try to avoid bowling with four people or more on one lane. When you have too many people on a lane, you get too much rest in between frames, and your heart doesn't really have time to become active to the point where bowling can be considered a cardiovascular activity. Instead, bowl a few games on your own or with a partner, or bowl with no more than four bowlers spread out between two lanes. Because of the smaller number of par-ticipants, you'll get up and down to bowl more frequently, which will get your heart pumping more.

Bowling as strength training

Whether you're carrying a 6-pound ball or a 16-pound one, your arms and joints are still working to carry that extra weight every frame (and sometimes twice a frame) for several games. If you bowl fairly regularly, your upper body strength will increase, and your shoulders, arms, and legs will improve in muscle tone, strength, and power.

The first few times you bowl, you're bound to experience some muscle sore-ness. That's normal if you're using muscles you've never used before. Pain, however, is something else. If any part of your body starts to hurt when you're bowling, you may be using a ball that's too heavy or you may have thrown incorrectly at some point and injured yourself. Stop bowling immediately and check with your doctor.

If you're concerned about injuring yourself while bowling, turn to Chapter 14, where we show you some warm-up exercises and tell you what to do if you pull a muscle or suffer another injury while at the center. Have a bad back? You can still bowl. Just follow the advice we include in Chapter 16.

Bowling on the big and small screens

Even Hollywood gets in on the bowling action. Feature films such as the Coen brothers' *The Big Lebowski* use bowling in key scenes. Probably one of the silliest movies featuring a bowling storyline is *Kingpin*, directed by the Farrelly brothers and starring Woody Harrelson and Randy Quaid.

Over the years, the characters of many hit television sitcoms have gone bowling too. One of the most popular sitcom duos ever, Laverne and Shirley, not only bowled competitively on the show, but Laverne's father owned the local pizza and bowling hangout. Ralph Kramden and Ed Norton from *The Honeymooners* is another pair of famous sitcom bowlers. Speaking of sitcoms, the show *Ed* revolved around Ed Stevens, a big-time lawyer who moved to his hometown and bought a rundown bowling alley after getting fired from his job. Shows such as *Roseanne, Malcolm in the Middle, The Simpsons, According to Jim,* and *Glee* have featured bowling scenes too. And who can forget cartoon legend Fred Flintstone's twinkle toes bowling performance or his granite bowling ball as it literally splits in half going down the lane in order to hit all the pins? Classic!

Chapter 2

Getting Down to the Basics of the Game

---

*B*owling is fun even if you don't know what you're doing, but if you want to do well, you should go to the center armed with some basic knowledge of how the game works. That's what this chapter gives you. In the next several pages, we explain the basic rules of bowling and show you how to keep score. (Even though almost all centers have computerized scoring that does the work for you, it's good to understand the fundamentals.) We also introduce you to the lanes and the pins because knowing what the various markings mean can help you become a better bowler. Finally, we give you some advice on what to do when something goes wrong in your lane or with your ball.

Dem's da Rules: Bowling 101

A game of bowling consists of ten frames. Your mission in each frame, should you choose to accept it, is to roll your ball down the lane and knock over the ten pins sitting at the end of it.

In order for the points to count, the ball must hit the pins directly. The points don't count if the ball jumps out of the gutter or hits the side wall and comes back onto the lane. If either of these scenarios occurs, you have to change the scoring manually because the computer doesn't know that those points don't count. Ask the center's staff to help you change the scoring.

You have two throws in each frame to hit all the pins. After your first throw, any pins you knock down are automatically swept away by a bar known as the *sweep.* While the sweep removes the fallen pins, any pins left standing are automatically lifted up and out of the way by the pinsetter. They're then placed back onto the lane for your next shot. ***Note:*** Sometimes the pins don't reset correctly for your second throw of the frame. We tell you how to handle this and other mechanical difficulties later in this chapter.

After you've completed your two tries, your turn is over for that frame, and your score is recorded. The next time you bowl, all ten pins are set up again.

Each pin you knock down is worth 1 point. If you knock down all the pins after rolling the ball twice, that's called a *spare,* and it gives you one opportunity to score bonus points. Knocking down all ten pins on your first throw of the frame means you bowled a *strike* — the best you can do in that frame. When you strike, your turn in that frame is over, but because you did such a great job, you're rewarded with two chances to add bonus points to your score. (We fill you in on the details surrounding bonus points in the later "Keeping Score" section.) If, however, the ball goes into one of the *gutters* (the alleys on the side of the lane), that's *gutterball.* You don't get any points for gutterballs. Nothing. Zip. Zilch. So keep your ball out of the gutter.

You can bowl as an individual or form a team and compete against other teams. If you're bowling with others, you take turns in each frame until every player has completed the game. If you're playing on your own, you just move on to the next frame when you're done with your turn. The winner is the individual or team that scores the most points by the end of the tenth frame.

Keeping Score

Bowling scores are supposed to be high — as close to 300 as possible — which means you do a lot of math while you keep score over the course of a game. Most bowling centers have computerized scoring machines that calculate your score for you; at a few centers, however, you still have to keep score by hand using pencil and paper. We explain how to keep score during a game in the following sections.

Diving into the basics

Each pin counts as 1 point, so if you knock over three pins on your first throw, for example, you get 3 points. If you knock down four pins on your second throw, you add those points to the points from your first throw to get your score for that frame. In this case, your total so far is 7. This number gets recorded by the computer or on a paper score sheet.

Both paper and electronic score sheets have ten squares, which represent the ten frames of a game. The first nine large squares contain two smaller squares, and the tenth large square contains three smaller squares (we explain why in the next section). Figure 2-1 shows you what a handwritten score sheet looks like.

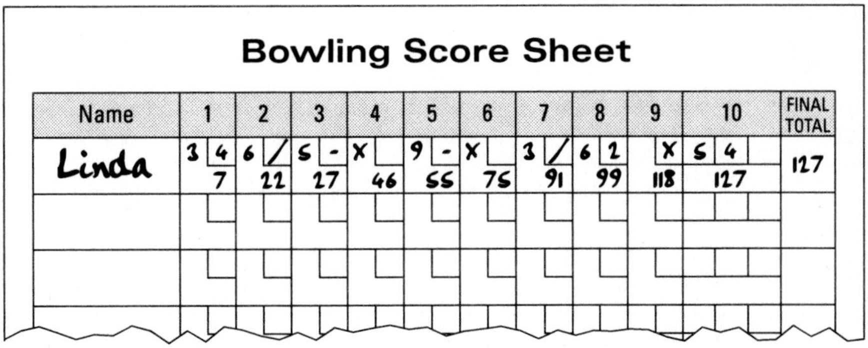

Bowling Score Sheet

Name	1	2	3	4	5	6	7	8	9	10	FINAL TOTAL
Linda	3 4 / 7	6 / 22	5 - 27	X 46	9 - 55	X 75	3 / 91	6 2 99	X 118	5 4 127	127

Figure 2-1: A handwritten bowling score sheet.

On a paper score sheet, note the number of pins you knocked down after each throw in the corresponding small squares. Then write the total score for each frame in the main part of the large square. So in the previous example, you'd write a 3 in the first small square and a 4 in the second small square. Then you'd write 7 in the main part of the large square.

If you don't knock down all the pins after your second throw and the pins that are left are separated from each other, you have what's called a *split*. (If the spare includes the *headpin*, which is the 1 pin, you shouldn't call it a split, no matter what else is left.) Whenever you wind up with a split, circle the first number in the frame on your score sheet so you can keep track of how many splits you get (for more on splits see Chapter 12).

If, to your dismay, you throw a gutterball or manage not to knock down any pins, mark the small box with a – or a 0, as shown in the third and fifth frames in Figure 2-1.

Scoring strikes and spares

Throwing strikes and spares is exciting because you earn extra points, but those points require you to keep score a little differently than you do when you don't manage to knock down all ten pins in one frame.

A strike is scored with an X in the first small box of the frame on the score sheet (see the fourth and sixth frames in Figure 2-1). You leave the second small box and the main part of the box for that frame blank until after your next two throws. Then you add whatever points you got in those two throws to the 10 points you earned for the strike.

Bowling strikes in the tenth frame is a little more interesting. For the first nine frames, your turn is over after you strike. However, if you strike on the first throw of the tenth frame, you throw the ball two more times for a total of three throws in one frame. This is the only frame where this happens.

As you improve your game, you're bound to start bowling more than one strike in a row. Two strikes in a row is called a *double,* and three strikes in a row is called a *triple* (or a *turkey*). Four and five strikes in a row are called a *four-* and *five-bagger,* and six strikes in a row is referred to as a *six-pack.* When you get on one of these strike streaks, be aware that the computer score sheet won't show your score until after your streak comes to an end.

A spare is marked with a / in the second small box of that frame, and it's worth 10 points plus what you bowl on your next throw. So if you scored a 6 on your first throw and knocked down the remaining four pins on your second throw, you'd write a 6 in the first small square of that frame and a / in the second small square (see Figure 2-2).

Figure 2-2:
This box shows the score for the first ball and the mark for the spare on the second ball.

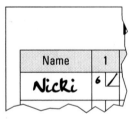

Name	1
Nicki	6 /

When scoring spares, don't record your total score for that frame until you know what you score on the first throw of the next frame. Add that number to the 10 points you earned for the spare.

Just like strikes, scoring a spare in the tenth frame is a little different than the other frames. If you bowl a 6 on the first throw and a spare on the second, you throw one more time for that frame, and the points from that throw get added to the 10 points from your spare. If you don't get a spare in the tenth frame, your game is over.

Fowl bowling

Why are three strikes in a row known collectively as a turkey? Supposedly years ago, when bowling scores were lower and strikes were rare, the owner of the bowling alley would give out a turkey to a bowler who achieved three consecutive strikes. We don't know whether that actually happened, but that doesn't change the fact that bowling a turkey makes the game exciting!

Walking through a frame-by-frame scoring example

Short of us dropping by your center to explain it to you, the easiest way to understand scoring is to follow a game frame by frame. That's why we're sharing a sample score sheet in Figure 2-3 and explaining what Travis scored in each frame and why each square is marked the way it is.

Bowling Score Sheet

Name	1	2	3	4	5	6	7	8	9	10	FINAL TOTAL
Travis	6 -	5 2	X	5 4	3 /	8 1	X	X	3 2	8 -	119
	6	13	32	41	59	68	91	106	111	119	

Figure 2-3: Travis's score sheet for a complete game.

✔ **Frame 1:** Travis knocks down six pins initially, but he gets the dreaded gutterball on his second throw. He marks his gutterball with a – to indicate zero; other bowlers mark an actual zero in similar scenarios. Travis's total score in the first frame is 6. **Running score: 6**

✔ **Frame 2:** Travis knocks over five pins on the first throw and two pins on the second throw for a total of 7 in the second frame. Those seven pins in the second frame are added to the six pins from the first frame for a total of 13 in the second frame. **Running score: 13**

✔ **Frame 3:** Travis nails a strike on his first throw. It's worth 10 points plus whatever Travis scores on the next two throws, so he has to wait and see what he bowls on the next two throws before he can add up this frame.

You add the next two *throws,* not the next two frames, to the 10 points you get for a strike.

✔ **Frame 4:** Travis bowls a 5 on his first throw and a 4 on the second for a total of 9 points. He adds those 9 points to the strike from Frame 3 to get 19. Then he adds 19 to the 13 from the second frame, which makes his score for the third frame 32. Now he can tally up the score for his fourth frame: 32 + 9 = 41. **Running score: 41**

✔ **Frame 5:** Travis knocks down three pins on his first throw and picks up a spare on his second. A spare is worth 10 points for that frame plus whatever Travis scores on the first throw of the next frame, so he must wait until he completes the first throw of the sixth frame before he can tally up his score for the fifth frame.

✔ **Frame 6:** Travis knocks down eight pins on his first throw. These eight pins plus the ten pins from the fifth frame equal 18 points. Travis adds those 18 points to his fourth frame total of 41 to find that his score for the fifth frame is now a 59. On the second ball of the sixth frame, Travis knocks down only one pin. He adds these 9 points to the previous frame for a current sixth frame total of 68. **Running score: 68**

✔ **Frames 7 and 8:** Travis strikes in both of these frames, but he has to be patient and see what he bowls in the ninth frame before he can score the seventh and eighth frames.

✔ **Frame 9:** Travis knocks down three pins on his first ball, so now he can add up the seventh frame. The seventh frame strike plus the score from the next two balls is 10 + 10 + 3 = 23. Travis adds those 23 points to the 68 points in the sixth frame for a total of 91 in the seventh frame. On the second ball of the ninth frame, he knocks down two pins, so now he can score the eighth frame: 10 + 3 + 2 = 15; 91 + 15 = 106 for the eighth frame. Add his five pins in the ninth frame and Travis's total is now 106 + 5 = 111. **Running score: 111**

✔ **Frame 10:** Travis scores an 8 on the first throw and then throws a gutterball on his second throw. Because he didn't pick up the spare, he doesn't get a third shot. Consequently, his final score is 111 + 8 = 119. **Final score: 119**

Letting the computer score for you

Almost all bowling centers use an automatic scoring system now, allowing you to focus on your bowling and let the computer worry about the math.

To use the computerized scoring system at your center (which should look something like the one in Figure 2-4), simply follow the directions on the screen to type in the names of the bowlers. The computer takes over from there. In fact, it even tells you whose turn it is to bowl. So keep an eye on the screen for when your name comes up on your lane and ask the staff for help if you get stuck.

Figure 2-4:
A computer does the work of scoring for you at most centers.

© istockphoto.com/Loretta Hostettler

Computers make mistakes. Keep an eye on the scoreboard after you bowl and make sure that your strike is marked as a strike, a spare as a spare, and so on. If the electronic score is wrong, you can either ask the manager to fix it by pressing a call button on your scoring monitor or by going to the front desk. You can also ask how you can make the change yourself in case the computer messes up again.

Calculating your bowling average

Want to know whether you're improving as a bowler? Keep track of your average. To calculate your bowling average, simply add up the total number of points you scored in each of your past games and then divide that total by the number of games you bowled. Say you bowled a 90, a 110, and an 84 over the course of three games for a total of 284 points. Divide 284 by the three games you played to find your average score, which is 94 (we cover averages in greater detail in Chapter 18).

Looking at the Lanes

Bowling is all about just giving the ball a roll down the lane, but you'll do much better if you take some time to understand what those funny-looking markings are and how they can help you become the best bowler you can be. The next sections fill you in on the structure of a bowling lane and demystify what those strange lane markings mean.

Walking through the parts of a lane

Although a lane looks pretty straightforward, it actually has several components. Check them out in Figure 2-5 and refer to the following list for details:

✔ **The approach:** This is the area between the seats and the foul line. (It's also the name of the combined motion of your arm swing and footsteps, as we explain in Chapter 6.)

✔ **The lane markings:** The dots beneath your feet when you're on the approach and the arrows on the lane are called *lane markings*. The dots guide you to your starting point, and the arrows act like a target.

✔ **The lane:** This is where the ball gets rolled down to the pins. A single lane is 60 feet long, and most were once made out of about 40 one-inch-wide wooden boards. Today, most centers, especially the newer ones, have lanes made from synthetic materials that last longer, are easier to maintain, and are less expensive to install than wood. The shiny stuff on a lane is oil, and it's used to protect the lane and help your ball roll smoothly.

Ask your center's manager whether her lanes are wood or synthetic. Knowing whether you're bowling on a wood or synthetic lane is important because your ball will react differently to each type of lane and the oil that has been applied to it. (We offer more details on how lane oil affects your game in Chapter 13.)

✔ **The gutters:** These are the alleys on either side of the lane. Whatever you do, steer clear of the gutters. If your ball lands in either one, you don't get any points for that throw.

✔ **The bumpers:** Sometimes you may see a padded edge, called a *bumper,* on both gutters. The ball is meant to bounce off of the bumpers and roll toward the pins. Little kids (and some bowlers with special needs) are the only people who need bumpers to help them hit the pins and enjoy the game. In fact, bumpers aren't even allowed in league bowling unless the league is a child's bumper league.

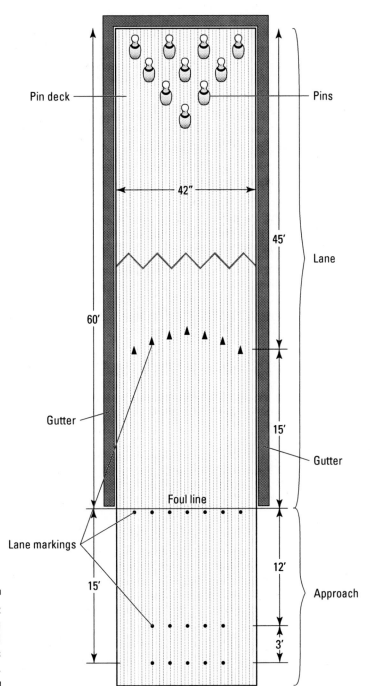

Pin deck

Pins

42"

45'

Lane

60'

15'

Gutter

Gutter

Foul line

Lane markings

15'

12'

Approach

3'

Figure 2-5:
A bowling
lane and
its various
parts.

✓ **The foul line:** This is the line that separates the approach from the lane. Step over it, and you may hear a loud buzz. In *open bowling* (when the lanes are open for anyone to come in and bowl), that buzz serves a cautionary purpose to keep you from stepping further onto the lane and falling due to the oil. In league or tournament play, that buzz means you just got a zero for that throw.

✓ **The sweep:** The bar that pushes the fallen pins away from the lane is known as the *sweep*. It also prevents you from throwing your second ball too early. After the sweep rises again, you can continue bowling.

✓ **The pins:** Each lane has ten bowling pins that are set up in a triangular pattern. We delve into the particulars of pins later in this chapter.

✓ **The pin deck:** This is the area where the pins are located. Pins are swept away by the sweep, and an automatic pinsetter picks up and places the remaining ones back onto the lane. The pinsetter also puts down a brand-new set of ten pins for each frame.

✓ **The ball return:** Your ball automatically comes back to you via the ball return so you can bowl again. Most ball returns have a fan to dry sweaty hands as well as a pin reset button on each side. Press this button if the sweep doesn't come down to do its job.

Deciphering lane markings

The two sets of markings on the lane — dots and arrows —help guide your throw so you can better aim at the pins, which are sitting a long, long ways away.

✓ **The dots:** Think of the dots on the approach as markers that help you figure out where to stand. Which dot you choose to stand on to start bowling depends on whether you're a lefty or a righty (we help you figure out your starting position in Chapter 6). After you find your starting mark, you know which dot to move to when you need to pick up a spare or when the lane conditions change.

✓ **The arrows:** The seven arrows on the lane are like targets that point the way your ball should go. Each arrow has a corresponding number. If you're a right-handed bowler, you count them by fives starting from the right: 5, 10, 15, and 20 (an arrow is placed on every fifth board). If you're a left-handed bowler, count them the same way but start from the left.

Pondering Pin Particulars

The pins standing in triangle formation at the end of the lane can be tough to topple. In the sections that follow, we give you an up-close look at the structure of a bowling pin and how the pins are arranged on the pin deck.

Curves ahead: Examining a pin's shape

Bowling pins (like the one shown in Figure 2-6) are made of hard maple wood inside and plastic outside. They stand 15 inches tall and weigh between 3 pounds 6 ounces and 3 pounds 10 ounces. They're almost always white with a red stripe (or stripes) around the neck.

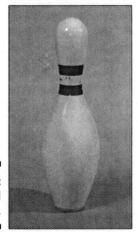

Figure 2-6:
A standard
bowling pin.

Triangles, splits, and pockets: Figuring out pin configuration

When you begin a frame, ten pins are set up in a triangle at the end of the lane, with each pin 12 inches apart from its neighbors. This distance provides enough room so the pins can act like dominoes — one tips or rolls into the other after it's hit. The first row has one pin, called the headpin; the second row has two pins; the third row has three pins; and the fourth row has four pins. Each pin has its own number (see Figure 2-7) starting from the headpin, which is 1. The numbers increase from left to right in each row.

As you become more familiar with the pins, you'll begin to recognize your splits and spares. Soon you'll be saying, "Oh, that's the 7-10 split," or, "I left the 4-7," to your bowling buddies.

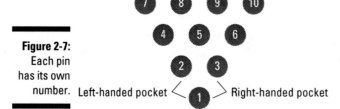

Figure 2-7:
Each pin has its own number.

To bowl successfully, you need to know how to hit the *pocket* — the space between the headpin and one of the pins in the second row. For right-handed bowlers, the pocket is between the headpin and the 3 pin. For left-handed bowlers, the pocket is between the headpin and the 2 pin. Hitting your respective pocket creates the most pin action and increases your chances for strikes. (Flip to Chapter 10 for more on pin pockets.)

Some centers replace one of the traditional white pins with a pin of another color during special promotions. When that pin becomes your headpin and you get a strike (or sometimes a spare), the bowling center awards a prize. Make sure the management sees you make the shot, or else you may be out of luck.

Coping with Mechanical Difficulties

Mechanical difficulties occur every now and then. That's just the nature of the beast. Following are just a few of the things that can happen and what you should do about them so you can get back to your game:

- **Your ball won't come back through the ball return.** The ball return is designed to automatically send your ball back to you after a throw, but sometimes the bowling balls get stuck rolling around in the back of the pin deck and can't enter the ball return. If a minute or two has passed and your ball hasn't reappeared, tell a staff member about the problem.

✔ **The ball is stuck in the gutter.** Try as you might to prevent this from happening, sometimes the ball lands in the gutter. If you can stretch and reach the ball without stepping onto the lane or into the gutter, then it's safe to try and retrieve it. However, if you'd have to step into the gutter or onto the lane to get your ball, ask the center's management to help you get it back.

✔ **The pinsetter sets the wrong number of pins or the pins fall down.** Perhaps this scenario has already happened to you: You're ready to bowl, but either all the pins aren't there or they've fallen after being placed on the lane by the pinsetter. Press the rerack button on your scoring console. A *rerack* removes the pins and resets them without interfering with your score.

Rerack and *reset* are two different things. A *rerack* provides a completely new set of ten pins; a *reset* is when you force the sweep to come down and do its job. Be careful not to hit your reset button when you need a rerack (or vice versa). If you hit the reset button, the computer takes this to mean that you've completed your throw. If you haven't thrown, the computer will miscalculate your score as a zero. Always take a moment to make sure you're pressing the correct button.

Bowling lanes take a beating, so if your lane isn't cooperating, ask to be moved. The center's managers are there to help you, keep you safe, and make sure you're having fun, so if other lanes are available, the management should be happy to accommodate your request to move.

Chapter 3

Heading to the Center

. . . .

In This Chapter

▶ Stepping into a bowling center for the first time

▶ Revealing everything you need to know about renting shoes

▶ Selecting a house ball that's the right weight and fit

▶ Keeping bowling etiquette and safety in mind at all times

*W*elcome to the bowling center! Unlike baseball or soccer, you can't practice your bowling hobby in an open field (well, maybe you could, but it wouldn't work too well). So unless you're lucky enough to have a couple lanes in your basement, a bowling center is the place to go when you want to throw a game.

In this chapter, we tell you how to dress for the sport, find a comfortable pair of bowling shoes, and, of course, select the perfect house ball. After you're dressed and ready to go, we explain bowling etiquette and safety. Why? Because knowing how to share a lane with other bowlers, take turns, and bowl safely is important so you don't hurt yourself or the people around you. Trust us: Bowling is much more fun when everyone follows the rules.

Going to the Center for the First Time

Before you hop into your car and head straight for the nearest bowling center, you may want to know what to expect when you step inside. Will it be crowded? Will it be loud? How much will you have to spend? What should you wear? The following sections help you find a place to go bowling, offer advice on when to hit (or avoid) the lanes, give some suggestions on bowling attire, tell you what to expect in terms of cost, and help get you oriented to your surroundings when at the center.

Finding a center near you

Maybe you know where every bowling center is in your town. Or perhaps you're aware of where one is but are curious whether any others are located nearby. Finding the bowling center or two nearest you out of the 7,000 alleys and centers in the United States isn't difficult; in fact, it's quite easy!

To find detailed information about bowling alleys and centers in your area (and possibly links to Web sites with pictures), visit www.gobowling.com. Plug in your zip code at the top of the page, adjust your search radius, hit the Search button, and get ready to receive the listings nearest you.

Don't be surprised if a bowling center's Web site lists activities other than bowling. Traditional bowling alleys — the kind that include just the lanes, a snack bar or vending machines, and possibly a bar — still exist. However, today's more modern and expansive bowling recreation centers include a variety of other activities such as laser tag, minigolf, sports bars, and upscale restaurants.

Choosing when to go

Every bowling center is different. They can be big or small, open only on weekends or until the wee hours of the night. Some open early for senior bowling; others don't open until the late afternoon when kids are out of school. To find out when a particular bowling center is open, call and ask, check out its Web site, or stop by and grab some flyers so you can become familiar with the times.

How busy or slow your bowling center of choice is depends on what activities it has going on. Following are some events that typically occur at bowling centers and can influence your decision of when to go:

✔ **League bowling:** *League bowling* is organized competitive bowling. Members of bowling leagues use a set number of lanes at the same time each week for a certain number of weeks. Some leagues use all the lanes in a center, meaning you can't bowl during league hours. Other leagues don't use all the lanes, so some are available for open bowlers. (*Open bowling* is when the lanes are open to anyone who wants to come in and bowl.) Whether or not you can bowl during league time depends on how big the league is, how many lanes the center has, and the center's policies, so ask your center about its league schedule and open-bowling policies. (And head to Chapter 18 for the full scoop on league bowling.)

If you're at the bowling center at the same time as a league, ask to be given a lane away from the league bowlers. Most centers do this automatically so the open bowlers aren't a distraction to the league bowlers, but it doesn't hurt to ask.

Glow-bowl: Some centers offer special types of bowling, such as glow-bowl, on the weekends (which, by the way, is apparently when all the teens and tweens decide to go bowling). For glow-bowl, the center lowers the lights; turns on the disco ball, neon lights, or other blinking lights; and turns up the music. Your white clothes, sneakers, and even the white parts on the bowling balls glow in the dark. Glow-bowl is a ton of fun, but it may not be for everyone. Call ahead to see whether the center you're interested in offers glow-bowl on the weekends.

Special events: Bowling centers are often reserved for special events such as birthday parties (mostly on the weekends), after-school bowling programs, and camp days (usually just during the summer). To get an idea of your center's special events schedule, head to its Web site or sign up to receive e-mail reminders of upcoming events.

Dressing for the center

Bowling doesn't have an official dress code (aside from the shoes, which we explain in detail later in this chapter); it's a casual sport. We do have a few suggestions, though:

- **Dress comfortably.** Bowling requires a lot of bending over, so try not to wear anything too short, too revealing, or too tight.

- **Prepare for temperature changes.** If it's summer, be sure to bring a sweater or sweatshirt because most centers are air-conditioned and can get chilly. The reverse is true for the winter; wear layers so you can take off your outer layer if you get too warm.

- **Wear or bring a pair of socks.** You don't need to wear socks to the center, but do bring a pair with you because you're renting bowling shoes that have been used by bowlers before you. Even though the shoes are disinfected with antibacterial spray, wearing socks helps protect your feet from any harmful bacteria or fungi.

   If you forget your socks, never fear. Many centers have vending machines or a section in the pro shop filled with bowling supplies you may have forgotten, including socks, gloves, powder, and towels. Vending machine socks cost just a few dollars; if you don't have change, ask for some at the front desk.

- **Leave your rings at home.** Wearing rings on the fingers that you put in the ball may cause your fingers to fit in the holes poorly. It may even hurt your fingers when you bowl.

- **Wear shoes that are easy to take off and put on.** You must wear regulation bowling shoes in order to bowl, so wear shoes to the center that you can slip off and on easily. This way, if you have to go outside or use the restroom, you can easily slip in and out of your street shoes. (Changing to your street shoes prevents water from getting on the soles of your bowling shoes. If water does somehow get on your shoes, whether they're rentals or your own, it can make you stick when you're bowling.)

If you don't want to deal with taking your shoes on and off, buy shoe covers at the pro shop, from the center's vending machine, or online. Shoe covers generally cost less than $10. They slip on easily and cover your shoe, saving you time from all that shoe switching.

Counting (and cutting) the costs

Bowling is an affordable activity for most budgets. The costs include your rental shoes, the games that you bowl, and any snacks or drinks you want. The average cost of shoe rental is around $3, and the average cost of a single game is about $3 to $4.

However, you should know that bowling costs vary depending on where you live. For example, upscale centers in Los Angeles and New York City charge $6 for shoe rental, $8 per game during the week, and up to $11 per game on a weekend. In contrast, a center in a smaller town may charge only 50 cents for shoe rental and $2 per game.

To free up part of your budget for some bowling fun, look for bowling specials on flyers at the center, on its Web site, or in local newspapers. These specials may include bowl-one-get-one-free coupons, hourly specials that allow everyone to bowl for one or two hours at a much more affordable rate than the cost of bowling per game, and special rates to get bowlers to come in at the quieter times. Centers may also provide other incentives, such as free soda or free shoe rental.

If you're bowling at a franchised bowling center such as a Brunswick or AMF center, search the Internet for coupons. Both Brunswick (www.brunswick. com) and AMF (www.amf.com) offer bowling coupons, birthday specials, and more if you sign up for their e-mail newsletters. Your local bowling center may offer something similar, so look into it.

Checking out what's where

We think it's helpful to have a general lay of the land and a sense of the ambience before you ever set foot in a bowling center. Usually when you enter a center, your first stop is the front desk. This is where you pick up your shoes and receive your lane assignment. If you're bowling with more than four people, you'll probably be assigned two lanes or more next to each other to ensure everyone has an ample amount of time to bowl.

Eating at the center

Eating at the bowling center is almost a tradition. You can order such fun finger foods as nachos, chicken fingers, fries, and pizza. Feeling like a full meal? Order up burgers, mozzarella sticks, grilled cheese sandwiches, and more. Or if you just want a snack, head to one of the many vending machines stocked with chips, candy, gum, juices, soda, and water. If none of that appeals to you, head to a bowling center that offers upscale food, like the one in Brooklyn, New York, that offers a mouthwatering chicken muffaletta, barbequed brisket, ribs, and chocolate chip bread pudding.

As you can see, you have plenty of options for bowling-center dining. The problem is, none of these options sound all that healthy, do they?

If you're watching your weight, it's best to steer clear of some (okay, most) of the foods offered at bowling centers. However, almost all centers *strongly* discourage you from bringing in outside food. So how are you supposed to eat healthy while bowling? Fill up a bit on the healthy stuff at home before you leave and then limit yourself to one snack and some water while you're bowling.

Here's an additional tip: If you decide to take a snack break while bowling and indulge in, say, some French fries, make sure you wash your hands after you eat and dry them well. Any residual grease from the food can cause you to drop your ball or throw it improperly.

Every center is designed differently, but most have lockers for storage, restrooms, snack stands and vending machines, and two sections of chairs near each lane. One set is in the bowling area, and the other is usually behind the bowling area. If you want to enjoy some food and drink while watching the action, you have to sit in this second area because no food is allowed in the actual bowling area.

Take a look around, and you may see other amenities, including a pro shop where you can find all of your bowling supplies, a bar area for the adults, and an arcade section with pinball games, pool, and toy vending machines for kids of all ages. Some centers even have a spare room that they use for community meetings or as a nursery.

So that's the scenery. What about the sounds and smells? Well, the first thing you may notice is the noise. Balls crashing into the pins, pins falling over, background music, and excited yelling combine to make a crowded bowling center a pretty stimulating place. You may also smell the food from the snack stand, but one thing you may not smell is cigarette smoke (many bowling centers are required by state law to be smoke free).

Renting Bowling Shoes

You must wear special shoes to bowl — it's bowling's only dress specification. If you don't own bowling shoes, you can rent them from the center. The average shoe rental fee is $3, but it can vary, as explained in the earlier "Counting (and cutting) the costs" section.

The following sections clue you in as to why bowlers wear special shoes, tell you how to get a good fit, and address concerns about wearing shoes other people have worn.

Discovering the benefits of bowling shoes

Rental bowling shoes may not be pretty (see for yourself in Figure 3-1), but they have many benefits for your game, including the following:

- **They're never worn outside.** Outside shoes and sneakers can track dirt and debris into the center, which can seriously damage the lanes.

- **They have soft leather soles that protect the lanes.** High heels, boots with spurs on the side, and children's soccer cleats can cause wear and tear on the lanes.

- **They allow you to slide, which is necessary when you complete your approach.** The soles of sneakers and other shoes are made of rubber and tend to stick to the lane, which can bring you to an abrupt halt. This sudden stop may hurt your back and your knees and cause you to fall or drop the ball on your toe. (For pointers on the proper bowling approach, head to Chapter 6.)

- **They protect your feet.** Bowling shoes aren't steel toed, but they're often thicker than your outside shoes. That's a darn good benefit if you accidentally drop a bowling ball on your foot.

Note: Don't be surprised if someone at the center asks you for collateral — a driver's license or one of your shoes, for example — to rent bowling shoes. The center is merely protecting its investment because the collateral guarantees you'll return the rental shoes when you're done and not drive off wearing them.

Making sure the shoe fits

Bowling shoes usually run the same size as regular shoes, so ask for your actual shoe size to start. For example, if you regularly wear a size 8, ask for a size 8 in bowling shoes. Don't worry if your feet are big or really tiny. Bowling centers carry all shoe sizes. Most centers offer shoes that start in infant or kid sizes and go up to a size-15 adult shoe.

Figure 3-1: A standard pair of rented bowling shoes.

Like regular shoes, all bowling shoes aren't created equal. They can stretch out with frequent use, so you may find yourself needing a smaller size than your usual one. If your toes are touching in the shoes, if the back of your foot is scraping, or if anything just feels wrong, return the shoes for a different pair or a different size. There's no extra charge for trying on more than one pair.

If your youngster is bowling but his feet are too small to fit into the center's smallest bowling shoes, don't worry. Most centers are willing to make exceptions for the wee ones and allow little Johnny to bowl in his street shoes, but be sure to check with management first. Whatever you do, don't just take your child's shoes off and let him bowl in his socks. Just like you, he can slip, fall, and get bruised.

Why not bowl in your socks?

Remember Tom Cruise's famous scene in the film *Risky Business*? The one where he slides across the floor in his underwear and socks? He seemed so cool and in control. Unfortunately, if you try to bowl in your socks, chances are you'll wind up sliding out of control and falling down — the absolute opposite of Cruise's smooth move.

Bowling lanes are much slipperier than your kitchen floor because they're shined and oiled (check out Chapter 13 for all the details on lane oil). Socks don't give you traction on a slippery lane, nor do they offer you any protection against dropped balls. Wear bowling shoes for your own safety — and to preserve your dignity!

Sharing shoes the safe and sanitary way

When you bowl, you're literally walking around in someone else's shoes. Bowling centers spray shoes with a disinfectant spray after each use, which kills germs and deodorizes, but if the idea of sharing shoes gives you the heebie-jeebies, consider purchasing your own pair. (We tell you how to go about buying bowling shoes in Chapter 4.)

Buying bowling shoes is a smart investment, especially if you want to become a regular bowler. You earn back the cost in no time because you don't have to rent shoes anymore. For example, say you pay $3 for shoe rental each time you go bowling, and you go once a week. When you invest in your own pair of bowling shoes at a cost of $30, the shoes have paid for themselves within ten weeks, and you're now saving money each time you go to the center. (You also have the added benefit of knowing you're the only person who's wearing those shoes.)

Choosing a House Ball

A *house ball* is a bowling ball found on the racks at the center. Each center provides a certain number of house balls that have already been drilled to fit a variety of hand and finger sizes. The house balls range in weight from 4 pounds to 16 pounds. It may take some time to find one that comes close to fitting you comfortably, but that's okay. Take as much time as you need to find the right ball because you'll bowl much better with a ball that fits. In the sections that follow, we help you find the house ball that's going to be the right fit for you all the way around, from the finger span and hole size to the size and weight.

If you pay to bowl by the hour, find your ball before you go to the counter to get your lane because some centers start the clock after you're assigned a lane and you don't want to waste that time (or money!) looking for a ball.

Get a grip: Seeking out the right finger span and hole size

You're not going to find a perfect-fit house ball because it's not drilled for your fingers, but you can make sure a particular ball has a close-enough finger span and hole size for you.

To check the hole size, insert your middle finger and ring finger into the two holes that are next to each other and your thumb into the other hole. Most house balls are drilled with a conventional grip, which means your fingers will ideally insert up to your second knuckle. If they do and it doesn't feel like the fit is too tight or too loose, the hole size is good enough for you. Figure 3-2 shows an example of a well-fitting house ball.

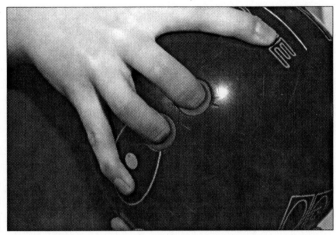

Figure 3-2:
This house
ball fits the
bowler.

If you're able to find a house ball with a great fit for you, try to remember something about it so you can track it down the next time you're at the center. Focus on the color, design, or a particular marking — basically zero in on anything memorable.

When you have a ball in hand with the right hole size, then you can examine the *finger span,* which is the space between your thumb and where your fingers grasp the ball. If this span is too far apart or too close together, you won't be able to grip the ball properly.

Here's a trick for finding the right finger span:

1. **Put your fingers into the holes in the ball.**

2. **Insert a pencil beneath your hand when you're gripping the ball.**

   Your hand should be just about touching the pencil (see Figure 3-3). If there's no space between your hand and the ball to insert the pencil, there's probably too much distance between your fingers and your thumb. If there's a lot of space and you can pick up the pencil and move it around, there's not enough span. In either case, that ball isn't right for you.

The pencil should just fit between your hand and the ball.

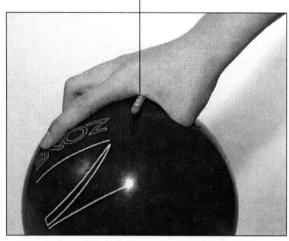

Figure 3-3:
Test your
finger span
by insert-
ing a pencil
between
your hand
and the ball.

Not too heavy, not too light: Finding a ball that feels just right

The "right" bowling ball is the one that feels right to you, plain and simple. Your fingers should fit in the ball comfortably, and you should feel like you can throw the ball frame after frame without tiring from the weight of it.

House bowling balls come in 1-pound increments ranging from 4 to 16 pounds. The weight of a house ball is engraved directly on the ball, and all ten-pin bowling balls are the same size, no matter what they weigh.

Traditionally, most beginning bowlers pick a very light (6- or 8-pound) ball because they think that a light ball thrown as hard as possible knocks down more pins. Beginners are also apprehensive about using a heavier ball because they think that the heavier ones are reserved for more advanced bowlers. In reality, getting strikes isn't about flinging the ball down the lane — it's about hitting the *pocket* (a point between two pins that, when hit at the right angle, speed, and power, knocks down all the pins, as we explain in Chapter 10). Flinging the ball down the lane doesn't guarantee that it's going into the pocket. A light ball can just as easily end up anywhere — including the gutter. Also, if you repeatedly throw a light ball very hard down the lane, you and your arms tire out more quickly, and your score ultimately suffers.

The formula for finding the perfect-weight bowling ball is to choose one that's 10 percent of your body weight. So, if you weigh 120 pounds, a 12-pound ball should be about right for you. However, if you find that weight to be too heavy — perhaps you had an arm injury or you're just not comfortable with the ball — try a 10-pound ball instead.

If you're trying to decide between two balls, bring both to your lane and try them both out to see which one feels more comfortable.

Do the best with what you can get: Accepting that your ball isn't perfect

The odds of finding a house ball that has the perfect hole size, finger span, and weight for you is about a million to one. That's because house balls aren't drilled to fit your hand specifically; they're drilled for various types of average-sized hands. Instead of seeking perfection, just look for a house ball that's good enough.

If you encounter any of the following when you pick up a house ball, put it back and try another one:

- **The finger holes are too big.** If the holes are too big, your hand may tire from squeezing the ball so it doesn't slip off of your hand. (Figure 3-4a shows finger holes that are too big.)

- **The finger holes are too small and tight.** You shouldn't have to jam your fingers into the holes to grip the ball. (See Figure 3-4b for an example of finger holes that are too small.)

- **The finger span is too far apart.** If you're stretching your fingers to reach the holes, then the span of the finger holes is too far apart for you.

- **The finger span is too close.** In this case, your hand will arch and you won't hold or throw the ball properly.

- **It's too heavy.** Lift the ball and swing it gently. If it pulls your arm into an uncomfortable position, consider a ball with a lighter weight.

- **It's too light.** The best ball is going to have a little weight on it. If the ball feels way too light, consider a heavier one (unless of course you have an injury or another reason for using a lighter ball).

Figure 3-4: Make sure the holes aren't too big (a) or too small (b).

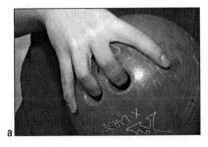

If you want that perfect fit, or if you can't find a house ball to fit your hand for the life of you, consider buying your own bowling ball. Doing so ensures that the ball fits you like a glove. For help purchasing your own ball, refer to Chapter 4.

Watch Yourself: Minding Bowling Manners and Safety

Mother always said to mind your manners when out in public; that goes for the bowling center too. Bowling is fun, but like any sport, it has its rules. Some are just common courtesy; others are designed for the safety of all bowlers and the people around them. The next sections fill you in on the basics of both.

Being a courteous bowler

The typical bowling center has enough distractions (music, chatter, the sound of pins falling down). You don't need to up the distraction level for yourself and those around you — and potentially damage the center or injure a fellow bowler — by being impolite. Here's how to be seen as a courteous bowler:

✔ **Give the "right of way," just like you would if you were driving.** When you're driving and you come to a stop sign, the driver to the right of you has the right of way. Bowlers practice this same concept. If the bowler to the right of you is ready to step up and take his shot, he has the right of way. *Note:* Respectful bowlers also grant the same courtesy to the bowlers to their left.

✔ **Wait your turn off the approach when a bowler to either side of you steps up.** Don't step onto the approach and prepare to bowl until after the other bowler has already taken his shot or is at the foul line watching his ball. Stepping up before the other bowler is done is distracting and can throw off his shot.

✔ **Be ready for your turn to bowl.** Because bowling is a social activity, you may be busy chatting with friends. That's perfectly fine (and encouraged!), but you still need to know when it's your time to bowl. Centers with automatic scoring display your name on the screen when it's your turn. Periodically glance up at the screen to watch for your name so you don't keep the next person waiting. (If you're at a center that doesn't have computerized scoring, just keep an eye on the score sheet.)

✔ **Always stay behind the foul line and in your own lane.** Don't walk over the foul line to try and get a better shot or to retrieve anything that has gone over it. (If something does cross the line, ask an employee to help you retrieve it because you can get hurt walking on an oiled lane.) Also, make sure you stay in your own lane. Never move over into the next person's lane to see your shot because you can be a distraction and cause that person to mess up his shot.

✔ **Bowl in a timely fashion.** Some bowlers stand on the approach for much longer than necessary. Complete your turn in a timely fashion and don't hold up the other bowlers.

✔ **Stay seated when it's not your turn.** Walking around the pit area when it's not your turn can be distracting to those who are bowling.

✔ **Say please and thank you.** If someone grants you courtesy and lets you bowl before he does, remember to say thank you and be sure to return the favor.

✔ **Ask before using someone else's bowling ball or other equipment.** If you want to try a person's ball, ask first, but remember that if it's his own custom-drilled ball, it's fitted specifically for his hand and not yours.

✔ **Watch your language.** Bowling is a family sport, and centers are often filled with children. Try to avoid bad language while at the center. If you don't and your language gets out of control, you could be asked to leave.

✔ **Be a good sport.** Nobody likes a poor sport, whether it's a bad loser or a cocky winner. Support your fellow bowlers. Give them compliments on their bowling or high-five them when they've made a good shot. Don't taunt or tease other bowlers.

✔ **Respect the equipment.** Bowling equipment costs money to buy and maintain, so don't damage the equipment unless you want to pay more to bowl in the future. Yes, this means you shouldn't sit on the ball return; it's not meant to hold your weight.

✔ **Make sure you return the bowling shoes and ball when you're done.** You'll probably need to return rented bowling shoes to get yours back, but even if you don't, it's easier for the center to clean and keep track of the shoes if they're returned. Besides, they're not a souvenir.

Keeping it safe

Bowlers get injured all the time simply because they aren't watching what they're doing or because they're goofing off. Follow these rules, and you'll be a safe bowler:

✔ **Use common sense.** Goofing around in the bowling center is just like goofing around anywhere else; someone usually gets hurt. Reckless behavior can get you kicked out of the center.

✔ **Walk, don't run — especially if you're holding a bowling ball.** If you trip while running with a ball, you can fall and injure yourself or someone else.

✔ **Wait until your ball emerges from the ball return before grabbing it.** You can easily get your hand stuck in the belt that returns the ball if you reach your hand into the ball return. Instead of risking a whole lot of pain, wait for the ball to completely pass the belt before you pick it up. And make sure your kids follow this practice too.

✔ **Avoid swinging the bowling ball in the common areas off the lane.** Just like a baseball player doesn't take practice swings near anyone, bowlers shouldn't swing their bowling balls when someone else is around.

✔ **Use the appropriate equipment.** Equipment that's too big or too small can cause you to fall and drop the ball or loft it onto another lane or approach and hit someone.

✔ **Watch your children.** Don't let young children roam on their own, kick or play with the equipment, purposely drop bowling balls, or run around the pit area. Not only can they get hurt, but the distraction to the other bowlers can also cause safety problems.

✔ **Make sure your area is clean and keep it clean.** You want a clean approach, so look down before you bowl. If you see black skid marks on the approach, someone may have bowled in street shoes before you. Ask the manager to wipe the marks up so you don't trip on them. Also, check for obstacles, such as candy wrappers, that could trip up you or other bowlers on the way to the foul line. When you're done bowling, be sure to throw away your trash.

Chapter 4

Buying Your Own Ball, Shoes, and Accessories

· ·

In This Chapter

▶ Scoping out the parts of a bowling ball

▶ Taking weight, grip, and more into account to select a custom ball

▶ Caring for, storing, and upgrading your ball

▶ Finding the best bowling shoes for you

▶ Checking out hand accessories (think gloves and gripping aids)

· ·

*T*o be really good at any activity, you need the right equipment. You're not required to buy a bowling ball or shoes in order to bowl (you can always use the center's, as explained in Chapter 3), but if you're serious about learning the game, having your own bowling ball and shoes really helps (not to mention it saves you money in the long run).

Having your own ball means no more searching through racks at the center feeling like Goldilocks and constantly saying, "This ball is too big," or, "This ball is too small," until you find one that's at least good enough for today. House bowling balls aren't one-size-fits-all. With your own custom-drilled ball, the Goldilocks in you will be happy because the fit will be "just right" each and every time you bowl. Plus, you'll have the joy of knowing you'll never again have to bowl with a house ball that may have dings and chips that prevent it from rolling properly.

The same goes for shoes. Owning your own bowling shoes means having a comfortable pair of shoes that fits your feet just the way you want. You can say good-bye to the days of renting bowling shoes that many other bowlers have worn.

In this chapter, you discover the ins and outs of buying your own bowling ball (and a bag to protect your investment). We also help you find bowling shoes you can call your own, and last but not least, we bring out the "stuff" — the extra equipment and products that make bowling easier.

What to Know Before You Buy a Ball

Although liking a particular ball's design is a great place to start, there's more to picking out a bowling ball than just choosing your favorite design and getting that ball wrapped up to go. In order to make an informed decision, you need to be aware of the different components of a bowling ball. The sections that follow touch on each part of a bowling ball so you can be in the know.

A bowling ball's makeup

Focusing on the look and feel of a bowling ball is all too easy to do, but if you take a minute to look past that and get acquainted with the innards of one, you can better understand what makes a bowling ball roll the way it does. Following is what you'd find if you were to crack open a ball (which, by the way, we don't recommend doing, even if you're really, really frustrated with your score). Figure 4-1 gives you the visual of all three parts.

- ✔ **Weight block:** The weight block is like the bowling ball's engine. When you turn your hand to create a hook shot (more on that in Chapter 9) and then release the ball, the weight block revs up and spins the ball down the lane, crashing it into the pins. The bigger the weight block, the faster the ball revs up as it goes down the lane. (Note that bowling balls weighing 8 pounds or less don't come with weight blocks.)

- ✔ **Core:** The core surrounds the weight block, filling up the remainder of the ball's interior and eliminating air pockets so that the ball is solid.

- ✔ **Coverstock:** This is the part of the ball that you see. Consequently, it's also the part that makes contact with the lane. Coverstock comes in three different materials: plastic, urethane, and reactive resin (we fill you in on all three in the next section). Each material causes a different amount of friction when it hits the lane. The more friction the coverstock material causes, the more of a hook you get.

Coverstock options

The surface, or *coverstock*, of a bowling ball is made from one of three materials: plastic, urethane, or reactive resin. Each one is geared to a different level of bowler.

- ✔ **Plastic:** A plastic coverstock is perfect for the beginner bowler or anyone who bowls using a straight form (described in Chapter 5). Plastic doesn't grip the lane oil well (see Chapter 13 for details on how oil affects the lanes and your bowling), and it doesn't cause a lot of friction.

Therefore, it hooks the least and ends up going right where you throw it. A plastic ball is also a perfect ball to bowl with on a dry lane. Most house balls are made of plastic.

✔ **Urethane:** A urethane coverstock kicks a ball up a notch in both quality and price. Urethane absorbs the lane oil and provides a medium level of friction (more than plastic but less than reactive resin). Urethane balls hook more than plastic balls and are a great choice for a beginning hook bowler. (Find out about the hook form of bowling in Chapter 5.) Occasionally you may find a urethane house ball, but don't count on it.

✔ **Reactive resin:** This is the most popular coverstock for advanced bowlers (which means you won't find a reactive resin house ball). Reactive resin digs into the oil on a lane, causing the ball to hook and react to the pins more (more pin action equals a higher score). The downside to reactive resin is that it isn't as durable as the other coverstock materials and can break down more easily, causing it to need replacement more frequently than other coverstocks. How often it needs to be replaced depends on how often you bowl.

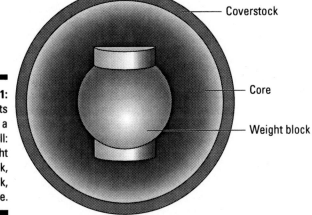

Figure 4-1:
The parts
of a
bowling ball:
the weight
block,
coverstock,
and core.

Coverstock

Core

Weight block

Choosing a Custom-Drilled Bowling Ball

From bowling balls that feature cartoon characters or sports team logos to those that sport wild designs, the choices available for custom-drilled bowling balls can be overwhelming — but they don't have to be. In the next sections, we fill you in on everything you need to know to make buying your own bowling ball a breeze. And after you find that perfect ball, you can have it drilled to fit your fingers. Pretty soon you'll be all set to bowl your heart out.

Buying a bowling ball shouldn't be a budget buster. You can find a ball that fits your skill level, weight requirement, and budget. As a beginner, you're better off starting with a lower-priced plastic or urethane bowling ball while you practice the basics of bowling and improve your game. Plastic bowling balls generally cost less than $80; urethane balls start around $120. Whatever you do, don't buy an expensive, top-of-the-line ball when you're first starting out. As your game improves, you can always move up to a higher-end ball.

Some pro shops buy back used bowling balls and resell them at a discount; ask whether yours does. (A *pro shop* is a store inside the center where you can purchase bowling balls, bags, and other supplies. Almost all centers have one.) A used ball will of course need to be redrilled for your hand, but buying one is a great way to save money. *Note:* Depending on the previous owner, the ball may have its share of dings, but the pro shop's staff can smooth these out for you.

Knowing where to shop

We recommend purchasing your first custom bowling ball from your local pro shop so you can build a relationship with the staff there. Getting to know the pro shop's staff enhances your chances of obtaining a ball that's the right fit for your needs. It also means the staff members can help you later on whenever you need the holes redrilled or the ball fixed, or when you have questions. Then if you want to purchase your next ball online, you'll know a little more about what you're looking for.

Note: Buying your bowling ball online may require additional drilling fees. Although you can supply the retailer with your finger measurements, there's only so much she can do without you there in person. That's why most online stores caution that their custom-drilled bowling balls may still need minor adjustments at your local pro shop for a small fee.

Before you buy a ball, the pro shop owner should see how you throw so she can recommend the best ball for you. To do this, the pro shop owner will usually stop by the front desk and ask to borrow a lane (at no cost to you) so she can see how you bowl.

Picking the perfect weight

Custom bowling balls range in weight from 6 to 16 pounds. Bowling with a ball that's either too light or too heavy isn't going to help you grow as a bowler. People have a tendency to throw a really light ball too hard and with less control. As for a heavier ball? Well, if it's too heavy, your arms may get tired, and you may drop it. Your best bet is to find a ball that's the right weight for you.

A bowling ball should weigh approximately 10 percent of your body weight. For example, if you weigh 120 pounds, you should bowl with a 12-pound ball. Use this 10-percent guideline as a starting point, but also consider

✔ **Your personal comfort level:** If the formula says you should use a 12-pound ball, but you're struggling to hold it and your arms are tiring, consider a lighter ball. On the flip side, a thin 130-pound man may have the arm strength to bowl with a 16-pound ball and not the 13-pound ball recommended by the formula. Go with the weight that feels right to you.

✔ **Any previous injuries or problems:** If you've had an injury to your bowling hand, shoulder, or elbow, or if you've had previous surgery, a lighter-weight ball can be easier to handle.

Before you commit to a weight for your custom ball, make sure you try out a few house balls of different weights so you can have a better idea of the weight you're most comfortable with.

Buying a ball that's made to hook or go straight

Wouldn't it be great if you had a ball that hooked when you wanted it to and went straight when you wanted it to? That dream can be a reality thanks to the weight blocks inside bowling balls (we cover weight blocks in greater detail in the earlier "A bowling ball's makeup" section).

The bigger the weight block, the more revolutions the ball can make, so if you're a hook bowler, buy a ball with a bigger weight block. We help you figure out your bowling form, whether that's hook or straight, in Chapter 5. The staff at your local pro shop can show you which bowling balls come with which weight blocks.

If you're a straight bowler, good news! The size of the weight block in a bowling ball isn't as important to you because straight bowlers can make nearly any type of bowling ball go straight. (Although it's worth noting that straight bowlers, especially beginners, tend to use a ball with a plastic coverstock and a small weight block.)

Getting a grip

A brand-new bowling ball doesn't come with the holes for your fingers already drilled. Those holes need to be drilled into the ball after you've purchased it, which means you need to know which grip you want to use before handing over your cash or credit card. Your *grip* is how you hold the ball, and it's determined by how far your fingers go into the holes as well as how far your hand stretches to reach those holes (this is known as your *span*). The ball will be drilled with the grip measured for your hand.

Bowling with a ball that you can't grip properly can cause sore, blistered fingers or even injuries.

You have two grips to choose from: conventional and fingertip. Which one you choose is based on your comfort level and skill level. (We give you even more details about grips in Chapter 7.)

✔ **Conventional grip:** Beginning bowlers typically start with a *conventional grip,* in which the thumb and the middle and ring fingers are inserted into the bowling ball up to the second knuckle (see Figure 4-2a). The conventional grip is actually the most common grip used in bowling.

✔ **Fingertip grip:** League bowlers and more experienced bowlers tend to use the *fingertip grip,* in which the middle and ring fingers are inserted up to the first knuckle only and the thumb is inserted all the way in (see Figure 4-2b). This grip provides you with the ability to rotate the ball; it also gives you a greater potential for throwing a hook.

Figure 4-2:
Conven-
tional grip
(a); fingertip
grip (b).

a   b

If you decide to switch from the conventional grip that you use on a house ball to a fingertip grip on your custom-drilled ball, the distance between your fingers and your thumb will actually increase a little. Give yourself time to adjust to the change.

Drilling the ball for a perfect fit

After you choose the weight and style of your ball, it's time to fit it to your hand. To do this, the pro shop measures your fingers, specifically their length and width, using a special device that determines the finger span as well as what size the holes should be. The shop's staffer then drills three holes, one for each finger that you put into the ball.

Depending on how busy the shop is, you can pick up your newly drilled ball the same day your fingers are measured or just a few days later. Regardless of when you pick up your ball, be sure to try it out and make sure it fits okay before walking out the door with it.

You spent your hard-earned money investing in the perfect bowling ball for you, so if the fit isn't exactly how you want it to be or if it hurts your fingers in any way, speak up. The pro shop can make adjustments to the finger hole sizes, including smoothing them out or making them bigger or smaller. When the ball feels right, you bowl better, plain and simple.

Adding a bag to store your stuff

The best way to protect your brand new custom bowling ball is with a special type of bag called (surprise, surprise) a bowling bag. Bowling bags, which can cost as little as $20, come in different colors and styles with single or multiple pockets to hold your ball, shoes, towels, rosin bag, good luck charms and other accessories. They can hold one or multiple bowling balls, and they come with or without wheels. (Check out the wheeled one shown in Figure 4-3.) Choosing a bag is a matter of personal preference and budget.

You can find new nylon bowling bags online or at your local pro shop. If you're not too picky about your bag or don't want to shell out cash for a new one, you can buy a used bowling bag at garage sales, flea markets, or online shopping sites such as eBay (ebay.com) or Craigslist (craigslist.com).

Figure 4-3:
A bowling
bag on
wheels.

Storm Productions, Inc.

Maintaining and Storing Your Bowling Ball

If you've spent hard-earned cash for a custom-drilled ball, you should keep your investment in tiptop condition. That means cleaning and storing your ball properly to protect it from outside dirt and grime, damage from oil buildup, and other things that could harm it.

But here's a dirty little secret: There's no one "right" way to care for your ball. Some bowlers whip out the cleansers and clean their bowling ball after each bowling session. Others don't clean them for months at a time (or at all). Although regular cleaning is recommended by the bowling ball manufacturers, there's no right or wrong answer as to how, or how often, you should clean your ball. All of that is up to you.

When you're not using your ball, store it someplace where it won't get damaged and where it isn't likely to cause harm to someone. (So forget about putting it on that upper shelf in the closet.)

We tell you what you need to know about cleaning and storage in the following sections.

Keeping your bowling ball cleaned and polished

The goal of cleaning your bowling ball is to get as much of the oil and grime off of it as possible. A ball that's clean of debris and oil slides quickly and hooks when it should. A ball that's caked with oil tires out, loses energy, and can hook too early.

You can use a cleansing product and/or a polishing product any time during open bowling. Try Ebonite Energizer Powerhouse cleansers or polishing products. Follow the manufacturer's directions for guidance on how often to clean or polish the ball, or just spruce it up on an as-needed basis.

Rubbing alcohol and the old standby, soap and water, make good cleansers for plastic bowling balls. Just be careful not to get liquid in the holes and don't soak the ball.

You can use bowling towels at any time during a game to help keep your ball free of oil and dirt. Bowling towels are perfect for wiping off any oil, grit, or residue that gets on your hands or on the ball. They're oil free, made of cotton or microfiber, and about the size of a kitchen towel. You can purchase one at your local pro shop or online at www.bowlersparadise.com. (Don't feel like spending the money on a special bowling towel? Use a kitchen towel or a small bath towel instead.)

If you're feeling fancy, you may want to invest in a seesaw towel (see Figure 4-4). To use one, place the ball in the seesaw, which is similar to a bag, and pull the handles up and down. This up-and-down motion helps clean and shine the ball. *Note:* If you have arm or shoulder difficulties, you may prefer the gentler motion of using a regular towel.

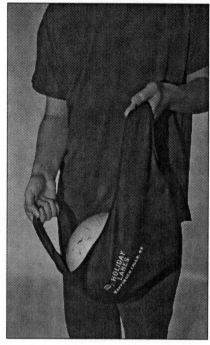

Figure 4-4:
Using a see-saw towel is an easy way to clean your bowling ball.

If you want to compete in tournaments or leagues, be aware that you can't use just any old cleanser. Some tournament and league operators limit the type of cleansers you can use and how often you can clean your ball during a game. They typically follow the guidelines put forth by the United States Bowling Congress (which you can find at `bowl.com`). Get into the habit of using approved cleansers and towels correctly now so you don't risk being disqualified. (We cover league rules and tournament play in Chapter 18.)

Letting a machine do the work

If applying cleanser and polish to your bowling ball is the absolute last thing you want to do, let someone else do the work. Place your ball into a cleaning machine at the center and then sit back and relax while it gets all spruced up.

Most bowling centers have polishing machines as well as cleaning machines. They cost from $1 to $5, depending on how long they last. Some machines require exact change, so ask the person at the front desk for change if you need it.

If you're just looking to clean your ball and you accidentally use the polisher, the shine you've added will make the ball hook less — that's not a good thing if you're a hook bowler. Read the signs carefully, or just ask the center's staff for advice.

Chances are your local pro shop will gladly clean your bowling ball for you using its special machines, but it may charge a fee for this service. If you're a regular customer or if you purchased your ball through the shop, you may be able to wriggle out of any cleaning fees.

Dealing with defects

Bowling balls take a lot of abuse, so they're bound to chip eventually and start looking like the ball in Figure 4-5. Any coverstock can break (we explain what a coverstock is earlier in this chapter), but reactive resin balls are softer than plastic and are at a higher risk for dings, chips, and cracks. These defects affect your bowling shot. For example, a chip can be on the ball's *track area,* the part of the ball that rolls on the lane and picks up oil. Each time the chip hits the lane, it moves the ball slightly and changes your shot.

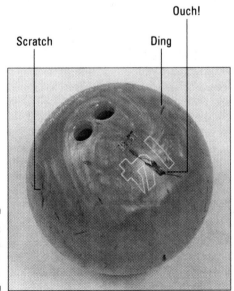

Figure 4-5:
Dings and chips on a house ball.

Dings and scratches that are imbedded with dirt and oil can be sanded down on an as-needed basis by your local pro shop for between $5 and $10. Sanding changes the surface of your ball, so definitely leave this task to the pro shop. You don't want to mess up your ball because you don't know what you're doing.

Another option for removing dings, especially if they're inside the track area, is to have your ball resurfaced, which costs $20 to $40. When a pro shop staffer resurfaces a ball with a special machine, she sands the ball down until all the damage has been removed and the ball is smooth again. Resurfacing really doesn't change the size of your ball, and if you own a ball for quite some time, it can be resurfaced several times as needed.

Pro shops have machines that can smooth out and fix most defects, except for cracks. A cracked ball is impossible to fix and must be replaced.

Where (and where NOT) to store your ball

When you're not bowling, safely store your bowling ball to protect it from dirt, debris, and accidents. If you want to keep your ball close by, store it in a closet at home, safely tucked away in your bowling bag. If you prefer to store your ball, bag, shoes, and other accessories at the bowling center so you don't have to lug everything back and forth all the time, rent a locker. You can usually rent storage lockers for an annual fee. Contact your local bowling center to ask about its specific policies.

Bowling balls can crack when subjected to really cold temperatures or warp when kept in a really hot storage area (like your car trunk during the summer — that's never a good idea). To keep your manufacturer's warranty intact, store the ball in an area of your home or the center that maintains a steady room temperature year-round.

Deciding When to Upgrade or Add Another Ball

Bowling balls have long life spans, sometimes lasting for decades, but at some point you may want or need a new ball. When's the perfect time to upgrade? It just may be when you walk into the pro shop and spot that brand-new, fire-red urethane ball. It looks cool, makes you feel good, and could very well take your game to the next level. If a ball inspires you, then that's just as good a reason as any to upgrade or grab a new one for your collection.

Following are other considerations that may factor into your decision to upgrade or add a new ball to your arsenal:

- ✔ **Your average has improved.** Say you started with a plastic or urethane ball, and after following our tips and suggestions, your average improves a whopping 30 points (flip to Chapter 2 for the basics on how to calculate your average and Chapter 18 for further details on averages). That means you're ready for a reactive resin ball that'll provide more power, more hook, and more pin action.

- ✔ **You can now handle a heavier ball.** If your current ball seems a little too light, you may just be used to its weight, or you may have improved your upper body strength. A ball that's too light for you doesn't necessarily travel where you want it to, so move up to a heavier ball without any reservations.

- ✔ **You're a hook bowler who can't make certain spares.** You use a urethane ball, but you're struggling with knocking down that elusive 10 pin. Consider adding another ball to your arsenal. A plastic ball meant for straight bowlers helps when a hook bowler needs to throw a direct shot to that single-pin spare.

If a new ball isn't immediately working out the way you'd hoped it would, relax. Adjusting to how a new ball reacts to the lanes, where to stand when you're throwing it, and so on takes time. Sure, your score may suffer while you're getting adjusted, but if you're patient, it should improve after you're familiar with your new ball.

When the old is new again

What if you're ready to hit the lanes again after a break from bowling and just found your old ball in the attic? Hold off on using it until you take it to your local pro shop. The staff there can inspect it, check to see whether it's in good condition, and make sure it still fits your fingers properly. You may be (pleasantly!) surprised to find out it just needs some minor adjustments to be as good as new, or you may need to invest in a brand-new ball.

Selecting the Right Accessories for Your Feet

Bowling shoes are essential for bowling because they help you slide during your delivery. Bowling centers rent shoes, but if you're bowling regularly, we encourage you to invest in a pair of your own. This investment pays for itself almost immediately. For example, say you purchase a pair of $36 bowling shoes and your center's weekly shoe rental is $3. Your shoes will pay for themselves after only 12 weeks of wear.

Another benefit of owning bowling shoes: You don't have to keep trying on and exchanging shoes that don't fit just to find the one pair that does. The sections that follow help you figure out how to purchase your very own bowling shoes and introduce you to some accessories that make your shoes even more functional.

Buying your own bowling shoes

Bowling shoes you buy at a pro shop look more like traditional sneakers and not like those oh-so-pretty bowling shoes you can rent at the center (see for yourself in Figure 4-6). They have soles that help you slide and can be either moderately priced or as expensive as high-priced sneakers. The styles and colors available are vast, so try them on like you would a pair of regular shoes and be sure to find a pair that fits both your feet and your personality.

Figure 4-6:
A pair of bowling shoes you can buy at a pro shop.

Some bowling shoes have soles you can replace when they wear down; others have interchangeable soles for different lane conditions. These types of shoes are of better quality than traditional bowling shoes, but they're also more expensive. However, the cost may be worth it when you consider that being able to replace your soles extends the life of your shoes. The average starting price for these special shoes is $100.

Some high-performance shoes have one sole that lets you slide and one that helps you brake. The shoe that slides is the one opposite your bowling hand. For example, if you're a left-handed bowler, your right shoe is the sliding shoe, and your left shoe is the braking shoe.

Outfitting your shoes

We suggest picking up the following items to keep your bowling shoes doing the job they're supposed to do:

- ✔ **Shoe covers:** Bowling shoes aren't meant to be worn outside or in the center's bathrooms, where they can pick up dirt, water, and debris and then track all that onto the lanes. Protect your shoes when you're planning on stepping outside or heading to the restroom by using specialized shoe covers. Bowling shoe covers cost about $10, are made from vinyl, and are elastic so they can stretch over your shoes.

- ✔ **Aids to smooth sliding:** Sliding is what you want to do when you're bowling, but if you're sticking because of debris or normal wear of the sole, apply a little baby powder to the bottom of the shoe, near the toes on your sliding foot, to get the groove back in your slide. You can also try using a wire brush to remove debris or file down the surface of the shoe enough to regain your slide. Some centers have wire brushes available for their customers to use. If yours doesn't, check out the pro shop. You can buy a wire brush for about $5.

Get Wise and Accessorize: Hand Gear

Even though you use your hands to bowl, the accessories available for hand protection while bowling aren't essential. The next sections highlight some hand-related bowling accessories you're welcome to try; you can find any of them online or at your local pro shop.

If your bowling hand or wrist is weak, you may want to invest in a wrist guard. This accessory provides support so you don't feel like your wrist is going to give under the weight of the ball. Wrist guards cost anywhere from $20 to $70.

Supporting your wrist with a bowling glove

Bowling gloves, which cost between $4 and $70 depending on the gizmos and gadgets you get with them, help keep your hand and wrist steady so you can throw the ball accurately and with more power. They come in either leather with metal posts that can hold your wrist in one position or elastic (which allows more flexibility). Figure 4-7 shows you one type of bowling glove.

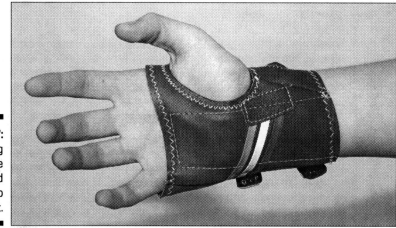

Figure 4-7:
A bowling glove can add support to your wrist.

Consider wearing a glove if you've had a previous injury or if your wrist tires out easily. You can choose from a glove that covers your hand completely, one that covers the fingers that aren't inserted into the ball, and a finger-less glove. Go with the one that feels most comfortable and best meets your physical needs.

You can use a batting or golf glove in place of a bowling glove and achieve the same support.

Avoiding slip-ups with gripping aids

If you don't have a good grip on the ball, you can drop it on the lane too early or too late. Sweaty or clammy hands can even cause the ball to slip right off of your fingers. The following gripping aids help keep the ball where it's supposed to be:

- ✔ **Rosin:** A *rosin bag*, shown in Figure 4-8, is a sealed pouch filled with powder that soaks up the moisture on your hands so the ball doesn't slip out. Simply hold the bag in your hand between frames, and it'll do its job. You can find rosin bags at pro shops or online for about $3 to $5.

- ✔ **Baby powder or bowling powder bags:** If the ball is sticking to your fingers, a little dab of baby powder — and we do mean a little — can solve the problem. Tap a tiny amount of baby powder onto one finger and then rub that finger around your hand or the part of the finger that feels like it's sticking. You can also use bowling powder bags such as Easy Slide on the bottoms of your bowling shoes (near the toes on your sliding foot) to help you slide better.

- ✔ **Tape:** Sometimes your fingers thin out from weight or water loss. This doesn't mean your ball needs to be redrilled or that it's time to buy a new ball. Just cut some bowlers tape to fit and put it into the hole that's too big for your fingers. Remove the tape from the ball and replace it when it gets too dirty or your fingers expand.

Figure 4-8:
Using a rosin bag keeps the ball from slipping out of your hands.

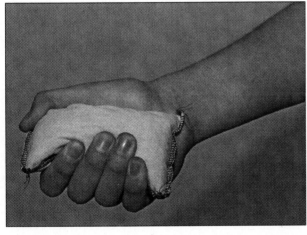

 If you're using rosin or baby powder, keep it away from the approach and the pit where other bowlers can step in it, get it on their shoes, and stick or slide — or worse, fall and get seriously injured. (See Chapter 2 for a rundown of the parts of a lane.)

 When you use powder on a shoe, slide the shoe back and forth a few times on the carpeted area of the center before your next turn in order to rub the powder into the shoe a bit and remove any excess that can get on the approach.

Part II

Body Basics: Throwing Yourself into the Game

The 5th Wave   By Rich Tennant

SID'S BOWLING CENTER

"Why don't we wait until they're done practicing and then pull the car down closer to the building?"

In this part . . .

Time to throw the ball and start knocking down some pins! In this part, you discover whether you naturally throw a hook or a straight ball, and you pick up everything you need to know about your form, your approach, and your throw. In other words, you find out how to hold the ball correctly, when to release it, and how much power and speed it needs to get down the lane.

This part is also a resource for correcting common problems that pop up after you've been practicing your bowling for a little while. We help you assess what you're doing right and where you need some improvement so you can become a better bowler.

Chapter 5

Finding Your Form and Style

. . . .

In This Chapter

▶ Discovering the importance of form and figuring out what your natural one is

▶ Reviewing the proper techniques for the three traditional forms

▶ Taking a look at bowling styles

. . . .

*W*hen you watch bowlers, you quickly realize that everyone has his or her own unique bowling style. Everyone stands, holds, and throws the ball a little differently. However, your style is different from your form. *Form* is how you throw the ball. Three traditional forms exist: the straight form, the hook form, and the backup form (also known as the reverse hook). We fill you in on all three in this chapter so you can find the form that's most natural for you and figure out how to achieve it (this is where the proper hold and release techniques come into play). We also touch on bowling styles and offer suggestions for adapting your style so that you always feel comfortable when bowling.

Understanding the Finer Points of Form

Your form consists of how you release the ball onto the lane, but it's more than just how your hand throws the ball. Believe it or not, every part of your body participates in the action of bowling.

✓ Your head and shoulders keep your upper body balanced.

✓ Your back keeps you steady.

✓ Your arms stay close to your sides so you can control your throw.

✔ Your wrist and hand provide the support you need to carry the ball (they also give you the ability to create spin for hook shots or stay steady for straight throws).

✔ Your fingers grip the ball.

✔ Your legs give you the strength you need to walk the approach, squat down, and release the ball.

✔ Your feet allow you to slide so you can finish your throw in style.

Bowling is a sport of geometry and physics. Roll a ball into pins spaced a certain distance apart from each other at the right angle and speed, and they should all fall down. Based purely on this concept, throwing a hook ball gives you a greater chance of knocking down more pins than throwing a straight ball, which is why many bowlers choose to learn how to throw a hook ball or, as they gain more experience, adapt their form to throw a hook shot (we cover the ins and outs of hook shots in Chapter 9).

The following sections explain the three basic forms, help you figure out which one comes naturally to you, and give you some advice on changing your form if and when you need to.

Getting a feel for the different forms

According to tradition, only three specific forms exist: the straight form, the hook form, and the backup form. Following is what you should know about each one:

✔ **Straight form:** A straight throw looks exactly how it sounds — the ball rolls in a straight, or relatively straight, line toward the pins and the pocket. The *pocket* is the space between the 1 and 2 pins for a left-handed bowler and the space between the 1 and 3 pins for a right-handed bowler (flip back to Chapter 2 if you need a refresher on how the pins are numbered and where the pockets are). If a straight ball hits the pocket properly, all the pins should fall down. Figures 5-1 and 5-2 help you visualize the straight form, which is a common form for most beginning bowlers.

A straight ball doesn't typically give you as much *pin action* (the number of pins that fall down) as a hook shot because it doesn't necessarily give you the perfect angle on the pocket. However, when you need to pick up single-pin spares, the straight form is your best friend.

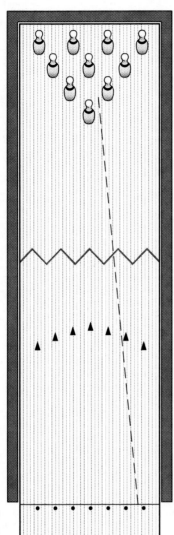

Figure 5-1:
A straight
ball thrown
by a right-
handed
bowler
travels in a
straight line
toward the
1-3 pocket.

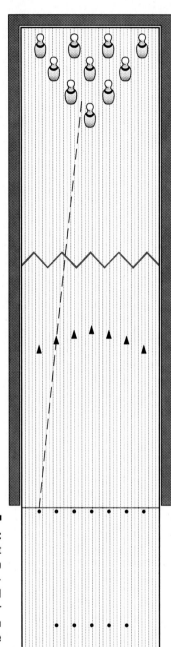

Figure 5-2:
A straight
ball thrown
by a left-
handed
bowler
travels in a
straight line
toward the
1-2 pocket.

- **Hook form:** When you throw a hook shot, the ball starts out straight but then curves toward the pocket, as shown in Figures 5-3 and 5-4. A left-handed hook bowler throws a ball that curves out to the left of the lane and then back in again toward the left-side pocket. A right-handed bowler throws a ball that hooks out to the right of the lane and then turns back in toward the right-side pocket. More experienced bowlers rely on the hook form because it increases their chances of getting a strike.

A hook shot is a hard, but not impossible, throw to master. It takes practice to perfect, but if you have the natural ability to throw a hook, you're off to a great start. This form is your best bet for scoring strikes because hook balls give you a better angle on the pocket than straight balls.

- **Backup form:** As you can see in Figures 5-5 and 5-6, a backup ball hooks in the opposite direction from a traditional hook ball. So a backup ball thrown by a right-handed bowler actually hooks out to the left before hitting the pocket on the left side, and a backup ball thrown by a left-handed bowler hooks out to the right and then swings back again to the pocket on the right side.

We know some bowlers who are quite comfortable using a backup form, but we don't encourage it. The backup form offers no additional benefits to your game when compared to a regular hook shot. Also, it goes against the natural movement of your wrist and hand, which can feel awkward. Stick with the regular hook form instead, at least when you're first starting out.

Determining your natural form

How can you find out what your natural form is? Go bowling. Don't worry about bowling a regular game or even keeping score. Just throw the ball several times and watch what it does. It'll either go straight toward the pins or curve to the outside and then head toward the pins.

Now that you know how your ball moves, think about how comfortable you felt throwing it. If throwing the ball straight down the lane felt natural, then your go-to form is the straight form. If your hand turned the ball and it curved as it traveled down the lane, you have a natural hook form. Determining your natural form is as easy as that.

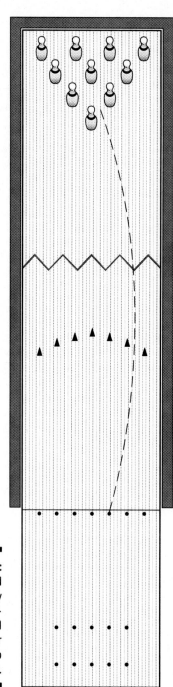

Figure 5-3:
A hook ball
thrown by
a right-
handed
bowler
curves to
the right.

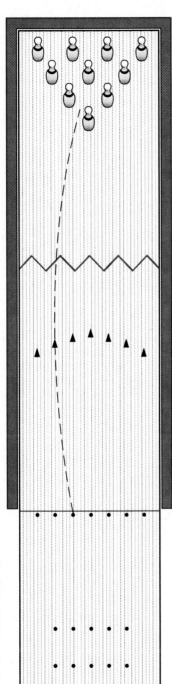

Figure 5-4:
A hook ball
thrown by a
left-handed
bowler
curves to
the left.

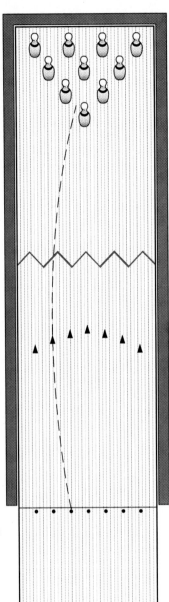

Figure 5-5:
When
a right-
handed
bowler
throws a
backup ball,
it hooks to
the left.

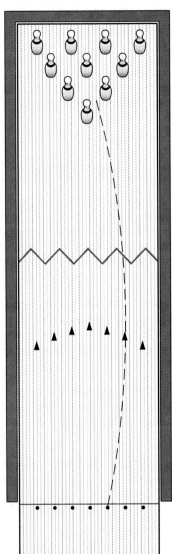

Figure 5-6:
When a
left-handed
bowler
throws a
backup ball,
it hooks to
the right.

When you're just starting out as a bowler, try to stick with the form that comes naturally to you. If you don't, you're not going to bowl well.

However, we do admit that now is the perfect time to learn how to throw a hook if you want, before you get too comfortable with one form (see Chapter 9 for pointers on perfecting the hook). If you'd rather stick to doing what comes naturally, remember that you can always change your form later on should you feel the need.

Using more than one type of form

As you gain more bowling experience, you may decide to augment your natural hook form by adding the straight form to your repertoire. Being able to switch between these two forms comes in handy when you're a hook bowler trying to knock down a single pin, such as the 7 or 10, and don't want the ball to curve away from it. (We give you pointers on picking up lone pins in Chapter 11.)

For example, Sam is a right-handed hook bowler who has been bowling for a number of years. However, he struggles with picking up the 10-pin spare. As you can see in Figure 5-7, Sam's hook looks like it's on a direct mission toward the 10-pin, but at the last minute it veers away from it, and Sam is foiled again.

So that he could finally conquer those daunting 10-pin spares, Sam used a straight form. His natural form (which he uses when delivering his strike ball) is still the hook, but being able to throw a straight ball on certain spares has improved Sam's score.

After you're comfortable with your natural form, you can start practicing a new form that'll help you improve your score. To adopt a new form, just follow our instructions on that form in this chapter. If you need additional instruction or can't seem to make the switch, work with a local bowling coach (we tell you how to find one in Chapter 15).

Don't get frustrated if you find that a new form isn't coming easily to you. Adapting your form for different spares and other lane situations is a little difficult, but it becomes easier as you gain more experience. So keep at it!

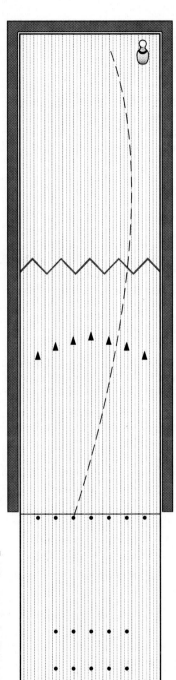

Figure 5-7:
A right-handed hook ball typically misses the 10-pin spare.

Holding and Releasing the Ball Properly for Each Form

To execute your natural bowling form for the best results, you should know how to hold and release the ball properly. The following sections walk you through how to do just that for each form. (Chapters 6 and 7 go into more detail on where to stand, how to start your approach, and how to follow through.)

Throwing a straight ball

When you throw a straight ball, it should go in a straight line (who woulda thunk it?), which is why this is the easiest and most comfortable throw for beginners to master. You can throw a straight shot using any type of ball, although the ideal type is plastic because it can come with a very light weight block or no weight block at all, depending on the ball's weight.

Here's how to throw a straight ball:

1. **Start with the proper positioning — middle and ring fingers and thumb of your bowling hand inserted in the correct holes, hand centered directly underneath the ball, and wrist straight (see Figure 5-8).**

   Your fingers should feel comfortable in the holes. If they don't, you need to select a different ball (see Chapter 3 for tips on finding the right one for you). As for your nonbowling hand, it should be supporting the ball by holding it underneath your bowling hand, on the side, or on the top. When you start moving, your body will automatically put your nonbowling hand out to the side to help you balance as you release the ball.

   A straight wrist increases the odds of your ball staying in a straight line when you let go of it, so don't bend or flex your wrist. If you find that your wrist is bending no matter how hard you try to keep it straight, try a lighter ball and see whether that corrects the problem.

2. **Push the ball away from your body slightly and swing it down by your side.**

3. **As the ball starts to come forward, let it roll off of your fingers while keeping your arm straight.**

   When you release the ball, your hand should still be in the same position as when you started (see Figure 5-9).

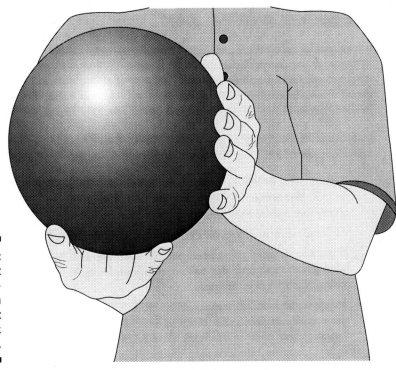

Figure 5-8:
The correct hand position for both the straight and hook forms.

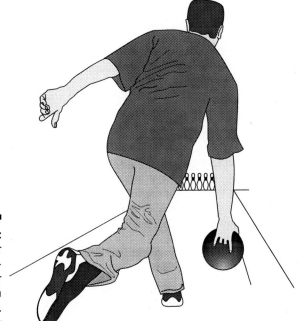

Figure 5-9:
The proper hand position for releasing a straight ball.

Throwing a hook shot

A hook ball actually starts out straight and then curves in the opposite direction of the hand you threw the ball with. So if you're left-handed, your ball starts out straight and then curves to the right. The source of the hook is a slight twist of the wrist and hand as you let the ball go. Urethane balls work best when you're just starting to throw hooks; they hook more than their plastic counterparts.

Following are the step-by-step directions for throwing a hook shot (make sure to focus on your hand position before, during, and after your release):

1. **Center your bowling hand directly beneath the ball, placing your fingers in the proper holes. Keep your wrist straight and use your other hand to support the ball.**

   Your hand positioning should look like the example in Figure 5-8.

2. **Continue to hold your hand underneath the ball with your wrist straight as you push the ball away from the front of your body and swing it down and back.**

3. **When your arm has swung forward far enough that it's parallel to your ankle, rotate your bowling hand toward the opposite side of your body so that your hand is on the side of the ball.**

   For example, in Figure 5-10, a left-handed bowler rotates his wrist toward the right. A right-handed bowler rotates his wrist toward the left. Either way, you don't want to rotate too much. When you release the ball, your goal is to end up with your hand ready to shake someone else's, not palm side down.

 If the ball isn't hooking toward the pocket, your hand may not be moving properly from the bottom of the ball to the side of it. Check to make sure you're rotating your wrist enough.

Throwing a backup ball

A backup ball hooks in the opposite direction of a regular hook ball. For example, when a righty throws a regular hook ball, it hooks to the left, but when a righty throws a backup ball, it hooks to the right. The steps for throwing a backup ball are the same as those for throwing a hook ball with one small exception — how you rotate your wrist.

1. **Position yourself properly — bowling hand directly underneath the ball and fingers in the appropriate holes.**

2. **Continue to hold your hand beneath the ball with a straight wrist as you push the ball away from the front of your body and swing it down and back.**

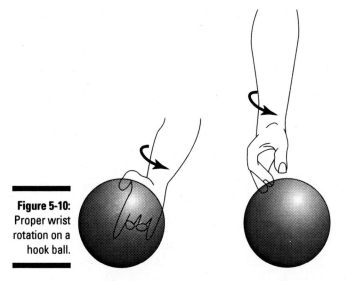

Figure 5-10:
Proper wrist
rotation on a
hook ball.

3. **As your arm swings forward, rotate your bowling hand toward the inside of your body.**

   A left-handed bowler rotates his wrist toward the right, and a right-handed bowler rotates his wrist toward the left.

Note: We suggest avoiding this form and sticking with the regular hook form. We've included the steps for throwing a backup ball to help you identify this form just in case it's your natural form. Throughout the rest of the book, though, we focus only on throwing straight and hook balls.

Putting Your Own Spin on the Game: Bowling Styles

Your personal bowling style is a combination of your posture, where you choose to hold the ball, and how you position your feet. No two bowlers have the same style, including us. Lisa keeps the ball in front of her; A.J. holds the ball low and down by his side.

Watch the differences in bowling styles at your center. Perhaps one bowler squats slightly and holds the ball down by his side, whereas another stands straight and keeps the ball near her chin. Someone else may lean back a little and bend one knee. None of these personal styles is wrong. After all, bowling styles really just come down to personal preference and comfort.

Look, Ma, two hands!

Check out the following picture of professional bowler Jason Belmonte. What's so unique about the way Jason's bowling? Take a close look at how he holds the ball. He throws a hook ball with two hands, thumb extended and not in the hole. He fires the ball down the lane with force, speed, rotation, and accuracy.

His style is unorthodox, but it works. Bowling two-handed gives Jason the ability to gain more power and rotation in his throw, allowing the ball to hit the pins with greater force, thereby creating greater pin action. (To find out more about Jason's form, go to www.jasonbelmonte.com).

Credit: Storm Products, Inc.

You may find that you change your style as you bowl. For example, perhaps you normally bend your knees slightly but your arthritis is acting up, so you stand straighter one day. Bowlers tweak their styles often to accommodate ailments, fatigue, and other comfort factors.

Where you hold the ball is purely about comfort, but we suggest you don't hold it too far away from your body because your arms can tense up and your grip may become too tight. (For more helpful pointers on the swing and the release, head to Chapter 7.)

Chapter 6

Positioning Yourself for a Smooth Approach

In This Chapter

▶ Setting your body appropriately and comfortably

▶ Walking through the traditional four-step approach

▶ Evaluating how your stance and approach are looking

*I*f you want to bowl well, you have to know how to position your body, which is why we start this chapter off by explaining how to get into a good bowling stance. Then we take you through the traditional four-step approach to bowling. What is the *approach,* you ask? Technically it has two definitions. It refers to both the floor you step up on when it's your turn to bowl and the physical steps you take to set yourself and throw the ball. When we mention the approach in this chapter, we're almost always talking about the four steps that not only get you ready to throw but also set you and your ball in motion.

In this chapter, we show you how your four-step approach starts as soon as you pick up the ball. You find out how to take your first step, push the ball away from your body, create your backswing, and smoothly release the ball onto the lane. And because finding a comfortable stance and mastering the traditional four-step approach are so important, we provide a checklist you can use to figure out what you're doing right and what you need to work on.

After you have these bowling basics down, you're ready to head to Chapter 7, which goes into more detail about throwing the ball (especially wrist rotation, an important concept for hook bowlers).

Getting into Position

Although a good approach sets you up for a strong, solid throw (as explained in the later "Moving through the Four-Step Approach" section), you can't achieve one without getting yourself into an appropriate and comfortable position. We show you how to do just that in the following sections.

While you're getting into position before you bowl, quickly scan the approach to make sure it's clear of any debris, such as little rocks, buttons, towels, pieces of gum or candy, or anything else that could cause you to trip and fall. Keep checking it every time you bowl because someone may have walked around the center and picked up something on the bottom of her shoes between frames. (While you're at it, check the bottoms of *your* bowling shoes to make sure they're clean, especially if you've stepped away from the pit. You may have picked up a crumb from a dropped French fry that could cause you or another bowler to stop short or slip and fall while bowling.)

Choosing a starting spot

Bowlers start their approach at the foul line, just before the seats, and at every point in between. So where's the right spot for you? If you're a beginning bowler, the best place for you to start is on the middle set of dots on the approach (flip to Chapter 2 for the full scoop on lane markings). The dot you should stand on depends on the length of your stride (longer strides should start on the dots at the back of the approach) and whether you're a righty or a lefty (whether you're a hook bowler or a straight bowler is a secondary consideration). We help you figure out what dots belong to you in the next sections.

The dots are just guidelines; they aren't set in stone. After you know how your particular ball rolls, you can make some minor adjustments to your starting dot (we help you figure out how to do that in Chapter 8).

Knowing the right spot for righties

If you're a righty who bowls a straight ball, start with your left foot on the second dot from the right (see Figure 6-1). Starting from this spot allows the ball to correctly angle into the pocket as it goes down the lane. (**Note:** When you look at the photos in this chapter, you may think that the bowler is standing at the foul line as she prepares to make her shot. Don't worry, she's not. The bowler is standing on the approach, not at the foul line. The bowling center where the photos were taken has two different shades of flooring, which makes it look like the bowler is already at the foul line.)

If you throw a hook ball, start with your left foot on the third dot from the right (see Figure 6-2). Starting here gives the ball enough room to hook out and back into the pocket.

Figure 6-1:
The starting spot for a right-handed straight bowler.

Figure 6-2:
The starting spot for a right-handed hook bowler.

Standing on the correct dot if you're a lefty

If you're a straight-throwing lefty, stand with your right foot on the second dot from the left (see Figure 6-3). Starting from this dot lines the ball up on the best angle with your pocket.

Figure 6-3:
The starting
spot for a
left-handed
straight
bowler.

If you're a left-hander who throws a hook, start with your right foot on the third dot from the left (see Figure 6-4). Doing so gives your throw ample room to hook out and back into your pocket.

Figure 6-4:
The starting
spot for a
left-handed
hook
bowler.

Setting your stance

After you know where to stand (as explained earlier in this chapter), you're ready to set your *stance* — how you set your body up to bowl. The idea is to make sure you stay balanced, like the bowler in Figure 6-5a. To do that, your body must be properly aligned — head and shoulders straight, eyes on your target, and feet planted. If you start out properly aligned, you have a better chance of keeping your body aligned as you release your ball (see Figure 6-5b).

Figure 6-5:
A balanced
stance (a)
leads to a
balanced
release (b).

a   b

You don't want to feel like you're tipping over when you assume your stance. If you tip too far to one side or bend too far forward, you won't throw the ball well. You also risk losing your balance and falling over after you release the ball. We suggest how to set your stance from your feet to your head in the sections that follow.

Although we make recommendations on your stance, the most important thing is to find the stance that works for you. Standing properly, and comfortably, helps you bowl better, so if you need to tweak one of our suggestions so you feel more comfortable, please do.

However you decide to set your stance, relax when you step onto the approach and assume it. The more relaxed you are, the better your shot will be.

Planting your feet so they face the pins

To stay balanced during your throw, you first need to make sure your feet are properly positioned and comfortable. Plant them in a forward position so they're facing toward the pins and not off to the side. As for the comfortable part, that's really up to you. Some bowlers find it more comfortable to have their feet slightly apart (as shown in Figure 6-6a), whereas others put them together (like in Figure 6-6b). Some bowlers have been known to put one foot slightly in front of the other one (check out Figure 6-6c); other bowlers keep their feet together and perfectly even. Try a few different foot positions on for size to see what feels good to you.

Figure 6-6:
You can set your feet in many different ways as long as they face the pins.

Setting your feet so that they face toward the pins is the foundation of a good stance. Take a few seconds to check your feet and make sure they're on the right dot and set the way you want them.

Keeping your head straight

Your head should always be positioned straight and pointed forward, as in Figure 6-7. Avoid tipping it to one side so you don't risk throwing off your balance. Your head affects the position of your shoulders too, so if your head is tilted, your shoulders start to tilt too, then your hips . . . you get the idea.

Keep your eyes focused on your target arrow on the lane, *not* the pins. The arrows are closer to you than the pins are; as a result, they're easier to hit.

Holding the ball comfortably

The proper way to hold a bowling ball is with two hands rather than just one. The middle and ring fingers as well as the thumb of your bowling hand should be inserted into the correct holes. Your other hand, which is there for support, can go underneath your bowling hand, next to it, or on the side or top of the ball — the choice is yours.

Figure 6-7:
Keep
your head
straight
and your
eyes on the
arrows.

Your other choice involves where you hold the ball, and it depends entirely on your comfort level. If holding the ball toward the outside of your body (like in Figure 6-8) is comfortable for you, that's fine. If you feel better holding the ball in front of your body, that's fine too. How high or low you hold the ball also depends on your comfort level, but remember that you need to swing the ball out to the side of your body before you throw it. Starting with the ball on the outside of your body and a little on the low side gives you a better chance of having a more controlled backswing and a good throw; it also reduces the odds that the ball will swing behind your back.

Whether you hold the ball to the side or in the front, keep your elbows close to your body to avoid having too much muscle tension in your arms. To see what we mean by muscle tension, try holding the ball with your arms away from your body. Do you feel your muscles tightening up? You never want to experience this feeling while holding your bowling ball.

Don't hold your ball down by your side while you're waiting to take your turn because the weight of the ball fatigues the arm muscles. Instead, leave it on the ball return until it's your turn to bowl. If you absolutely have to hold it, do so with your opposite hand (as in the nonbowling one) and cradle it instead of letting it hang.

Figure 6-8: Hold the ball to the side of your body, if you can.

Bending your knees — or not

Whether or not you bend your knees really is a personal preference, but we can tell you that a slight bend brings you a little closer to the lane (see Figure 6-9 for proof). Being lower helps you release the ball more smoothly onto the lane instead of dropping it and increases the power of your throw, but you don't have to keep your knees bent the whole time (or at all) to achieve this. Many bowlers who keep their legs straight at the beginning of their approach slowly bend down through the approach until they're down lower on the final step and still smoothly release the ball onto the lane.

If you have knee or back problems, you may not want to (or even be able to), bend your knees due to the risk of possible injury. That's okay. Go ahead and stand with your legs straight and concentrate on making the other parts of your throw the best they can be.

Figure 6-9:
Bending
your knees
slightly gets
you closer
to the lane.

Moving through the Four-Step Approach

The most traditional way of bowling is what's called a *four-step approach*. This means that you take four steps while swinging the ball and then releasing it onto the lane. The four-step approach is a great way to get a handle on the basics of setting yourself up for a successful throw.

How you make the four-step approach has nothing to do with whether you throw a straight or hook ball. The process is almost exactly the same for everyone; the only difference is the foot you lead off with. If you're right-handed, you start on your right foot; if you're left-handed, you begin with your left foot.

Here's how the traditional four-step approach is done:

1. **Simultaneously take your first step with your bowling foot and push the ball out from your body to start your arm swing.**

   Your *bowling foot* is the one that's on the same side of your body as the ball. So if you're a right-handed bowler, take your first step with your right foot, like in Figure 6-10a (Figure 6-10b shows the first step for lefties). As for the arm motion, it helps to think of your arm as a pendulum swinging down and back (however, your arm makes this motion only once).

Figure 6-10: Take your first step and push the ball out.

a   b

2. **Take your second step with your lead foot and keep the ball swinging back with your arm and wrist straight (see Figure 6-11).**

   Your *lead foot* is the one opposite your bowling foot. When it hits the ground, the ball should be at its lowest point in the swing.

3. **Take your third step with your bowling foot and make sure your ball is at the peak of your backswing (see Figure 6-12).**

   The ball shouldn't be too high or behind your body.

Figure 6-11: The ball should be swinging back on your second step.

a

b

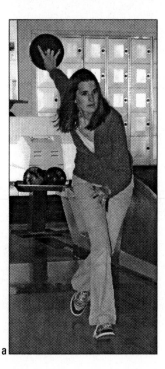

Figure 6-12: The ball should be at the peak of your backswing on your third step.

a

b

4. Swing the ball forward and release it down the lane as your lead foot slides toward the foul line on your fourth and final step.

At this point, your lead foot should be bearing most of your weight. Check out Figure 6-13 for reference. Your bowling foot will automatically kick behind you, toward the opposite side of your body. This is an automatic reflex to make sure you stay balanced.

Be sure to keep a good grip on the ball when you're releasing it. If you're squeezing the ball because the grip is too loose or your fingers are stuck because the grip is too tight, your throw isn't going to be good. Also, remember that the release should be smooth. Imagine laying the ball down on the lane rather than dropping it there.

After you release the ball, make sure to follow through on the motion with your arm and your hand. We give you the complete lowdown on follow-through in Chapter 7.

A good approach creates a powerful throw that sends the ball down the lane in a controlled fashion so it can push the pins aggressively. If you make a poor approach, your ball's speed will peter out by the time it gets to the end of the lane, causing the ball to miss the pocket and drift off into the gutter.

Figure 6-13:
Release and follow through on your fourth step.

a

b

Nailing the timing is essential for a good four-step approach. Reaching the foul line when your arm is low to the ground and releasing the ball at the right time (when it's near your ankles) increases your chances of throwing a ball that gives you a strike or a spare. (For more tips on timing, see the "Assessing Your Stance and Approach" section later in this chapter.)

You can shorten the steps to the traditional four-step approach by saying something like this to yourself as you're waiting for your turn or standing on the approach:

- ✔ Push (the ball away)
- ✔ Swing (the ball back)
- ✔ Hit (the peak of your swing)
- ✔ Release (the ball) and follow through

Assessing Your Stance and Approach

After you've been practicing your stance and approach for a little while, it's a good idea to find out whether you're doing them right. You can either evaluate yourself or ask for constructive criticism from a more experienced bowler; we help you figure out how to do both in the next sections.

Doing a little self-examination

To assess your stance and approach on your own, ask yourself the following questions. If you have problems in any of these areas, refer to the corresponding section earlier in this chapter.

- ✔ Are my feet on the right dot? (See "Choosing a starting spot.")
- ✔ Are my feet keeping me balanced? (Refer to "Planting your feet so they face the pins.")
- ✔ Is my head straight, and are my eyes focused? (See "Keeping your head straight.")
- ✔ Am I holding the ball close enough to my body? (Refer to "Holding the ball comfortably.")
- ✔ Am I pushing the ball out when I start to take my first step? (See "Moving through the Four-Step Approach.")

✔ Am I swinging the ball on my second step? (Refer to "Moving through the Four-Step Approach.")

✔ Am I starting to power the ball on my third step? (See "Moving through the Four-Step Approach.")

✔ Am I finishing with a smooth release and follow-through? (Refer to "Moving through the Four-Step Approach.")

✔ Am I falling to the side when I complete my approach? (See "Setting your stance.")

Asking for a critique

If you just can't seem to get your stance or approach (or both) right on your own, don't be afraid to ask for a more experienced bowler's help. Ask the center's manager or the pro shop owner whether she can observe your stance and watch your approach to pinpoint what you're doing wrong and what you're doing right. If you need more assistance than she can provide, she may suggest asking a local bowling coach to give you a lesson (we fill you in on bowling coaches in Chapter 15).

It's best to ask the center's manager or pro shop owner to watch you when the center is slow so she can actually take time to guide you.

Chapter 7

Throwing the Ball

. . . .

In This Chapter

▶ Finding the proper placement for your fingers, hand, and wrist

▶ Perfecting your arm swing

▶ Observing how your ball moves so you can control its speed and spin

. . . .

*T*hrowing the ball properly is the key to getting strikes and spares, but it's more complex than simply chucking the ball down the lane. You need to know how to hold it correctly, how to swing your arm, and how to let go of the ball at just the right moment so that it sails down the lane and knocks down all the pins.

This chapter focuses on all of these important points and more. Prepare to pick a comfortable finger grip and understand how to position your hand and wrist for both a hook and a straight shot. Then get ready to discover how your hand motion creates the rotation your ball needs for an awesome hook shot and how much speed you need to put on the ball to get it down the lane. By the end of this chapter, you'll be throwing a bowling ball better than you ever have before.

Setting Your Fingers, Hand, and Wrist

The fingers, hand, and wrist on your bowling arm (as well as your nonbowling hand) all work together to support the bowling ball during your throw. If they aren't set properly, your throw — and the results you get from it — will be off. In the following sections, we show you the proper way to position these body parts to execute a good throw.

Sticking your fingers into the ball

How you position your fingers in the ball is your *grip*. The right grip helps you hold and control the ball when you throw it. You have two options to choose from:

- ✔ **The conventional grip:** A *conventional grip* is when your middle and ring fingers are in the ball up to the middle knuckle and your thumb is inserted all the way into the ball (see Figure 7-1a). Because this grip places more of your fingers in the ball, it gives you better control, which makes it the best grip for beginners. Straight bowlers also typically use a conventional grip because it reduces the amount of hook you can get on the ball. Most house balls are drilled to fit a conventional grip, which means the holes are deeper than they are on a ball that has been drilled for someone who uses a fingertip grip.

- ✔ **The fingertip grip:** In a *fingertip grip,* the fingertips of your middle and ring fingers are inserted into the ball up to the first knuckle, but your thumb is inserted all the way in (see Figure 7-1b). A fingertip grip lets bowlers hook the ball. Most urethane or reactive resin bowling balls are drilled to fit a fingertip grip because they're used for throwing hooks.

To understand how the fingertip grip lets you hook the ball, think of a spinning top. When you want to spin the top, you use your fingertips to hold it, spin it quickly, and then release it. If you were to put more of your fingers on the top, this spinning action would be harder to do. It's the same concept in bowling. Using your fingertips alone allows you to spin the ball and quickly release your fingers.

Figure 7-1:
A conventional grip (a) is perfect for beginners; a fingertip grip (b) is great for hook shots.

a   b

Note: If you're a beginner who starts with a conventional grip, you can move on to a fingertip grip after you have the basics down and feel comfortable with your throw.

Giving alternative grips a go

The conventional and fingertip grips aren't the only types of grips used in the bowling world. There's also the *semifingertip grip,* which is when you insert your middle and ring fingers into the appropriate holes about midway between the first and second joints. The semifingertip grip is the least common grip, but if you find jumping from the conventional grip to a fingertip one to be too much to handle, then the semifingertip grip may be a good option for you.

Then again, you may want to try *palming* the ball. To do this, put your middle and ring fingers into the bowling ball but leave your thumb out. Palming the ball allows you to throw either a straight ball or a hook shot.

What do you do with your pointer and pinkie fingers after your grip is set? Just place them where they feel most comfortable (which is usually on the ball right next to your middle and ring fingers).

Positioning your hand and wrist

Your hand and wrist must both be positioned correctly if you're going to throw the ball properly. Think of your wrist, hand, and fingers as a tree. The wrist is the trunk of the tree; it gives support to your hand (the middle part of the tree) and your fingers, which are the limbs. Without a strong trunk, the limbs would just topple over.

How you position your hand and wrist depends on whether you're a hook bowler or a straight bowler. (If you're not sure, turn to Chapter 5 for help figuring out your form.)

The proper positioning for a straight bowler

To throw a straight ball, position your hand and wrist directly underneath the ball, palm up and with the correct fingers in the holes (see Figure 7-2).

Your other hand is an extra support for the ball, but where you put it is your choice. Some bowlers put their nonbowling hand on the side of the ball, others place it on the top, and some put it under the hand that's holding the ball. Find what's comfortable for you and keep your wrist strong so the ball doesn't move from this position.

Figure 7-2:
Proper hand
and wrist
position-
ing for a
straight or
hook ball.

The proper positioning for a hook bowler

If you're a hook bowler, where you position your hand and wrist depends on how much hook you want the ball to have. Most hook bowlers start in the same hand-and-wrist position as a straight bowler — bowling hand and wrist directly beneath the ball with the hand palm up (see Figure 7-2) — and use their nonbowling hand to support the ball. This starting hand-and-wrist position gives you even more room to rotate your hand from the bottom of the ball to the top when you're throwing it, thus creating your hook.

The difference between a straight bowler and a hook bowler is the position the hand and wrist end up in after the ball is released. A straight bowler's hand and wrist remain in the same position they started out in, whereas a hook bowler's hand winds up in the handshake position (palm facing the inside of the lane and thumb pointing upward).

Bowlers who want to put even more spin on the ball place their hand in the regular starting position and then shift their hand and wrist a little toward the inside of their bodies. This is known as the *crank* position, and it gives a hook bowler more room to turn, or crank, the ball for a bigger hook (flip to Chapter 9 for how to rotate your hand when throwing a hook).

Want even more hook? Cup your hand (as shown in Figure 7-3) to create additional room so you can rotate the ball.

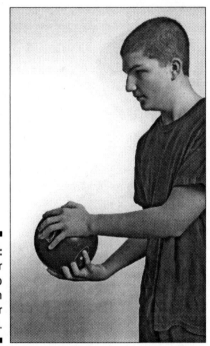

Figure 7-3:
Cup your
hand to
throw an
even bigger
hook.

Putting Your Arm through the Motions

Your ball isn't going to zoom down the lane without a little momentum behind it. The swing of your arm is what provides the ball with the momentum it needs to hit the pins. Of course, your arm isn't the only part of your body that's moving. As your arm swings, the rest of your body is also in motion. This forward movement of your body toward the lane is called your *approach.* We break down this motion in Chapter 6, but in the sections that follow, we just want you to focus on how your arm should move throughout your throw.

Swinging your arm forward, back, and forward again

Some people think all they have to do to throw a bowling ball is move their throwing arm backward and then forward again. However, the correct arm swing is actually a threefold movement. First, you push the ball out and to the side, then you swing your arm backward to build up momentum, and finally you bring your arm forward to prepare for the release and finish out your throw.

To start your arm swing, hold the ball in a position that's comfortable for you. That may be on your side, near your hip, upper thigh, or chest. Or it may be in front of you, either up by your chest or down by your waist. The more comfortable you feel, the better you'll throw.

Holding the ball higher in front of your body may give you room to create more momentum, but keep in mind that you must be able to control your arm swing so it doesn't go wildly to the side or around your back. Starting with the ball lower and on your side gives you greater control over your arm swing.

You begin your arm swing as soon as you take your first step. With that step, push the ball forward and away from your body. (Push just hard enough to swing your arm out and to the side.) This movement gets your arm swinging back on your second step, back behind you on your third step, and coming forward on your fourth step, which is when you release the ball.

Whether your arm is moving forward or backward, your arm swing should always be natural.

Releasing the ball

How and when you release the ball are vitally important aspects of a great throw. After all, your release sets up exactly where the ball goes on the lane and how fast it makes it down to the pins.

The correct moment to release your ball is when it's crossing the ankle of your sliding leg so that it's lower to the lane (see Figure 7-4).

Figure 7-4:
Exactly
when to
release
the ball.

Here are a few things that should happen when you release the ball:

✔ Your sliding leg should be bent to help bring the ball closer to the lane. (If you can't comfortably bend your knees, go ahead and stand straight, but still release the ball at the same spot.)

✔ You should roll the ball onto the lane, not drop it, so that you can barely hear it hit the lane.

✔ Your arm should continue swinging forward after the ball has been released. When you're done following through, your hand should be in the handshake position if you're a hook bowler or the palm-up position if you're a straight bowler.

Perfecting your release takes some time. For a while, you may release the ball too soon or too late, both of which affect how your ball hits the pins. We help you deal with these common problems in Chapter 8.

Following through

After you release the ball, your throwing arm should follow through, not stop midswing. Stopping your arm short gives you an incomplete throw, which reduces your odds of hitting all the pins.

How high up your arm comes depends entirely on your comfort level. However, the best form is to stop your upper arm at shoulder level but keep your forearm and hand moving up and back.

If you're a hook bowler, your hand should end up in a handshake position, as shown in Figure 7-5a. If you're a straight bowler, keep your arm straight and your wrist and hand in the same position throughout your entire throw. (So when you release the ball, your wrist and hand should still be facing up toward the ceiling, as in Figure 7-5b.)

Figure 7-5:
Following through on a right-handed hook (a) and a left-handed straight shot (b).

a   b

Seeing How the Ball Rolls

When you go to the bowling center, watch how your bowling ball rolls down the lane. Does it go faster or slower than others? Does it hook in the right direction as it rolls toward the pins, or is it hooking in the opposite direction from what you wanted? How your ball rolls and hooks is the direct result of how you threw it. And, of course, the speed and spin (or lack thereof if you're a straight bowler) you put on the ball affect where it goes and how many pins fall down.

We tell you what you need to know to make your ball move the way you want it to in the next sections.

Knowing your ideal ball speed

Bowling is all about physics. A ball that's moving at the right speed and coming in at the right angle creates a perfect chain reaction when it hits the pins. In contrast, a ball that's moving too slowly usually deflects off the standing pins, and a ball that's moving too quickly tends to fly through the pins without creating the right amount of pin action.

The ideal speed of a bowling ball is 16 miles per hour. This speed allows the ball to hit the pins and create the right pin action necessary for strikes. Yet just because the ideal ball speed is 16 miles per hour doesn't mean you absolutely have to throw your ball that hard. The strength of your throw depends on several factors:

✔ **Your body size:** A child or a small adult may not have the body strength to throw a bowling ball 16 miles per hour.

If your center has a computerized radar program and it shows that you're comfortably throwing your ball at, say, 12 miles per hour, don't try throwing the ball any harder. Throwing at a speed that isn't comfortable for you can mess up your form and cause you serious injury.

✔ **Hook potential:** When throwing a hook shot, you don't want the ball to go too fast. If it does, it'll get down to the pins before it has time to hook. Of course, you don't want the ball moving too slowly either. When that happens, you risk the ball hooking way too early.

Experiment with the speed of the ball to see what works for your throw. Too fast? Slow down a little (we explain how in the next section) and give the ball the time it needs to hook into your desired pocket. Too slow? Give the ball a little extra oomph and see whether that works.

✔ **Drifting straight throws:** If you throw a straight ball without enough speed to get it down to the pins, the ball will peter out and drift off to the left or right of your pocket. Make sure your throw has enough speed to get into your pocket. (We share ideas on how to speed up your throw later in this chapter.)

✔ **Lane conditions:** Lane conditions affect your shot too. On an oily lane, a bowling ball rolls more slowly, so you may want to throw a little harder. When the lanes are dry, the ball tends to pick up speed, so you may need to slow it down a little. Oil typically doesn't affect a straight shot, but you should still keep lane conditions in mind if your ball isn't hitting the pocket.

Throw some practice shots before you start keeping score in order to figure out the conditions at your lane.

In the following sections, we offer suggestions for slowing down and speeding up your throw as necessary.

Slowing it down

If you're throwing the ball a little too fast and not getting the pin action you want, reconsider how you're swinging your arm. Say, for example, that you normally carry the ball in front of you, push it out, and swing it back, but you're getting too much speed on the ball anyway. Instead of holding the ball in front of you, try holding it next to your hip and not pushing it out as far. These adjustments cut the amount of arm swing down, which reduces the ball speed.

Don't forget about your feet. To slow down the speed of the ball, you may need to slow your feet down too. Bowlers tend to rush up to the foul line and release the ball. Taking slower, more deliberate steps should help curb your ball speed.

Speeding it up

You may actually need more ball speed if your ball is slowing down and moving off to the side (or even the gutter!) before it reaches the pocket. To make your ball roll a bit faster:

✔ **Have a larger backswing.** The more backswing you get with the ball, the more momentum and speed the ball will have. Start by holding the ball in front of you. On your first step, push the ball out in front of you and then swing it back. This bigger arc helps rev up the ball.

✔ **Move your feet faster.** No, we don't want you running to the foul line, but do try walking a wee bit faster. You'll have to experiment to see how much faster you need to go.

✔ **Combine a larger backswing with faster feet.** A larger backswing paired with faster steps is an ideal way of creating a faster, more effective throw.

Putting a little spin on your hook shot

You may hear bowlers talk about rotation and spin when it comes to a hook ball. Don't let the terms confuse you. *Rotation* and *spin* are the same thing. As you throw a hook shot, your hand moves from the bottom of the ball to the side of it before you let it go, forcing the ball to rotate, or spin. The more spin you give the ball, the more it hooks as it rolls down the lane. (We cover the other factors that affect how much a ball hooks in Chapter 9.)

The more spin you want, the more wrist rotation you need to have. Of course, how much spin you need to give the ball depends on the lane conditions. A drier lane requires more spin, whereas an oily lane requires less spin. As the game goes on and the amount of oil on the lane begins to change, you may need to adjust your throw.

If your ball is hooking too much, move your hand a little bit to the outside of it to reduce the spin. If the ball isn't hooking enough, consider cupping your hand or spreading out your pointer and pinkie fingers on the ball to help create more spin.

Just because one technique works at the start of a game doesn't mean it'll still work in the middle of your third straight game. You may need to change your throw slightly in order to compensate for fatigue or changes in the lane conditions.

Chapter 8

Correcting Common Approach Problems

As you get comfortable with the basics of bowling, you're going to encounter some problems with your approach and want a quick fix. Finding what works for you takes time. We want to help you cut some of that time down a bit, so in this chapter we're sharing several of the most common bowling problems we've seen over the years. Rest assured that this chapter also has solutions to help you improve your delivery.

In the next several pages, we break down the problems you may be having in every part of your approach. We talk about how the conditions of the lane can alter the way your ball travels down the lane and what to do if your equipment fails you. Troubleshooting your problems is a great way to find solutions, make changes, and become a better bowler.

Reevaluating Your Equipment

Sometimes your game is only as good as your equipment. When your form is perfect, your timing is impeccable, and your release is right on the mark, but your score is going nowhere fast because the ball isn't making it to the pocket for some odd reason, the problem may lie with your ball or the shoes you're wearing. Grab your ball and shoes and compare them to the descriptions we give in the following sections. Then make a quick fix if necessary. (For more on equipment, see Chapter 4.)

Correcting the bowling ball blues

You've had your bowling ball for years and love it like a child. Over time, though, both you and the ball have changed. You may've become a better bowler, or perhaps you've gained or lost weight and your fingers are now too big or too small to fit into the holes properly. As for your ball, it has hit the lanes hundreds or thousands of times and likely has some damage. Consider these questions to determine whether the ball you own (or your favorite house ball) is what's causing you problems:

- ✔ **Do my fingers still fit properly in the ball?** By now you may be so used to the way your ball fits on your fingers that you don't notice small but important changes. Take a closer look. Are your fingers squeezed a little too much, or does there seem to be extra room around them? Even the slightest change in how you hold the ball can throw off your shot. This is especially important if you throw a hook and need your fingers to fit properly so you can create the right amount of spin on the ball. Visit your local pro shop and have someone there take a look and see whether redrilling is necessary.

- ✔ **Is my ball too heavy or too light?** If you're releasing the ball too early, your arm may be tiring out because the ball is too heavy. On the contrary, if you're lifting the ball into the air (called *lofting*) instead of rolling it onto the lane, the ball may be too light. Remember that the weight of the ball should equal 10 percent of your body weight (for bodies up to 160 pounds, that is). Weigh yourself, check the weight of the ball, and see how close the two weights come to the 10-percent guideline. If the numbers are off significantly, head to your pro shop to find a ball that's the proper weight for you.

The 10-percent guideline is one of several factors to consider when determining whether a ball is the right weight for you. You also need to take into account your personal comfort level and any arm or shoulder injuries you've had. If throwing a ball hurts, then switch to a lighter ball and think of other ways you can improve your game, such as hitting your target and picking up spares.

- ✔ **Does my ball need to be resurfaced?** Bowling balls take a lot of abuse. They're dropped, thrown onto a hard lane, and banged into by the other bowling balls when on the ball return. If your ball is filled with nicks and dings and is looking a little worse for wear, it's due for a makeover. That's because nicks and dings can interfere with what's otherwise a great shot, especially if they're on the track where the ball rolls down the lane. Having your pro shop resurface the ball removes those little divots and makes your ball smooth again. *Note:* Nicks and dings are one thing; if your ball is cracked, stop bowling with it immediately and invest in a new one. A cracked ball doesn't roll properly and can split completely in half (we've seen it), ruining the lane.

Why getting a ball that fits like a glove is worth it

What do you do if you're a small woman with big hands and you want to use a house ball, but the holes in the lightweight bowling balls aren't big enough for your fingers? Whether you're a small woman with big hands or a big man with thin fingers, this is one of the best reasons to own a custom-drilled ball. Investing in an inexpensive (less than $100) plastic ball that's drilled to fit your fingers can solve your problem. Even if you only go bowling once in a while, having a ball that fits you like a glove makes the experience much more enjoyable.

Don't bowl with a house ball that's filled with nicks. Rummaging through all the racks can be a bit tedious, but we assure you that taking the time to find a smoother house ball is beneficial.

Solving shoe troubles

Perhaps you put on your bowling shoes and tie them up without giving them a second thought. That's usually fine, but if you're not seeing the score you want, take a good look at your shoes before stepping onto the approach. Ask yourself the following questions:

- ✔ **Do my shoes fit right?** If your feet hurt because the fit isn't right, you won't complete your approach properly. You may hesitate or limp to one side without even realizing it. If you own your own bowling shoes, you may have outgrown them, or they may be too old and worn down on the bottom. Consider purchasing a new pair. As for rented bowling shoes, they should fit as comfortably as your sneakers or other shoes do. If they hurt when you put them on or after you start walking around, they aren't the right fit and should be exchanged for a better-fitting pair.

   You can exchange your rented bowling shoes at the counter as often as you want until you find a pair that fits properly. However, if you're renting a lane by the hour, ask to try on the shoes before you're assigned a lane so you don't waste precious bowling time.

- ✔ **Are they clean?** Clean bowling shoes are vital for a good, safe game. Imagine how tripped up you'll be if you step outside (a huge bowling center no-no) or in the food area and get debris on the soles of your shoes. Step on the approach and that debris can force you to stop short and maybe even fall. Not only can this mess up your game because your throw will be off but it can also cause you serious injury. Residue from excess powder (which bowlers use to help their shoes slide) can also dirty the soles of your bowling shoes and cause you to slip.

Foul line behavior

Some bowlers start their approach on the right marks but end up *fouling* — sliding over the foul line a lot. If you're bowling in a league, fouling can hurt your score (and bruise your ego). Every time you foul in league play, you hear a loud, annoying buzz that lets everyone in your area know you just went over the line. You get zero points for that throw, which can really smart, especially if you got a strike (strikes don't count when you foul).

To stop fouling, you need to change your foul line behavior. If your feet feel out of control when you bowl, check the bottoms of your shoes for excess powder or dirt and make sure you remove any debris. If they're house shoes, consider switching to a new pair and let the center know you're exchanging the shoes because they're too slippery. The center's staff will know which shoes have soles that are less worn down and therefore not as slippery.

If your shoes aren't the reason you're fouling, the simplest change you can make is to move back a little from your starting position. Try a half-step at a time until you find where your new starting position needs to be to stop fouling.

After you find your new starting spot, watch and see whether your shot needs adjusting. For example, by starting farther back, you may need to adjust your target arrow because your break-point is different. Whatever you do, avoid taking smaller steps to stop yourself from going over the foul line, especially if you're already comfortable in your approach; taking smaller steps changes your timing and your throw.

Always do a quick check of your shoes. Turn them over and look at the bottoms to make sure they're clean before you step onto the approach, especially before you bowl in the first frame and each time you return from leaving your bowling area.

Sizing Up Your Stance

Each throw of the ball begins with your stance. You don't just grab the ball from the return, keep walking to the foul line, and take your shot. Instead, you take a moment to set yourself and your body and think about what you're going to do next. The next sections help you correct common stance problems.

Standing in the right spot

When you step up to the approach, plant your feet on the dots. Which dot you should stand on depends on several factors, including whether you throw a hook or straight ball, whether you're a left-handed or right-handed bowler, and your comfort level.

We give you the basics on where to stand in Chapter 6, but it's important to note that they're merely a starting point. If the position we suggest for you just isn't working, simply move over a board or two to the left or right. If you still can't hit your target, try changing your target arrow.

Of course, how you adjust your starting point also depends on how much oil is on the lane. All centers use oil to condition and protect the lanes, but they don't all apply that oil the same way. Sometimes there's too much oil on the sides or in the middle of the lane; other times there may not be enough oil anywhere. How much or how little oil is applied and in what pattern (see Chapter 13 for the full scoop on oil patterns) can make the ball slide this way and that, messing up what you thought was a perfect shot. Take a few practice throws, and if you're not hitting your desired pocket, adjust your starting spot.

The "right" starting spot for you is the perfect combination of dots and arrows that allows you to hit your intended target every time. Finding it requires some trial and error, so take your time and keep on trying.

Holding the ball properly

Make sure your middle and ring fingers (or fingertips, depending on which grip you're using; see Chapter 7) are in the two side-by-side holes in the bowling ball and your thumb is in the thumb hole. Your other two fingers (the pointer and the pinkie) should be flat on the ball.

Next, hold the ball wherever it feels comfortable, whether that's in front of you, down by your side, or up high near your chin. As long as you're not having any issues with your throw, keep holding the ball there. If, however, you discover that holding the ball under your chin, for example, causes you to swing the ball wildly out to the side and makes your backswing go out of control, then you should adjust where you're holding the ball.

To reserve power for your backswing, try holding the ball either a little lower or to the outside of your body.

Aligning the rest of your body

When you set yourself up for your shot, be sure to stay straight. You don't want to be tipped to one side or feel like you're off balance. Keep your head straight, looking down the lane at your target. If your head is tipped, it can throw off your shot.

To break the habit of tipping your head, ask yourself this question each time you bowl: "Is my head straight?" Pretty soon you won't even have to think about keeping your head straight.

After you're certain that your head is straight, take a mental picture of the rest of your body. Are your knees slightly bent? Are your hips under your body and not sticking too far out to the side? Are your feet facing the pins? If you can answer "yes" to all of these questions, your body is aligned, and you're ready to bowl.

Improving Your Approach

In Chapter 6, we outline how to complete the traditional four-step approach. It seems pretty simple, but several things can go wrong in those four quick steps. We review some of the more common approach problems and give you the tips you need to know to keep your feet and arms in sync and your timing solid in the sections that follow.

Fixing footwork fumbles

Good bowling involves some fancy footwork, but not the kind that makes you a dandy dancer. Rather, it's the kind that keeps you strong, balanced, and walking straight to the foul line so you can throw a great ball.

For some bowlers, the process of taking several steps, swinging the ball back, gaining momentum, and then releasing the ball all in the same motion can make them feel like they have two left feet. Some bowlers even fall and land on their backsides when they get their feet mixed up. Fortunately, footwork fumbles can be easily corrected by making a few minor adjustments. We explain how to correct feet-related problems in the next sections.

Don't forget to check the soles of your shoes before making your approach. See the earlier "Solving shoe troubles" section for pointers on what to look for when examining your soles.

Starting with the correct foot

Failing to lead off with the correct foot can cause you to wobble when you reach the foul line. If you're wondering which foot you should start your approach with, the answer depends on whether you're right-handed or left-handed. If you're a right-handed bowler, start your approach on your right foot; if you're left-handed, begin your approach with your left foot.

Walking straight while looking at the correct target

When it comes to bowling, you may *think* you're walking in a straight line from your starting spot to the foul line, but you may actually be veering to the right or to the left. To fix this, get yourself on the straight and arrow. In other words, make sure you're not looking at the pins but at your target arrow. Looking at the pins while you're bowling may throw off your approach. Stay focused on your target arrow because it's pointing you in the right direction. (See Chapter 10 for help figuring out which arrow to look at.)

The target arrow for your strike ball might be different than the one for your spare. The arrow you use as your target depends on which spare you leave. Either way, you'll still need to hit that mark in order to knock down your pins.

Some bowlers suffer from balance problems that make walking in a straight line difficult. For them, teetering slightly to one side or another may be perfectly natural. If you're among this group, don't give up on bowling. Instead, just slow down your walk to the line and focus on hitting your target.

Bettering your backswing

Swinging a bowling ball down and back seems easy, but if your arm goes too far out to the side or too far behind your back, your ball will end up in a different part of the lane than you intended it to go. The goal is to keep your arm straight along the side of your body so that it's still straight when you release the ball. The following sections offer easy backswing fixes that can improve your bowling.

To get the hang of the correct backswing motion, swing your ball (or a gallon jug filled with water) back and forth in a controlled motion while standing in front of a mirror. Simply pay attention to how your arm moves. The more you practice, the more strength and control you'll build up.

Holding the ball at your side

If you're holding the ball in front of your body, your problems may be caused by swinging the ball too far out to the side when you push off. To keep your backswing under control, start your approach with the ball by your side instead, about hip or upper thigh level, and make sure to keep your elbow pressed against your body.

By starting your approach with the ball to your side rather than in front of your body, you're giving yourself better control.

Preventing the ball from hitting your leg

Okay, okay, we admit it. Even we hit our legs every now and then on our backswings. After all, it's easy to do. During your backswing, the ball is only inches away from your leg, so it's only normal that occasionally you'll cut it too close and bang your leg. When you do, you're almost guaranteed to be left with a bad frame and a possible black-and-blue mark for your troubles.

To stop this problem from happening in the future, you need to get your wild backswing under control. If you start your approach with the ball in front of you and you find yourself hitting your leg more than occasionally, start with the ball down by your side instead. Doing so gives you more control over your swing and reduces the chances that you'll smack your leg.

The best way to clear your hips and have a lesser chance of hitting your leg with the ball, whether you hold it in front of your body or to the side, is to clear your nonsliding leg. Finish with the nonsliding leg behind you and to the opposite side of your throwing arm while maintaining your balance. (So if you're a righty, put your right leg back and off to the left; if you're a lefty, put your left leg back and off to the right.)

Tweaking your timing

Proper timing is the key to a successful four-step approach. As you take your first step, your arm (and consequently the ball) should be in motion. Each step after that brings the ball closer to the point where you can let it go. If your timing is off — meaning you're moving too slowly or too quickly with either your feet or the ball — so are your backswing, release, and overall shot. Practice your timing by counting the steps so your backswing keeps in perfect pace with your steps. Check out the photos in Chapter 6 to get a better idea of where your ball should be in relation to your feet as you're making your approach.

Recognizing Release Problems

To hit your desired pocket, you need to release the ball at just the right spot on the lane. That perfect spot is as the ball passes your ankles, about 3 or 4 inches beyond the foul line. Sounds easy enough, but when you're just starting out as a bowler, you may have trouble letting the ball go at the right time. The sections that follow reveal how to correct any problems you may have with releasing the ball.

Be careful to always lay the ball down on the lane; don't drop or loft it.

For early releasers

Sometimes you're so eager to bowl that in your excitement you release the ball too early; other times the ball just slips right out of your hand (you can see an example of an early release in Figure 8-1). If you're releasing too soon, the ball will drop behind your body, not down by your feet. Because the ball's speed and power rely on an effective arm swing, an early release reduces the amount of speed and rotation you can get on the ball.

Figure 8-1:
This bowler is releasing the ball too early.

How can you make sure you're releasing the ball at just the right spot? Well, if you feel like the ball is dropping out of your hand, go ahead and check

- ✔ **The fit:** Are the holes too big for your fingers? Maybe you just lost some weight and your fingers got a bit skinnier, making it harder to hold the ball. Time for a checkup with the pro shop.

  If the finger holes feel slightly too big, try inserting tape into the thumb hole or using rosin, which removes all moisture and leaves your hands dry so you can secure your grip. *Note:* If you're using a house ball, please don't insert tape into the thumb hole; try to find a ball with a better fit instead.

✔ **The weight:** Even though the 10-percent guideline (see the earlier "Correcting the bowling ball blues" section) says that a 16-pound ball is the perfect weight for a 160-pound person, that same person just may not have the arm strength to throw that heavy of a ball. Always use a ball that's light enough that you can throw it comfortably.

✔ **The holes:** Powder dust can fly and get onto the ball and into the holes, making them slippery. Check that the holes are clean of powder and other debris before you begin your approach.

If you're consciously letting the ball go before it has reached your ankle, check your timing. If your feet are going too slowly, your backswing may start too early. As a result, you'll release the ball before your feet have caught up. See the "Tweaking your timing" section earlier in this chapter for help fixing timing problems.

For late releasers

With a late release (like the one pictured in Figure 8-2), you're either reaching out onto the lane before you let go of the ball or holding onto the ball for so long that you're lofting it into the air. Holding the ball too long also means you have too much time to rotate the ball and create your spin. As a result, your hand may end up on top of the ball rather than in the handshake position. Your entire hook shot will be thrown off. Releasing the ball too late may also result in pulling the ball across your body, which changes the direction of your hook.

Never loft the ball on purpose. Doing so damages the lanes.

Varying your distance to the foul line

Occasionally bowlers ask us whether it's wrong to release the ball farther back from the foul line and whether their average will climb if they move up and release the ball closer to it. Your score won't necessarily change simply because you move closer to the foul line. If your throw feels natural to you, then you don't need to change your approach. We know bowlers with a 210 average who throw a foot back from the foul line. If you're throwing from a distance that feels comfortable and works for you, then continue doing what you're doing and don't worry about what other bowlers are saying.

However, if you want to move closer to the line, give it a try. You can do so by simply moving your starting position up a little. Of course, you may need to make some minor adjustments after you start bowling from your new spot, but don't worry about changing your form or how many steps you take just yet.

Figure 8-2:
Don't be
afraid to let
the ball go.
Holding onto
it can lead
to lofting.

Here are a few adjustments you can make to ensure you're releasing the ball a little earlier:

- ✔ **Rethink your grip.** If you're a hook bowler and you're using a conventional grip (the grip that goes to your middle knuckle on your fingers), that grip may be causing you to hold the ball too long. A fingertip grip (which goes up to your first knuckle) encourages a slightly earlier release because your fingers don't have as far to go to slide out of the ball.

- ✔ **Check your timing.** Your arm swing should match the speed of your footsteps. If your arm is reaching out before your last step, your release will be late. Make sure your timing is right so you're releasing the ball at the same time that your feet are at the foul line. Refer to the earlier "Tweaking your timing" section for suggestions on how to sync up your arm and feet movements.

- ✔ **Check your hand position.** If you throw a hook and your hand is coming over the top of the ball when you release it, then you're holding the ball too long. You should release the ball when you're in the handshake position: thumb pointed up and palm facing the interior of the lane.

- ✔ **Relax and don't overthink.** Second-guessing your shot causes you to either hold the ball too long or release it too early. Take it easy and try not to think about your shot too much. Just get up on the approach, set yourself, focus on your target arrow, and throw. The more relaxed you are, the smoother your release will be.

Teaching a child to let go of the ball

When children start out bowling, they often hold the ball too long. When they finally release the ball, it bounces (sometimes into other lanes). So how do you help your son or daughter get the hang of letting go earlier? First things first: Make sure he or she is using a ball that's the right weight. When a child is able to throw a ball all the way to another lane, the ball is probably too light. Consider moving your child up to a heavier one. For example, if your little gal is lofting a 6-pound ball, she may be ready for an 8-pound ball.

Kids also have a tendency to run to the foul line and fling the ball. Have your child work on slowing down her approach, bending down during the release, and laying the ball down closer to the lane. To help a child slow down her approach, show her the correct timing and have her count her steps out loud at a slower pace.

Assessing Your Throw

Small movements that you execute during your throw determine how your ball moves down the lane. For instance, if you throw a hook ball, over- or under-rotating your wrist can cause your ball to head away from the pocket. If you throw a straight ball, moving your wrist from the straight position can cause a straight throw to hook and, again, miss the pocket. With the information in the following sections, you can assess your throw to get an idea of why your ball isn't hitting the pocket and then fix the problem.

Assessing your throw is a little harder to do on your own because you can't see yourself bowl. Have a friend or bowling coach videotape you or point out anything you're doing incorrectly.

Sending your ball spinning (or not)

For a hook to do its job, the ball needs to have enough spin. You put spin on your ball by rotating your hand. This movement generates revolutions that cause the ball to break at a certain point on the lane and hook right into your desired pocket, creating the pin action needed for a strike or spare. We cover hook shots in great detail in Chapter 9, so flip forward a few pages to find out how to increase or decrease the amount of spin on your ball.

If you're a straight bowler, however, spin is the last thing you want. If you find that you're twisting your wrist as you release the ball, change your starting hand position. Begin by placing your hand in the correct position for throwing a straight ball: palm up, facing the ceiling. Then turn your wrist just a hair clockwise. This way, as you release the ball, you may find your hand back in the correct starting — and releasing — position.

Throwing the ball with consistent force and speed

We can't tell you what the right speed is for you, but you do need to hit the pins at such a speed and with such force that all the pins fall down (if you want to score well, that is). If you're hitting the pins too softly, boost the power of the ball by pushing through your backswing a little harder or increasing your backswing a bit. Hitting the pins with too much force? Decrease your power by reducing your backswing slightly or moving the starting position of your ball down and back a tad.

If you throw too hard, your momentum may cause you to tip to one side. The solution? Don't overthrow. Throw a steady shot with enough power to knock down the pins and make sure you aren't dropping your shoulder (if you do, you can send your entire approach off balance).

Being consistent with your speed is more difficult. As you bowl, your arm is bound to tire, so your ball speed may decrease. To increase the speed of the ball, try walking to the foul line a little faster, increasing the size of your backswing, or putting a little more power on the ball. If you find that you need to slow down the ball's speed, you can try walking more slowly to the foul line during your approach, or you can try to make your backswing a little smaller.

Following through for strong throws

If you want to bowl well, you have to see your throws through all the way to the end. A throw isn't complete until your hand comes up after the ball has been released. If you're releasing the ball at your ankle and that's where your hand stays after you let go of the ball, you're not following through.

When you release the ball, your arm should be straight, whether you're throwing a hook or a straight ball. If your arm goes across your body on the follow-through, that means your backswing is probably out of control. To fix this problem, head to the earlier "Bettering your backswing" section.

Checking for Problems, Point by Point

Sometimes you're not quite sure what you're doing wrong, but you know you're not bowling well because your score isn't going up and you're not throwing strikes and picking up spares. To figure it out, you need to break down every aspect of your game, from your equipment to your throw. Following is a handy ten-point checklist you can use to help identify areas where you may be experiencing problems:

- ✔ **Equipment:** Without the right equipment, your game isn't going to be spot on.

- ✔ **Starting spot:** If you're starting in the wrong spot, you're off on the wrong foot.

- ✔ **Hand position:** Whether you're throwing a hook or a straight ball, the wrong hand position can send your ball down the wrong part of the lane.

- ✔ **Approach:** If your approach isn't clean, your entire shot will be off.

- ✔ **Timing:** In bowling, your steps should be timed to your swing. If the timing is off, your game will suffer.

- ✔ **Ball speed:** If your ball heads down the lane at the wrong speed, you're never going to knock down all the pins.

- ✔ **Target on the lane:** When you don't aim for the arrows on the lane, you can't hit your ultimate target — the pins.

- ✔ **Releasing the ball:** If you let go of the ball too early or too late, you probably won't hit the pocket.

- ✔ **Follow-through:** When you don't follow through, you're basically stopping short. Always finish your throw.

- ✔ **Pin action:** Bowling is about angles, force, and speed. Find the right combination of all three, and you get perfect pin action that results in a strike.

To prevent these common problems from occurring, you need to focus on getting your mechanics down and making sure you repeat a great form each time you bowl. After you master the proper form, be sure to bowl like that each time. Naturally, you'll have some adjustments to make when you have spares to pick up or lane oil is affecting your shot, but the basics remain the same: Your start, throw, and follow-through should all be done in one fluid motion.

If you're really interested in improving your bowling, you need to practice. Set aside some regular practice time at your local bowling center, either with a friend or by yourself. Focus on your form, not your score, and stay committed to becoming a better bowler.

Part III

Time to Get Rolling: Making Your Shot

The 5th Wave   By Rich Tennant

@RICHTENNANT

"I'm never sure if he's concentrating on his shot
or just loves smelling his bowling ball."

In this part . . .

If you throw a hook shot, here's a closer look at what you can do to perfect it. Also, because success in bowling means throwing strikes and picking up spares, this part shows you what you need to know to get as many of these as you can. Prepare to find out what it means to throw a strike ball into the pocket and why it's just as important to pick up those spares.

Speaking of spares, no bowling how-to book would be complete without sharing how to deal with the worst spares of all: splits. This part explains how to try and avoid a bad case of the splits and includes tips on converting them when you inevitably face one, including the downright-near-impossible 7-10 split.

Chapter 9

Everything You Ever Wanted to Know about Hook Shots

In This Chapter

▶ Understanding the hook shot and your personal throwing style

▶ Having the right equipment to throw a hook

▶ Knowing what to do, from rotating your hand to following through

▶ Adjusting your hook shot to make it better and more consistent

*B*eing able to throw a hook shot makes even a beginning bowler look like a pro. Bowlers who can throw hooks also tend to have higher scores and averages than those who can't. Yes, mastering the hook shot takes some skill (and a great deal of patience), but it's not impossible, especially with the tools we give you in this chapter. We show you exactly what you need to do to throw a perfect hook. Get ready to understand how to move your arm, wrist, and hand in perfect unison in order to make your ball hook; what to do when the ball's just not hooking the way you want it to; and more.

Getting Acquainted with the Hook Shot and Your Form

Throwing a hook is the best way to increase your chances of hitting the pocket at the right angle so you can score a strike. When you throw a hook, the ball first rolls toward the outer part of the lane (that's to the right if you're right-handed and to the left if you're left-handed), but then it curves, or hooks, into the pocket (we cover the pocket in detail in Chapter 10). Figures 9-1 and 9-2 show you the path of a hook shot thrown by a righty and a lefty.

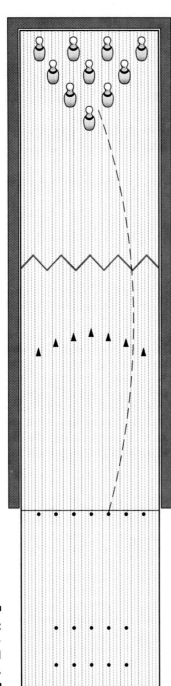

Figure 9-1:
A right-
handed
hook shot.

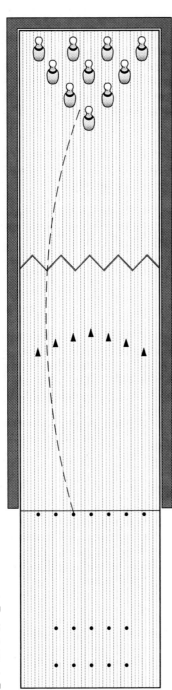

Figure 9-2:
A left-
handed
hook shot.

If you've been to your local bowling center and thrown a few practice shots, you may already know whether your natural form is a straight ball or a hook. If throwing a hook feels comfortable and comes naturally to you, you're in luck. All you have to do is practice and refine your technique so that the ball gets into the pocket at the right angle and speed. If you don't naturally throw a hook, forcing yourself to throw one may feel awkward at first, but if you'd rather throw a hook than a straight ball, you can master hook shots with practice.

To figure out your natural form, try throwing a straight ball and a hook shot during practice sessions (we give you the how-to for both in Chapter 5). The way that feels most comfortable for you is your natural form.

If you're brand-new to bowling and don't yet have a set way of throwing the ball, practice throwing a hook. Getting used to throwing a hook early on makes the process of growing as a bowler much easier.

Creating a Hook

Although it's an impressive throw that gets results more often than not, a hook isn't a mystical part of the sport reserved only for the elite. Anyone can throw a hook, including you. That's because creating a hook is really just a matter of combining the right ball with the right grip, adding in a little hand and wrist rotation and leg power, and following through on your release.

In the next sections, we fill you in on what you absolutely have to have for a successful hook and walk you through the process of throwing one.

Hook shot must-haves

You can't throw a solid hook without the right bowling ball. Having the right grip on the ball is also important because your grip is what helps you put spin on the ball. If done properly, the spin you put on the ball is what hooks it into your desired pocket. We fill you in on the ball and the grip that are best for throwing a hook in the sections that follow.

The right ball

The perfect bowling ball for a hook shot is one that has a weight block inside. The bigger the weight block, the more spin you can put on the ball. Bigger weight blocks can be found in bowling balls with urethane and reactive resin coverstocks, both of which cause friction on the lane (the more friction, the more the ball hooks). You can try to throw a hook using a house ball, but the coverstocks of most house balls are plastic, which doesn't hook well (if at all). You may be able to find a gem among the racks — a house ball with a urethane coverstock — but that's pretty rare (for more information on bowling balls, weight blocks, and coverstocks, see Chapter 4).

If you're planning to buy your own ball, keep in mind that bowling balls with reactive resin coverstocks are pricier than those with urethane coverstocks, so starting with a urethane ball is definitely easier on the wallet. You can always invest in a reactive resin ball as you progress. If buying your own bowling ball is out of your budget, try practicing on a plastic ball and do what you can to make it hook. After you see how it reacts, you can find the right target arrow and starting spot to accommodate that ball (we cover these technical details in the later "The how-to" section).

The right grip

Having the right grip is extremely important for throwing a hook. Of the two main grips — *conventional,* which is where you put your middle and ring fingers as well as your thumb in the ball up to the second knuckle, and *fingertip,* which is where you only insert your fingers up to the first knuckle (but your thumb still goes in to the second knuckle) — the fingertip grip allows you to create more spin on the ball.

By inserting only the tips of your fingers, your fingers slide out of the ball faster. This is why most advanced bowlers who throw a hook shot use a fingertip grip.

The how-to

The following sections walk you through the actions you take when throwing a hook in the hopes of getting a strike. (If you want to know how to adjust your hook for picking up spares, head to Chapter 11.) The last section then puts it all together for you in a nice, neat package.

Rotating your hand

The secret to a successful hook is how you spin the ball. The more spin you give the ball, the more it hooks. So how do you get spin? By rotating your hand, wrist, and fingers in unison before releasing the ball onto the lane.

Your bowling hand should start out underneath the ball, and your wrist should be straight in order to support it. Push the ball out and then start to swing it back. As your arm begins to come forward out of your backswing, turn your hand and wrist so that the back of your hand (not the palm side) is turning toward the outside of your body. (For a right-handed bowler, this means you're turning the ball in a counterclockwise position; for a left-handed bowler, turn the ball in a clockwise position. Either way, your hand rotation stops when you release the ball down near your ankle.) Follow through on your throw and keep your hand in the handshake position after you let go of the ball.

Don't forget about your fingers for the sake of focusing on your hand rotation; their positioning is important too. When you start your approach, your thumb is in the bowling ball, but it's your fingertips that give the ball its hook. During your throw, your thumb should come out of the ball first so your fingers can rotate the ball and release it.

Figure 9-3 shows what a hook shot looks like for a right-handed bowler; Figure 9-4 shows the same thing for a left-handed bowler. Pay special attention to the positioning of the bowler's hand in whichever photo applies to you.

Figure 9-3: The direction the wrist rotates for a right-handed hook shot.

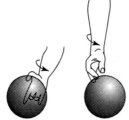

Figure 9-4: The direction the wrist rotates for a left-handed hook shot.

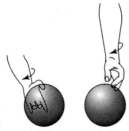

You can control the amount of spin you put on the ball by moving the starting position of your hand. If you want the ball to hook more, you can *crank* it — which means starting with your hand in the starting position and then turning it just a little further toward the inside of your body (as shown in Figure 9-5). By turning your hand this way, you give yourself more space to create spin on the ball during your throw. If you want the ball to hook less, do the opposite —

simply move the starting position of your hand and wrist slightly toward the outside of your body (as shown in Figure 9-6). Doing so limits how much room you have left to create spin on the ball; it therefore hooks less.

Figure 9-5:
Start with
your hand
slightly to
the inside
for more of
a hook.

Figure 9-6:
Start with
your hand
slightly to
the outside
for less of
a hook.

Whatever you do, never rotate your hand over the top of the ball (see Figure 9-7). Many beginners who're trying to learn how to throw a hook make this common mistake. They think that over-rotating the ball gives them more of a hook, but in reality, over-rotating just isn't as effective as making sure your hand is always left in the handshake position at the end of your throw.

Figure 9-7:
Never rotate
your hand
over the top
of the ball.

Eyeing the target

The arrows on the lane are your target, not the pins. Which arrow you look at depends on your individual hook (we suggest target arrows for a hook strike shot in Chapter 10). By keeping your eyes on the target arrow, you have a much better chance of creating the right breakpoint (see the later "Improving Your Hook" section for more on this).

Using your legs for power and balance

Your legs help give your body momentum on your approach, which explains why your leg power affects the speed and power of your ball. The faster you walk through your approach, the more ball speed you generate. However, you don't want to run. Instead, you want to generate the right amount of speed on the ball to hit your target and, ultimately, your pocket.

Your legs are also key to maintaining your balance on the approach. If you're off balance when you throw, your entire throw will be off. More importantly, your hook won't break when and where you want it to (which usually means no strike).

When you release the ball, be sure your front leg is bent. Doing so brings you closer to the lane for a smoother release. Also, try to avoid overextending the leg that's going behind you so you don't lose your balance.

If you have knee or back problems, don't risk possible injury by bending your knees. Keep your legs in a naturally comfortable position and focus on making your approach, arm swing, release, and follow-through as good as they can be.

Following through

One of the easiest things you can do to help your hook succeed is to make sure you follow through. To do this, release the ball down by your ankle and then continue the motion of your arm (how high you go depends on your own comfort level), making sure to keep your hand in the handshake position. If you find that your arm is still down by your ankle even after your release, you're not following through.

Putting it all together

Are you ready to assume your stance, make your approach, and throw a great hook shot? We hope so! Here's how all the steps we cover earlier in this chapter come together:

1. **Grab the right ball for you and begin your approach.**

2. **When the ball is coming down from your backswing, start to turn your bowling hand and wrist to create spin on the ball.**

3. **Release the ball down by your ankle, keeping your hand in a hand-shake position.**

4. **Follow through with your arm, keeping your hand in the handshake position and maintaining your balance.**

Reverting to a reverse hook

If a regular hook just isn't working out for you, you may want to try throwing a reverse hook, also called a *backup ball*. A *reverse hook* is a hook that goes in the opposite direction. For example, when a right-handed bowler throws a hook shot, it hooks out to the right and then turns left to enter the pocket. A reverse hook for a right-handed bowler would hook out to the left and then hook right to enter the pocket. You can achieve a reverse hook by turning your hand in the opposite direction. So if you're a right-handed bowler, you'd rotate your hand clockwise; if you're a lefty, you'd turn your hand counterclockwise. Everything else that goes into a hook shot — the ball, the grip, and the follow-through — remains the same.

Note: If you're comfortable throwing a reverse hook and you're successfully hitting the pocket, don't worry about forcing your body to master the traditional hook shot. Just go with what feels best and is giving you the results you want.

Improving Your Hook

Keeping your hook under control is essential if you want to bowl well. If you consistently throw too hard, you're inevitably going to tire out by the middle of the game, causing your hook to suffer even more. The idea behind a great hook is to be steady and consistent. If your ball hooks too much on some days and not enough on others, you need to evaluate how you're throwing it so you can achieve better consistency.

To evaluate your throw, watch what your ball does after you release it. The hook shot is like the Goldilocks of bowling. The ball can't hook too much, and it can't hook too little; it needs to hook "just right." A ball that hooks too little won't make the pocket; in most cases, it'll shoot right past your pocket and head to the back of the pins. A ball that hooks too much will turn or break too early, miss the pocket, and head to the opposite side of the pins.

When your ball isn't hooking the way you want it to, you need to adjust your throw. To know what to adjust, ask yourself the following questions (if you can't answer them, ask a bowling coach, pro shop owner, or more experienced bowler to watch you and give you some feedback):

  ✔ **Am I starting on the correct spot?** Use the dots on the lane to help you figure out where to stand when you begin your approach. We guide you to the right starting spot in Chapter 6. Make sure you stand on that spot each time you bowl your strike shot, unless of course the lane conditions require you to change it. In that case, make sure you note the change so you know where to move when the lanes are dry or overly oily.

✔ **Is the ball coming off of my hand at the right time?** If you notice that your timing is off and the ball is rolling off of your hand too early or too late, you may need a quick refresher on the basics of the hook shot. After all, a proper release is essential for a good hook.

✔ **Is the ball hitting my targets?** You have two targets to hit — the arrow (or arrows) on the lane that you're aiming for and the pocket. Are you hitting both targets, just one, or neither of them?

✔ **Is the ball speed too fast or too slow?** Does the ball have enough speed to make it down the lane, or is it petering out early? Are you giving the ball enough time to hook, or are you throwing a bomb down the lane that's slicing through the pins?

✔ **Where's my breakpoint?** The *breakpoint* is the spot on the lane where your hook ball starts to change direction on the lane after you throw it. For example, in Figure 9-8, the bowler releases the ball and it looks as if it's headed straight for the gutter, but then it suddenly hooks toward the pocket. That spot where the ball changed its direction and headed toward the pocket is that bowler's breakpoint. Your breakpoint will be different from any other bowler's.

Ask yourself this question: Is my ball breaking toward the pocket at the right time, too late, or too early? If your ball breaks too early or too late, you're missing your pocket. Determine the perfect breakpoint for your hook shot by taking a few practice throws and noticing where the ball changes direction. You may need to move your starting position a little to the left or the right or change target arrows until you find the perfect spot that matches up with your breakpoint. How will you know? Your ball will hit the pocket almost every time.

If you need to make adjustments to your hook, try them out during practice rather than during an actual game. This way you can get more comfortable with them and focus on how you're throwing without having to worry about your score. However, if you're already in the middle of a game and need to make adjustments, make them as soon as you realize there's a problem so you can still salvage your score.

What works for your friend or fellow bowler may not work for you. Keep making adjustments until you can throw a hook that feels comfortable for your type of throw and goes where you need it to.

In the next sections, we help you make adjustments to a hook shot that's hooking a little too much and one that's not hooking nearly enough. We also give you the inside scoop on how to read the lanes so you can make the proper adjustments.

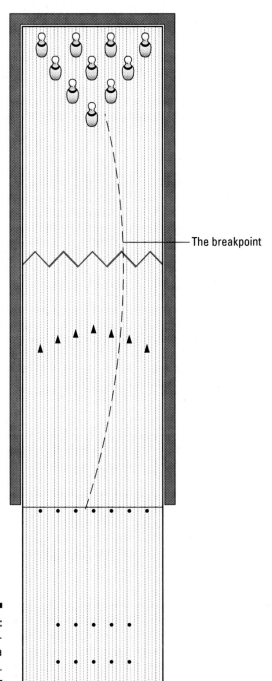

The breakpoint

Figure 9-8:
The break-
point of a
hook ball.

Fixing a throw that's hooking too much

If your ball is hooking a little too much (like the ones in Figures 9-9 and 9-10), the culprit could be anything from poor hand or foot positioning to an inaccurate target or a slow throw. We describe adjustments you can make for each of these scenarios in the sections that follow. (**Note:** You may need to experiment with a combination of these adjustments before you find what works for you.)

Change your hand position

Poor hand position may be one reason why your ball has more spin on it than intended. For example, your hand may be turned too far to the inside of your body. Always make sure your hand is positioned directly beneath the ball to start. To reduce spin, and therefore how much the ball hooks, turn your hand to the outside of your body ever so slightly (go counterclockwise if you're a righty and clockwise if you're a lefty).

Switch your starting position

Bowling is a game of physics and angles. The ball must enter the pocket at the right angle with the right amount of speed and power to give you a strike. If the ball isn't hitting the pocket at the proper angle even when you stand in the starting position that we recommend in Chapter 6, consider moving your feet a board or two to the left if you're a right-handed bowler or to the right if you're a left-handed bowler and see whether that helps.

Pick a different target

You set your eyes on the target arrow, but maybe your ball is hooking too much and you keep missing the pocket. When your ball hooks too much, you miss the pocket (and then, unfortunately, you miss the strike).

The good thing about bowling is that you aren't committed to a target or a starting spot. If one target isn't quite working for you, move your target arrow over one to the right if you're a right-handed bowler or to the left if you're a left-handed bowler. If that doesn't work, keep moving your target over one by one until you find the target that helps you nail your hook shot.

Speed things up a little

One reason why a ball hooks too early is that it's moving too slowly and losing steam before it reaches the pocket. If your ball is hooking much sooner than you want it to, try speeding it up a little. To add speed to your throw, walk a little faster to the line, increase your backswing a bit, or put just a tiny bit more power on the ball.

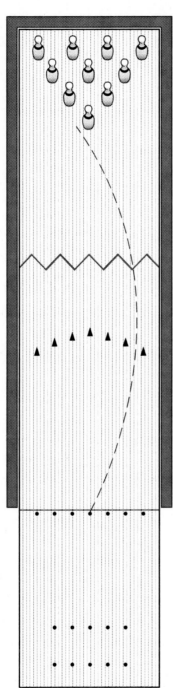

Figure 9-9:
This right-
handed
throw is
hooking
too much.

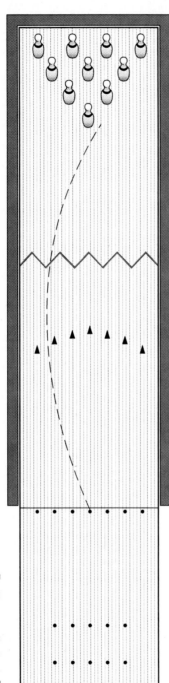

Figure 9-10:
This left-
handed
throw has
too much
of a hook.

Correcting your breakpoint

If your throw hooks too much, the ball may be breaking too early. Move your feet to a new starting position and change your target arrow until you find the right combination to fix your breakpoint.

Pumping up a throw that isn't hooking enough

A ball can hook a little bit (as in Figures 9-11 and 9-12) and still miss the pocket for a number of reasons, including a lack of spin or too much speed. In the next sections, we offer adjustments you can make to add more hook to your hook shot. (*Note:* You may need to try a combination of these adjustments to perfect your hook.)

Crank 'er up

If your ball isn't hooking enough, you may need to give it some more spin. First things first: Make sure your hand position is correct. If your hand starts too far to the outside of the ball, you aren't going to have enough room to create enough spin.

However, if correcting your hand position doesn't help, try using the crank hand position, which gives you a little more space to add spin to the ball. To crank the ball, place your bowling hand directly beneath the ball with your wrist straight. Then turn your hand toward the inside of your body a little, almost like you're twisting your wrist. Turn it in a clockwise position if you're right-handed and a counterclockwise position if you're left-handed (see Figures 9-5 and 9-6 earlier in this chapter for an example of the crank position).

Move over

Correcting your hook may just take a little shuffle of your feet. Move over a board or two in the same direction of your bowling hand (so go left if you're a lefty and right if you're a righty). Keep moving over a board at a time until you find the foot position that works for you.

Reconsider your target

Try a new target arrow if your ball isn't hooking enough. It's going to take some experimenting before you can know for sure which arrow works for your throw, but eventually you'll find the right one.

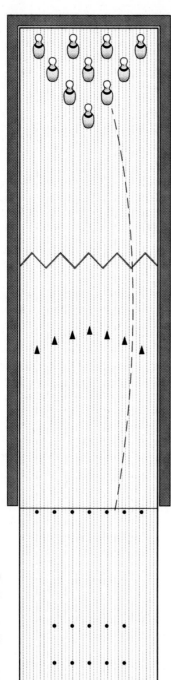

Figure 9-11:
This right-
handed
throw isn't
hooking
enough.

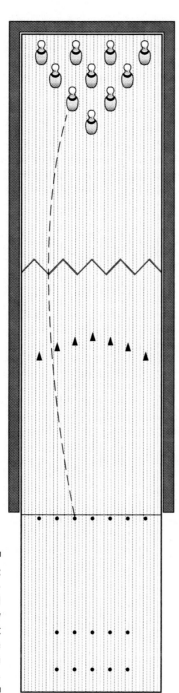

Figure 9-12:
This left-
handed
throw
doesn't
have
enough
hook.

Slow the ball down

If the ball is sailing clear past the pocket without hooking at all, you may be throwing it too hard. Slow your throw down just a little by either reducing your backswing or slowing your steps in order to give your ball more time to hook on the lane.

Fixing a bad breakpoint

If your throw doesn't hook enough, the ball may be breaking too late. To solve this issue, you first need to adjust your starting spot by moving to the right if you're a right-handed bowler and to the left if you're a left-handed bowler. If that doesn't work, try decreasing the speed of your throw a little by carrying the ball a tad lower to reduce your backswing.

Understanding what the lanes are telling you

Believe it or not, the condition of a lane can affect your hook. That's because some lanes are oilier and some are drier; both conditions send the ball in a slightly different direction than where you intended it to go. So just when you think you have your hook shot down, you may bowl on a lane that's too dry or has a new oil pattern that you're not used to, which means you have to adjust your shot.

Depending on whether your ball is hooking too much or too little, make your adjustments based on the recommendations we share in the earlier "Fixing a throw that's hooking too much" or "Pumping up a throw that isn't hooking enough" sections. Just be careful not to overdo it — try our pointers one at a time until you find the right combination.

Lanes often have more oil in the center than on the sides. More oil means less hook, so if your ball is hooking too much, aim for a target that's closer to the middle of the lane so the extra oil can help reduce your hook. On the other hand, if your ball isn't hooking enough, aim for a target that's closer to the outside of the lane, away from the oil.

Chapter 10

Knocking 'Em All Down: The Secrets to Bowling Strikes

In This Chapter

▶ Finding the strike pocket

▶ Throwing a great strike ball

▶ Improving your chances of getting a strike (almost) every time

▶ Problem-solving when good shots don't work

Strikes are like the jackpots of bowling, especially if you're good enough (or lucky enough) to knock down all ten pins in every frame and achieve the sport's Holy Grail — a perfect 300 game. Of course, when you're bowling for fun, and especially as a beginner, you're happy just to be knocking down any pins, much less bowling strikes!

Strikes are a great reason to high-five your bowling buddies, but they're also the best way to give your score a huge boost. Strikes are worth a full 10 points plus the points for your next two throws (see Chapter 2 for the full scoop on scoring). Just one strike can quickly improve your score.

In this chapter, we explain how to throw the perfect strike ball, taking into account whether you tend to hook the ball or throw it straight. We also share tips on how to tweak your approach if strikes just aren't happening for you.

The Key to Strikes: Hitting the Pocket

Many beginners feel that the best way to get a strike is to throw the ball as hard as they can right down the middle of the lane, aiming straight for the headpin. Unfortunately, hitting the headpin head on is more likely to split the pins down the middle — leaving you with a difficult spare to make — than give you a strike.

The best way to consistently throw strikes is to throw the ball into the *pocket* — the area between the 1 pin and the 2 pin if you're a lefty or between the 1 pin and the 3 pin if you're a righty. Check out Figure 10-1 to see exactly which pocket you should be aiming for.

Getting strikes in bowling is all about physics and chain reactions. Sure, that sounds intimidating, but all you need to know is that hitting the pins with the ball creates a chain reaction where one pin falls, then the next one falls, and so on. The angle that the ball hits the pins determines the direction in which the pins fall.

If you were to slow down a strike for a right-handed hook bowler and take a closer look, the chain reaction of the pins might go something like this: The ball first hits the 1-3 pocket. The 1 and 3 pins fall, creating a chain reaction with the headpin knocking down the 2, 4, and 7 pins and the 3 pin toppling into the 6 pin, which takes out the 10 pin. Of course, the bowling ball does part of the work too. It hits the 1 and 3 pins and continues to roll into the 5 pin before hitting the 8 pin and then taking out the 9 pin. By the time the ball reaches the back of the pin deck, all the pins have fallen, resulting in a strike.

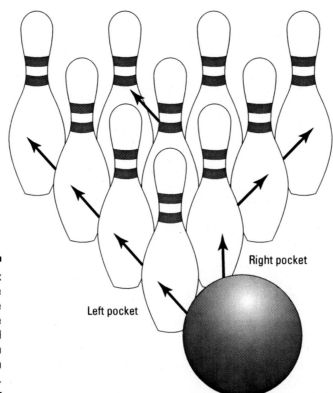

Right pocket

Left pocket

Figure 10-1:
When the ball hits the pocket, the pins fall down in a chain reaction.

How to Throw a Strike

Sending your bowling ball into the pocket with the right combination of speed and strength should result in a strike. How you get the ball to the pocket depends on several factors:

- ✔ Do you throw a straight or hook ball?
- ✔ How much hook does your ball have?
- ✔ Are you a righty or a lefty?
- ✔ How hard do you throw the ball?

In the following sections, we break down the steps for throwing strikes by hand (right or left) and type of throw (straight or hook), so skip to the section that describes you. If you're not sure which type of throw you have, head to Chapter 5; there we guide you in determining your bowling form.

Note: What we tell you in the following sections are merely guidelines. Try them out by taking a few practice throws and see how they work for you. If you don't hit the pocket, move your starting position over a little to the left or a little to the right and try again. Still not working? Move a little more or change your target arrow (or do both) and then try again. Keep going with this trial-and-error process until you find the starting spot and target arrow that works for your particular throw. It's not a scientific method, but it does work.

You don't need to throw your strike ball too hard or too fast to score a strike. Even bowlers who roll a slower ball often strike when they hit the pocket.

Before you begin your approach (we walk you through the traditional four-step approach in Chapter 6), take a second to think about your shot. Most importantly, picture yourself throwing a strike.

The Brooklyn strike

A *Brooklyn strike* is when you cross your shot over the middle and hit the opposite pocket. If you want to try throwing one, follow the steps listed in the "If you're a right-handed straight bowler" or "If you're a left-handed straight bowler" sections; just change your starting position. Righties should move a few boards to the right, and left-handed bowlers should move to the left a couple boards.

If you're a right-handed straight bowler

If you're a righty who throws a straight ball:

1. **Start your throw by standing with your left foot on the seventh board from the right side of the lane.**

2. **Focus your eyes on the second arrow on the right side of the lane.**

3. **Make your four-step approach, being careful to keep your eyes between the arrows and not the pins.**

   Flip to Chapter 6 for pointers on making your approach.

4. **With your wrist straight and your hand underneath the ball, release the ball by letting it roll off of your fingers.**

5. **Follow through on your approach and watch the ball roll down the lane and knock down all the pins.**

   If you rolled the ball correctly, it should sail over the second arrow and head straight to the 1-3 pocket (see Figure 10-2).

If you're a left-handed straight bowler

No big surprise here, but left-handed straight bowlers prepare for throwing a strike by standing on the left side of the approach.

1. **Stand with your right foot on the seventh board from the left side of the lane.**

2. **Aim for the second arrow on the left side of the lane.**

3. **Make your four-step approach, keeping your eyes between the arrows and not on the pins.**

   Refer to Chapter 6 for tips on making your approach.

4. **With your wrist straight and your hand underneath the ball, release it by letting the ball roll off of your fingers.**

5. **Follow through on your approach and celebrate as you watch all ten pins topple.**

   A properly thrown straight ball will roll over the second arrow on the left side and head straight to the 1-2 pocket (see Figure 10-3).

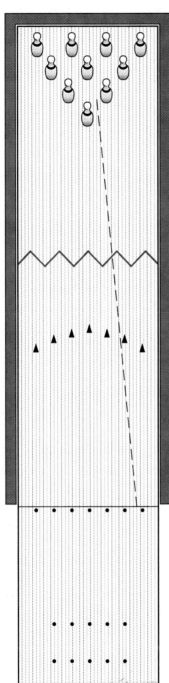

Figure 10-2:
A right-
handed
straight
bowler
hitting the
1-3 pocket.

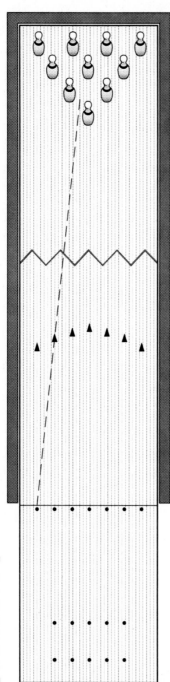

Figure 10-3:
A left-
handed
straight
bowler
hitting the
1-2 pocket.

If you're a right-handed hook bowler

If you throw a hook with your right hand, hitting the 1-3 pocket gives you the best shot at a strike. Here's how to do just that:

1. **Start with your right foot on the 25th board, counting from right to left (refer to Figure 10-4).**

   The 25th board from the right is also the third dot from the right.

2. **Keep your eyes on the second arrow from the right on the lane.**

   This is also known as the tenth board because there are arrows every five boards.

3. **Begin your approach to the foul line, focusing on that second arrow.**

   Your arm should push out and back while you're taking your steps to throw the ball; see Chapter 6 for more information on making your approach.

   Your goal is to throw the ball so it rolls directly over the second arrow, so don't look at the pins. Doing so will only throw you off.

4. **Turn your hand and wrist as the ball comes forward and release it onto the lane as it reaches your left ankle.**

   Are you in the position to shake someone's hand after you've released the ball (meaning your thumb is pointing straight up)? If so, your hand is in the correct spot, and your ball should roll over that second arrow, curve, and hit the 1-3 pocket. (Of course, whether it does this all depends on how much spin you've put on the ball as well as your power and speed.)

5. **Follow through on your approach and watch as all the pins fall down.**

If you're a left-handed hook bowler

A lefty who throws a hook should follow these steps to hit the 1-2 pocket:

1. **Place your left foot on the 25th board from the left (see Figure 10-5).**

   The 25th board from the left is also the third dot from the left.

2. **Focus your eyes on the second arrow from the left on the lane.**

3. **Start your four-step approach to the foul line, keeping your eyes glued on the arrow rather than the pins.**

   Head to Chapter 6 for the how-to on making your approach.

   Make sure you prepare to throw the ball with enough power and speed so it rolls over the second arrow and curves to hit the pins.

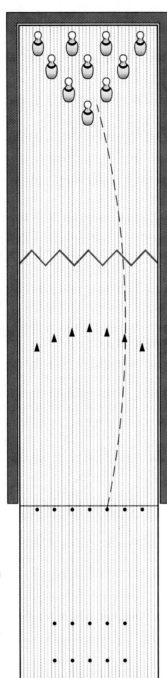

Figure 10-4:
A right-
handed
hook bowler
hitting the
1-3 pocket.

4. **As the ball comes forward, turn your hand and wrist and then release the ball onto the lane as it reaches your right ankle.**

   You know you've thrown the strike correctly when your hand is in a handshake position (meaning your thumb is sticking straight up) after you let go of the ball. The ball then rolls over that second arrow, curves, and hits the 1-2 pocket.

5. **Follow through on your approach and give yourself a pat on the back for throwing a perfect strike.**

Increasing Your Odds of Throwing a Strike

We know of bowlers who bowled a strike the first time they gave it the old college try. But if that didn't happen to you, that's okay, because there are steps you can take to increase your chances of throwing a strike. For instance, if your ball is hooking too far to one side, you may just need to adjust how you throw. Then again, you may need to increase your pin action or work on throwing the same shot time and time again. We give you the lowdown on all three tactics for increasing your odds of throwing a strike in the sections that follow.

Adjusting how you throw

Everyone bowls a little differently, so what works for one bowler may not work for you. If you notice that you're not getting strikes, you have to be able to stop and adjust how you bowl.

The following tips can help you adjust your throw:

- ✔ **Pay attention to where your ball hits the pins.** Where is it hitting the pins if not the pocket? Is it rolling too far to the left or too far to the right? Move your starting spot a few boards to the right or to the left and see whether that fixes the problem.

- ✔ **Put it on paper.** Ask a bowling coach or a member of the bowling center's staff to show you on paper what you're doing wrong and how to adjust it. This way you can see what you're doing and get an overview of where the ball is going, which gives you a better understanding of how you need to adjust your shot.

- ✔ **Watch where the ball rolls over the arrows.** Lane markings give you a precise idea of how far to move over if you're missing the mark. Depending on the hand you bowl with and whether you're a straight or hook bowler, move a little to the right or left and keep adjusting until the ball rolls exactly where you want it to.

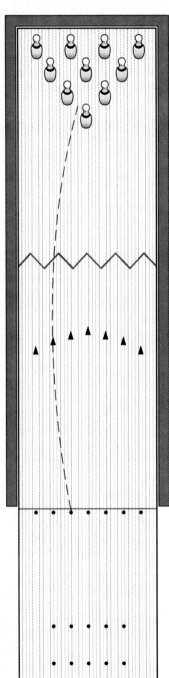

Figure 10-5:
A left-
handed
hook bowler
hitting the
1-2 pocket.

Increasing your pin action

Sometimes good pin action can overcome a shot that's a little off the mark. *Pin action* describes how the pins react to being hit by the ball, whether that's flying to the back, shooting off to the side, or spinning around and knocking the other pins down.

Some shots result in more pin action than others because they hit at different speeds and angles. You can increase your pin action by

- ✔ **Throwing the ball faster:** Just be careful not to throw the ball *too* fast. That can actually decrease your pin action. Chapter 7 tells you how to increase your speed without overdoing it.

- ✔ **Putting more spin on the ball:** Pins are like dominoes — they fall down because one pin falls into another one. The more spin, or *rotation,* your ball has, the more power your ball has when it hits the pins. (Chapter 7 also tells you how to put more spin on your ball.)

Being consistent

Consistency is the name of the game in throwing strikes. If you throw the perfect strike ball time and time again and hit your pocket, you're going to see strikes. Of course, the only way to achieve this is with practice, practice, practice.

Our advice? Head to the bowling center, get a lane, and bowl. Forget about the score. Just focus on sending the ball into the pocket and hitting your mark at the same speed each time. The more you try, the better you'll get.

Each lane is different due to oil patterns, the number of bowlers who've used the lane that day, the weather, and so on. The throw that works on one lane may need to be adapted for another lane. We explain how to adapt to different lane conditions in Chapter 13.

I Was Robbed! What to Do When You Can't Buy a Strike

Just about every bowler experiences it at one time or another — the excited rush after throwing what feels like a perfect strike ball followed by the crash back to earth when it falls short. Before you heave your bowling ball out the front door of the center, take a deep breath and remind yourself that bowling is a game of angles. If you didn't score a strike, there's a reason. It may be something you're doing, or it may have something to do with lane conditions, the weather, or your ball (and no, the problem isn't that your ball has a mind of its own).

With a little effort, you can find the reason why you're not throwing strikes and fix the problem. The following sections note some of the common causes of strikes gone bad and how you can problem-solve around them.

Looking into the lane conditions

Much like the conditions on a golf course can affect a game of golf, the condition of the bowling lane you're on affects how you bowl. Bowling lanes are treated with special oil to protect the surface from nicks and scratches, and that oil affects how your ball travels down the lane (see Chapter 13 for the full scoop on oil patterns).

How much, or how little, oil the lane has when you're bowling can determine whether you must make adjustments to your approach. In the next sections, we fill you in on how dry and freshly oiled lanes can change your game and how to deal with either type of lane so you can score strikes.

You can figure out whether your center's lanes are oiled or relatively dry by doing one of the following:

- ✔ Ask a staff member at the center when the lanes were last oiled.
- ✔ Look at your bowling ball after it comes through the ball return. The oilier it is, the more recently the lanes have been oiled (or the heavier the coat of oil that was applied earlier).

Striking on a dry lane

A dry lane can cause your ball to hook too much. (You can see what we mean in Figure 10-6.) You especially need to watch out for dry lanes in the summer because the oil that's applied on the lanes may dry up faster on hot, humid days.

You can't change the amount of oil on the lane, but you can change how you bowl on that lane. If your ball isn't hitting the pocket, move your starting position to the right a bit if you're a righty or to the left a bit if you're a lefty. Keep moving over slightly until you find the spot that works for you.

Striking on a freshly oiled lane

Bowling on freshly oiled lanes may sound like a bowler's paradise, but too much oil can cause your ball to slide rather than hook. It's like rolling your bowling ball on ice because there's no friction to help the ball roll. Figure 10-7 illustrates this.

You can adjust for the lack of a hook by starting out a little more to the left if you're a righty and a little more to the right if you're a lefty to give yourself a better angle on the pocket you're targeting.

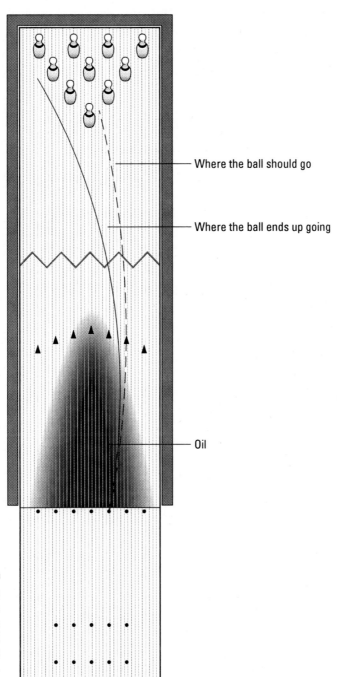

Where the ball should go

Where the ball ends up going

Oil

Figure 10-6:
A dry lane
can make
your ball
hook too
much.

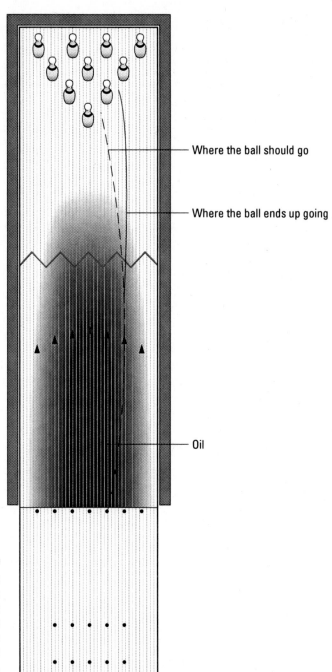

Where the ball should go

Where the ball ends up going

Oil

Figure 10-7:
A freshly
oiled lane
can keep
your
ball from
hooking.

Double-checking your form

If strikes aren't happening like you think they should, go back to square one and double-check your form by asking yourself these questions:

- ✔ **Am I starting from the right spot?** Count your spaces and make sure your feet are planted in the right spot every time you get up to bowl.

- ✔ **Am I standing properly?** Most people have a tendency to slouch when they're tired. If you find that as the games go on your ball is feeling heavier and you're drooping down to hold it, force yourself back up straight. And remember that any change in your stance or form can affect your throw.

- ✔ **How's my timing?** Are you pushing the ball away from your body at the same time as you're starting to take your steps, or are you a little delayed? The timing of your feet and arm swing should be synchronized for the best results.

- ✔ **Is my arm straight?** Carrying a heavy bowling ball game after game can wear out your arm, which means you may start getting a little sloppy in your throws. Don't hold the ball when it's not your turn, take a break when you need to, and consider switching to a lighter ball if the problem persists.

- ✔ **Am I using too much speed or not enough?** Too much speed can cause your ball to zip right through the pins before it has a chance to knock many of 'em down. Slow it down a little. On the other hand, if you're not giving your ball any momentum, it could run out of steam before it reaches the pins. Try adding more speed by increasing your backswing just a little bit.

- ✔ **Am I following through?** If you're hooking the ball, is your hand finishing in the handshake position, or are you literally releasing the ball onto the lane near your ankle and stopping there? Follow-through is vital in bowling. You should let go of the ball and then continue moving your arm up. How far you move it up is your call. Some bowlers move their arm higher than shoulder level; others stop at the height of their shoulders. The important thing is that the movement should come naturally and be comfortable.

- ✔ **Am I tired?** When you start a game, you're excited and have a tendency to throw a little faster and harder. As the frames wear on, you slow down. That's okay because you don't have to throw hard to get strikes. Just concentrate on getting the ball into the pocket for now and take breaks when you need to.

- ✔ **Am I staying focused?** Even the slightest distraction can throw you off, so stay focused. Keep a clear mind and create a tunnel vision to the pins. Concentrate on your target arrows and focus on the ultimate goal — throwing a strike!

Chapter 11

Picking Up Spares

*O*f course you want to get strikes. They make your score and your average higher, and you feel great when you get one. But odds are good you're not going to throw a strike every single time you bowl. Occasionally you're going to be left with some pins to knock down on your second throw. If you get all the pins down on the second throw, you've "picked up" your spare.

One of the biggest mistakes bowlers make is underestimating the importance of picking up spares. If you don't know how to pick them up, you're hurting your score. In our opinion, knowing how to pick up spares is even more important than knowing how to throw strikes. In this chapter, we explain why spares are so important, and show you how to change (or not change) your approach depending on which spare you're facing. Finally, we present you with important points you should keep in mind to master spares.

Seeing Why Spares Are Essential

Say you throw your first ball down the lane and you knock down nine pins and leave one. You take a deep breath, grab your ball for your second shot, eye your target arrow, and throw the ball again. When you knock down that remaining pin, you've rolled yourself a *spare* (because you've knocked down all the pins after two throws).

Picking up spares is important to you as a bowler for two reasons: it makes you a better bowler and boosts your overall score.

Picking up spares makes you a better bowler

The key to knocking down all the pins on your first shot is to hit your respective *pocket,* the space between the 1 and 2 pins for lefties and the space between the 1 and 3 pins for righties. Do this consistently at the right angle and with the right combination of power and speed, and you'll be a strike machine. But if you don't get a strike, it doesn't mean you're a bad bowler. It simply means you missed the pocket on that throw for a variety of reasons. Your angle may have been slightly off, your speed may have been a little slower or faster than what you normally throw, or some other unknown factor may have occurred. You can give up and just throw the ball down the lane and hope for the best, or you can become a better bowler by adjusting your shot, throwing a second ball, picking up the spare, and saving your frame (which means adding bonus points to your score).

To pick up a spare, you have to hit a smaller target (that is, fewer pins) more accurately. Accomplishing this takes a good deal of skill and practice (and occasionally some luck). When you can consistently and easily pick up spares, you're on your way to becoming a much better bowler.

Picking up spares is essential for high scores

If you want a higher score — and that *is* the name of this game — you must be able to pick up spares because they add more points to your score and, ultimately, to your average.

When you bowl a strike, you get 10 points for that frame, plus whatever you knock down on the next two throws. When you bowl a spare, you get 10 points for that frame, plus whatever you bowl on your next throw. If you miss the spare, you've bowled what's called an *open frame* because you didn't get a strike or a spare in that frame, but you also lose the chance to add the points from the next throw to your score. For every open frame you have, you're losing about 11 points off of your score.

Identifying Spares and Adjusting Your Shot Accordingly

How you tackle a spare (meaning where you start from, how you throw the ball, and so on) depends on the type of spare you're facing. Good bowlers can identify a particular spare and recognize exactly how to adjust their throw in order to pick it up.

You identify a spare by looking down the lane and noticing which pins are left standing after your first throw. If a solitary pin is left behind, you have a *single-pin spare;* if several pins are left, you have a *multipin spare.* If they're clumped together, you have a *cluster spare.* And if you're left with pins on each side of the lane, you're looking at one version of a *split,* a special type of spare that we cover in Chapter 12.

After you know the type of spare you're dealing with, it's time to consider all the options you have for picking up that spare. For example:

✔ Should you move your starting position a few boards to the left or to the right?

✔ Should you aim at a different target arrow?

✔ Should you throw the second ball harder than you threw the first one?

✔ Should you throw a straight ball rather than a hook?

✔ Should you just stay right where you are and throw your strike ball again?

In the following sections, we help you figure out how to identify and adjust for a variety of single- and multipin spares.

Whatever spare you're facing, always take the time to picture where your target is and what you should be doing, but don't overthink your shot. Too much thinking about any throw can put you at a higher risk of messing up. Just relax, let the ball go, and trust yourself.

If you've left pins after your first shot, quickly look up at the computerized scoring monitor. Some centers have video monitors that feature animation that shows where the ball should go so you can pick up that spare.

Single-pin spares

All but two single-pin spares are considered easy spares to make because you're aiming for just one pin. But if you listen closely on league nights, you'll hear the frustration that bowlers feel when two particular pins are left behind. For some bowlers, no matter how well they throw their strike ball, the pin action doesn't take out the 7 pin or the 10 pin. We show you how to conquer the 7- and 10-pin spares, as well as several other single-pin spares, in the sections that follow.

Whichever single-pin spare you're facing, remember that you need to cross the lane to throw the ball at it, regardless of which way you bowl. For example, if the lone pin is on the right side of the lane, throw from the left side; if it's on the left side of the lane, throw from the right side.

The 7- or 10-pin spare

If you're a hook bowler, the 7-pin and 10-pin spares can seem incredibly difficult. If you're a right-handed hook bowler trying to hit the straggling 10 pin, your ball will probably hook just before it gets to the pin. If you're a left-handed hook bowler, the same thing happens to you when you're trying to nail that slacker 7 pin. The good news is that with a few slight adjustments, the 7-pin and 10-pin spares don't have to be so hard to pick up. (The 7-10 split, in which both pins remain standing, is a whole other story that we cover in Chapter 12.) The next sections offer tips on picking up the 7- and 10-pin spares for righties and lefties.

If you want to get better at picking up either spare, visit your local bowling center, mentally block out all the pins except for the 7 pin or the 10 pin, and practice hitting the pin that's giving you trouble.

Tips for righties

To pick up the 7-pin spare, a right-handed hook bowler should move one or two boards to the right and aim for a different arrow than his strike target arrow (we help you figure out your strike target arrow in Chapter 10) until he finds the right combination (see Figure 11-1). *Remember:* Where you stand depends on your hook and its breakpoint; we explain what a breakpoint is in Chapter 9.

Picking up the 10-pin spare is a little tougher. Start by moving to the left and aiming at an arrow on the right, as in Figure 11-2. (Again, the arrow you choose depends on your hook.) Then throw your strike ball.

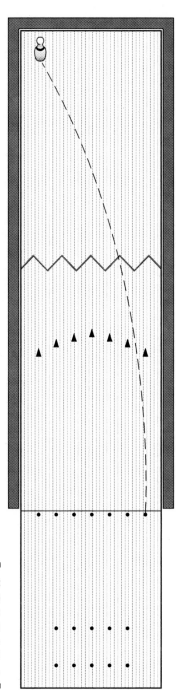

Figure 11-1:
Picking up
the 7-pin
spare with
a right-
handed
hook shot.

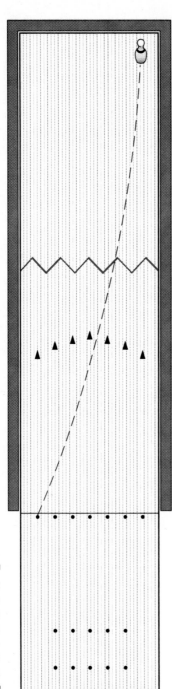

Figure 11-2:
Picking up
the 10-pin
spare with
a right-
handed
hook shot.

For either pin, you also have the option of throwing a straight ball. To throw a straight ball, position your hand and wrist underneath the ball as you would for your hook. Push off and start your backswing, but as the ball comes forward, don't turn your wrist and hand like you would when throwing a hook. Instead, keep your wrist and hand straight the entire time. When you release the ball, let it roll right off of your fingertips so that your wrist and palm remain face up toward the ceiling. (**Note:** With a straight shot, you may need to move your starting position to the left or right a bit so you can find a direct line to the pin. Practice until you find the starting spot that works for you.)

If your ball still hooks too much and misses the pin even when you try to throw it straight, you may need to invest in an extra plastic ball that doesn't hook and use it solely for picking up spares, especially the 7- and 10-pin spares.

Tips for lefties

Left-handed hook bowlers have a slightly easier time picking up the 10-pin spare than righties because their hook turns in the direction of the 10 pin instead of rolling away from it. To pick up the 10-pin spare as a left-handed hook bowler, shift your starting point one or two boards to the right and aim for a different arrow until you find the right combination for your hook that picks up the 10 pin (see Figure 11-3). Where you stand depends on how much your ball hooks.

The 7-pin spare is arguably the toughest spare for a left-handed hook bowler to pick up because the ball hooks away from the pin. To get it, start by moving to the right and aiming at an arrow that's farther out on the left (see Figure 11-4). Remember that the arrow you aim for depends on your hook.

You can also try throwing a straight ball to nail the 7-pin spare. Move to the left to create a direct line to the pin (you may need to move over even more to find the proper angle, so practice, practice, practice). Throw a straight ball by positioning your hand and palm underneath the ball as you would for your hook, but don't turn your hand or wrist as the ball comes forward. Keep it straight and let the ball roll off of your fingers. When you release the ball, your hand and wrist should remain face up through your follow-through. Do the same things to throw a straight ball at the 10-pin spare, but move over to the right instead.

The 4- or 6-pin spare

If you're a hook bowler and you leave either the 4-pin spare or the 6-pin spare, you may have to move your starting position over a few boards. Play with different starting positions during a practice game so you know exactly where to move when the points really count. You can also pick up these single-pin spares by throwing a straight ball instead.

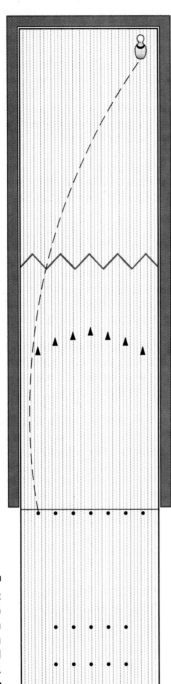

Figure 11-3:
Picking up
the 10-pin
spare with a
left-handed
hook shot.

The 5-pin spare

Because the 5 pin is directly in line with the headpin, it's kind of in the pocket, but it's a little farther back than it looks. To nail the 5-pin spare if you're a hook bowler, try your strike shot and aim for the now-imaginary pocket. (So righties should aim for the invisible 1-3 pocket, and lefties should aim for the invisible 1-2 pocket.) Your strike shot should send the ball smack into the 5 pin; if for some reason it doesn't, move over a board the next time you face a 5-pin spare.

Whether you're a righty or a lefty, if you prefer to bowl straight, just throw your strike shot. Flip to Chapter 10 if you're not sure how to throw a straight strike ball.

The headpin spare

The headpin, or 1-pin, spare is generally the easiest one to make because the headpin is part of your pocket whether you're a righty, lefty, hook bowler, or straight bowler. Because the headpin is one half of your pocket, just throw your strike ball again without making any adjustments to your throw, approach, or feet placement (trying, of course, not to repeat the mistakes you made on the first strike shot that missed the headpin). If you do that, you should be able to pick up the headpin spare.

The 2- or 3-pin spare

The 2 pin is part of the pocket for a left-handed bowler, and the 3 pin is part of the pocket for a right-handed bowler. When you're left with either spare, simply throw your strike ball; it should pick up the spare regardless of whether you're a right-handed hook bowler or a left-handed straight bowler (or any other combination).

The 8- or 9-pin spare

You may occasionally encounter the 8- or 9-pin spare. Approach the 8-pin spare the way you would the 7-pin spare and tackle the 9-pin spare as you would the 10-pin spare (see the earlier "The 7- or 10-pin spare" section for tips). However, you may need to make a minor adjustment to your starting position. For a right-handed bowler, you can move three boards to the right for the 8 pin. A lefty would also move to the right. For the 9 pin, righties and lefties can move four boards to the left. You still aim at your strike target.

Multipin spares

If you leave more than one pin behind after your first throw, you're left with a multipin spare. These spares are a little harder to pick up than single-pin spares because there's a greater chance of *chopping the spare,* which means throwing a good ball that knocks down some, but not all, of the pins. Then you're left with an open frame and no chance to add more points on your next throw. In the next sections, we give you strategies for picking up common multipin spares so you can avoid chopping them.

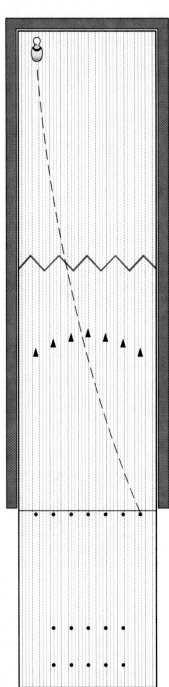

Figure 11-4:
Picking up
the 7-pin
spare with a
left-handed
hook shot.

To boost your chances of picking up a multipin spare, try increasing your ball speed, particularly if you don't want your ball to hook too much. A faster ball hooks less than a slower ball.

The cluster spares

A *cluster spare* is when just a few pins are left standing adjacent to each other on one side of the lane. Possible cluster spares include the

- ✔ **3-5-6:** If you're a righty, move two boards to the left to pick up this spare. If you're a lefty, shift two boards to the right. These adjustments should work regardless of whether you throw a hook or straight ball.

- ✔ **2-4-5:** To pick up this spare, move two boards to the right if you're a right-handed bowler and two boards to the left if you're a left-handed bowler. It doesn't matter whether you throw a straight or hook ball; just follow these adjustments.

- ✔ **4-7-8:** Shift five or so boards to the right if you're a righty and eight boards to the right if you're a lefty if you want to pick up this spare. Again, these adjustments go for either straight or hook bowlers.

The simplest advice we can give you for picking up a cluster spare is to aim for the front pin. For example, if you were left with the 4-7-8 spare, you'd aim for the 4 pin. If you hit the 4 pin properly, it should slide right into the 7 pin and the 8 pin (see Figures 11-5 and 11-6).

The 3-6 or 2-4 spare

The best way to pick up the 3-6 spare or the 2-4 spare is to aim for the pin that's in front and throw your strike ball. Of course, you may need to move over a board or two or aim at a different target. (Refer to Chapter 10 for help perfecting your strike ball.)

The 1-2-4-7 or 1-3-6-10 spare

The 1-2-4-7 and 1-3-6-10 spares are sometimes called *clothesline spares* or *picket fence spares*. The idea behind picking up these spares is to hit either the 1-2 or the 1-3 pocket. Hitting the 1-2 or 1-3 pocket increases your chances of hitting or carrying the 4 and 7 pins or the 6 and 10 pins, respectively. See Chapter 10 for pointers on how to aim at the right pocket; check out Figures 11-7 and 11-8 to see how to pick up the 1-2-4-7 spare.

Most bowlers tend to chop these spares, so if you bowl with a right- or left-handed hook, try to take some of the hook off of your ball by throwing a little faster or adjusting your starting position. See Chapter 9 for more pointers on correcting a ball that hooks too much.

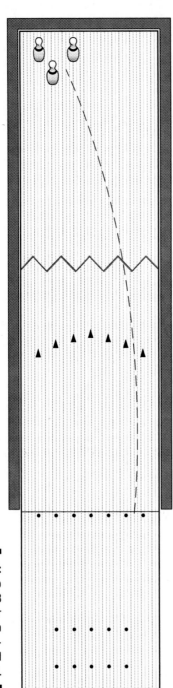

Figure 11-5:
Picking up
the 4-7-8
cluster
spare with
a right-
handed
hook.

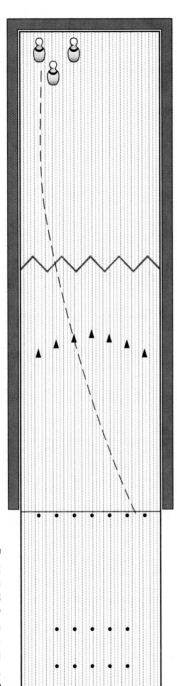

Figure 11-6:
Picking up
the 4-7-8
cluster
spare with
a left-
handed
hook.

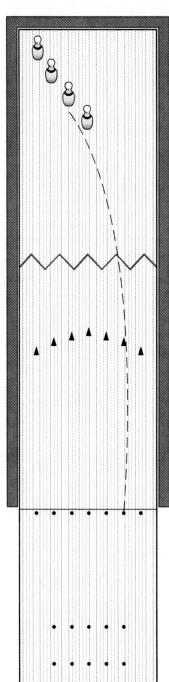

Figure 11-7:
Picking up
the 1-2-4-7
spare with
a right-
handed
hook.

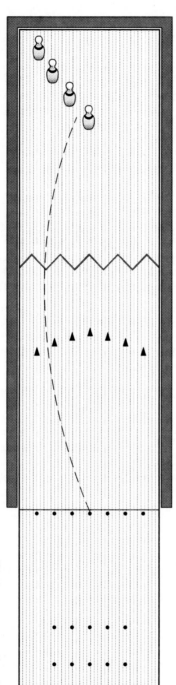

Figure 11-8:
Picking up
the 1-2-4-7
spare with
a left-
handed
hook.

Mastering Spares

Picking up spares requires you to exercise some patience before making your second throw. Take a few seconds to look at what pins are still standing and then think about what angle the ball needs to approach the pins in order to hit them all. When you know these two facts, you can figure out where you need to stand, what target arrow to look at, and whether you'd be better off throwing a straight ball if you're a hook bowler.

Here are some other pointers to keep in mind to help you truly master spares:

✔ **Recognize that making spares depends on how you throw.** We can't stress it enough: How you make your spares depends on whether you're a left-handed or right-handed bowler. If you're a right-handed bowler and you leave a spare to the left of the 1-3 pocket, you usually need to move your starting point a little to the left to get it. If the spare is to the right, you need move your feet a tad to the right. Left-handed bowlers should usually do the reverse in both cases, although their strike pocket is the 1-2 pocket.

✔ **Stay focused.** Your mental game is important. Don't allow yourself to become frustrated when you don't get a strike. Instead, stay focused and remember that you can easily turn a missed strike into a spare and pick up more points than if you leave an open frame.

✔ **Work around obstacles in your way.** In some cases, it may seem like you have to move so far to the left or right that you bump up against the ball return or even the bowler in the next lane. Don't give into this misconception; moving to such an extreme interferes with a good shot. Instead, move your target on the lane until you find a new one where your ball breaks the right way to pick up your spare. You find this new target by practicing and playing around with your target arrow and starting position.

✔ **Don't turn away.** How your ball reacts on the lane is a clear indication of how you should bowl to pick up your spares, so make sure you watch your ball after you let it go. For example, certain areas of the lane are more oiled than others, a fact that affects how your ball grips the lane (see Chapter 13 for more on oil and lanes). If you don't watch your ball all the way down the lane to see how it's moving, you won't know how to adjust your throw to pick up the spare next time.

✔ **Be consistent.** After you know how to pick up a particular spare, remember where you stood and the particular target you looked at. Also, remember whether you needed to throw a hook or a straight ball. Consistency is key to picking up spares, but because lane conditions always play a part in your throw, you may still need to make minor adjustments.

Chapter 12

Conquering Classic Splits

. . . .

In This Chapter

▶ Discovering why splits are a bowler's worst nightmare

▶ Steering clear of Splitsville

▶ Categorizing the various kinds of splits

▶ Doing your best to convert splits into points

. . . .

*I*t's a situation no bowler wants to face: You throw what you think should be a strike, but something goes awry and the ball cuts through the pins. What you're left with makes you cringe. You've taken a wrong turn and ended up in Splitsville. *Splits,* when the pins left standing are separated from each other, can ruin an otherwise good game. They're generally difficult to pick up, and in some cases, they're nearly impossible.

Whenever you wind up with a split (trust us, it *will* happen), take a deep breath and have faith that not all hope is lost. With a lot of practice and skill, you can indeed *convert* some splits; in other words, you can make spares out of 'em. In this chapter, we explain why splits occur and how you can avoid them (or at least try to). We then show you how to identify splits and provide recommendations for adjusting your aim and your feet for the one you're facing so you can successfully convert it.

Splits — Why Every Bowler Hates 'Em

Bowlers hate splits. If you don't believe us, sit back and watch them (especially league bowlers). We bet you see some pretty animated faces when bowlers realize they ended up in ever-dreaded Splitsville. Some bowlers sigh and throw their arms up in exasperation, others grunt in frustration, and a select few tend to laugh in sheer desperation because they know the odds of picking up a split are significantly lower than any other type of spare.

But for every bowler who has been left clutching her hands to her head and saying, "Why, oh why did I have to get that split?" is another bowler who has successfully knocked down the same split. It can be done, but it helps to first have an idea why you got a split in the first place and what a split means for your score. We shed some light on both topics in the next sections.

Understanding how you wound up in Splitsville

When you're left with a split, something went wrong either with your throw or your pin action (or maybe even both). Following are the top three reasons why bowlers wind up with splits:

✔ **An "off" throw:** A split happens for almost the same reasons that a regular spare happens — the ball you threw hit the pins at the wrong angle or at the wrong speed (or with not enough spin if you're a hook bowler) to create the necessary pin action. As a result, your ball cut right through the pins and left some standing with varying distances between them.

Some people wind up with splits more often than others. Straight bowlers have a tendency to hit the headpin head on more frequently, which splits the pins right down the middle. Other bowlers throw the ball so hard it slams right through the middle of the pins. Take some time to figure out your bowling form/style (see Chapter 5 for help with this) and make adjustments if you're ending up with too many splits.

✔ **Incorrectly set pins:** Pinsetting machines are just that — machines. They can break down and do things incorrectly. They may lift up the pins after your first shot only to drop them on the lane, or they may fail to release the pins at all. Other times the pinsetter may position the pins back onto the lane but not quite on their mark. Even the slightest change in pin position can affect your game.

If you notice that everyone is having the same difficulty with a split or spare on a particular lane, ask the center's management to check the equipment. Good managers want their customers happy and will be willing to check whether the machine is setting the pins down properly.

✔ **Bad luck:** Bowling is about the physics of hitting pins at the right angle so they all knock each other down, but even physics can stir up a bit of trouble from time to time. Sometimes the pins just fall in a different direction and miss the other pins, even if you hit the pocket the right way. If you're doing everything else in your form properly, you can't control whether this happens. All you can do is hope your bad luck clears up in the next frame.

Recognizing how splits affect your score

The harder the split, the less of a chance you have of picking it up. Unless you are, or can become, an amazing split converter, we're sorry to tell you that getting a split can almost guarantee you an *open frame* (which is when you don't bowl a strike or a spare in that frame). Open frames can knock 11 points off of your score each time you get one.

Avoiding the Splits

Even though some of the factors that cause splits are out of your control (as explained earlier in this chapter), you can take a few steps to reduce your chances of getting one. Here they are, in all their simple-yet-powerful glory:

- ✔ **Be consistent in your throw.** Each time you step up for your approach, throw your strike ball with the same speed and power (and spin if you throw a hook). When you find the right mark, hit it each time. (See Chapter 10 if you need help figuring out how to throw a strike ball.)

    Some bowlers make the mistake of overpowering their throws — especially with splits — to try and bump up a low score. They falsely believe that muscling the ball will knock down more pins and give them more points. Big mistake. Although you may need to bump up your power or speed on certain splits, overthrowing doesn't really work. It also tires out your arm faster and tends to cause your score to suffer even more. Consistency is key. If you're regularly hitting your mark at the same power and speed, you'll reduce your odds of getting a split and end up with a higher score.

- ✔ **Watch the ball.** Don't turn around and walk away after you release the ball. Instead, watch it go down the lane. Analyzing the ball's path gives you valuable information as to whether or not you're throwing it correctly. Is it hooking too much or too little? Are you missing the pocket and hitting the headpin? Are you missing your target arrow? By watching what the ball does, you can figure out which adjustments to make to reduce your chances of splits.

- ✔ **Make adjustments.** Take what you know about how your ball moves and tweak your form. If you're missing your mark and that's what's causing the splits, move over a board or two and try again. Still not hitting the mark? Pick a new target until you find the right combination that works for you. After you make these adjustments, you'll be hitting your target and the pocket more frequently while reducing your odds of seeing splits.

Identifying the Different Types of Splits

You can group any split into one of three categories: easy, not-so-easy, and almost-impossible. Note that we said *almost* impossible. No split is considered *completely* impossible. In the sections that follow, we introduce you to the specific splits that fall into each category.

Easy splits

In an *easy split*, the pins that are left are either in front of each other at a diagonal or right next to each other. Splits that fall into this category include

✔ The 3-10 split (see Figure 12-1a)

✔ The 2-7 split (see Figure 12-1b)

✔ The 7-8 split (shown in Figure 12-1c)

✔ The 9-10 split (see Figure 12-1d)

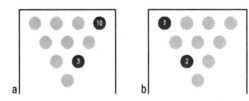

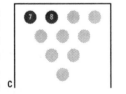
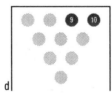

Figure 12-1: Four splits that are pretty easy to pick up.

Easy splits (also called *baby splits*) earn their name because you can convert them into spares by throwing the ball right between the two pins or by hitting one of the pins on the outside edge so that it falls into its neighbor.

Not-so-easy splits

A *not-so-easy split* is when the pins are a little farther away from each other and on such an angle that it's harder to get one to knock into the other. Splits that fall into this category include

- ✔ The 4-9 split (see Figure 12-2a)
- ✔ The 6-8 split (shown in Figure 12-2b)
- ✔ The 5-10 split (see Figure 12-2c)
- ✔ The 2-4-10 split (see Figure 12-2d)
- ✔ The 3-6-7 split (shown in Figure 12-2e)
- ✔ The 4-7-10 split (see Figure 12-2f)

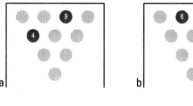
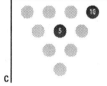
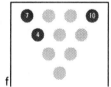
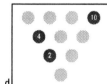
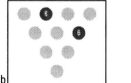
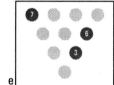

Figure 12-2: Six splits that are a little tougher to pick up.

Bowling a field goal

Bowlers who roll a ball right down the middle of a split without touching any of the pins often put their hands up and exclaim "Field goal!" in an homage to football. In football, you kick the ball through two posts to score an extra three points. Unlike football though, a field goal in bowling is worth absolutely nothing — sorry. Yelling "Field goal!" is just a way to make light of an unfortunate split.

The trick to hitting any of the not-so-easy splits is to hit one of the pins at such an angle that it goes across the lane and knocks down the other pin(s).

Almost-impossible splits

Not surprisingly, *almost-impossible splits* are the most difficult splits to make out of the many possible split combinations. They're supertricky because it's more difficult to send one pin into the other when the angle between them isn't quite right. Splits that fall into this challenging category include

- The 7-10 split (see Figure 12-3a)
- The 4-6 split (see Figure 12-3b)
- The 7-9 split (shown in Figure 12-3c)

Figure 12-3:
Three of
the most
challenging
splits.

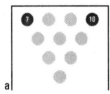 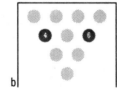 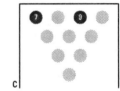

a | b | c

When faced with an almost-impossible split, most bowlers just decide which pin seems easier to hit and let the ball rip. Yes, you read that right. This is the one and only time that it's okay to throw the ball a bit harder because you're hoping a) that the ball can hit the first pin and b) that that pin either bounces out of the gutter or ricochets off the side wall to come back and knock over the lone standing pin.

Converting Splits

You *convert* a split by making a spare out of it. How you convert a split depends largely on what type of split you're facing (see the earlier "Identifying the Different Types of Splits" section if you're not sure). It also depends on whether you bowl left-handed or right-handed and whether you're a straight bowler or a hook bowler. In the following sections, we explain how to convert the easy, not-so-easy, and almost-impossible splits.

Note: The changes to your starting spot that we note in the following sections are just recommendations. Your exact starting spot depends on your hook, ball speed, and other factors. Use our suggestions simply as a starting point and play with them until you find the spot that works best for you.

When you're left with a split, don't give up and just throw the ball in the gutter. Even if you knock down just two pins of a three-pin split, you still get 2 whole points added to your score. If you're competing in a league, those 2 points can make a big difference.

Picking up the easy ones

A split is considered easy when the pins are close enough that you can throw a ball between them to make the spare. To convert easy splits, all you have to do is move your starting spot slightly.

The 3-10 split

Although any bowler can end up with any split at any time, right-handed bowlers tend to encounter the 3-10 split (shown in Figure 12-4) more often than lefties. The basic strategy for converting the 3-10 split is to aim the ball to the right of the 3 pin. The ball should hit the 3 pin on the left and the 10 pin on the right.

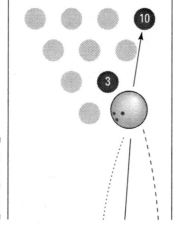

Figure 12-4:
Picking up
the 3-10
split.

Key:
―――― Straight ball
- - - Right-handed hook ball
······· Left-handed hook ball

Following are some tips for picking up this split if you're a

- **Right-handed hook bowler:** Move your starting spot five boards to the left so you can have a better angle between the pins.

- **Left-handed hook bowler:** Position your feet six boards to the left and aim for the 3 pin.

- **Right- or left-handed straight bowler:** Move a little to the left so you can aim the ball directly between the pins with your straight-as-an-arrow throw.

The 2-7 split

The 2-7 split (see Figure 12-5) is more common in left-handed bowlers, although there's always a chance that a righty will see this split too. The 2-7 split is the mirror opposite of the 3-10 split (covered in the preceding section). When facing this split, remember that you want the ball to hit the left side of the 2 pin. The the ball continues on its way to knock down the 7 pin.

Here's how to nail this split if you're a

- **Right-handed hook bowler:** Move your starting position six boards to the right and throw your strike shot.

- **Left-handed hook bowler:** Move your starting position five boards to the right and throw the ball so it goes between the 2 pin and the 7 pin.

- **Right- or left-handed straight bowler:** Righties should move their starting position six boards to the right and aim at their original target for their strike shot. Lefties should slide their starting position four boards to the right and aim at their strike target.

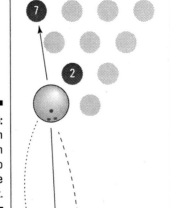

Figure 12-5: Aim between the pins to convert the 2-7 split.

Key:
—— Straight ball
- - - Right-handed hook ball
······ Left-handed hook ball

The 7-8 and 9-10 splits

Every bowler has a chance of seeing the 7-8 split (shown in Figure 12-6) and the 9-10 split from time to time, as well as other splits that are similar to them (such as the 4-5 and the 5-6), which means that all of these splits provide just enough space to throw the ball directly between the pins. Do it right and the ball will knock down both pins at the same time.

Following are some suggestions for picking up both the 7-8 and the 9-10 split if you're a

- ✔ **Right-handed hook bowler:** To convert the 7-8, move your feet five boards to the right and aim at your same strike target. To pick up the 9-10, move ten boards to the left and change your aim a tad so that you're shooting for the third arrow from the right

- ✔ **Left-handed hook bowler:** For the 7-8, move ten boards to the right but aim at the third arrow from the left. To convert the 9-10, move five boards to the left and throw your amazing strike shot.

- ✔ **Right- or left-handed straight bowler:** If you're a right-handed bowler, convert the 7-8 split by moving eight boards to the right and throw your strike shot. For the 9-10 split, move six boards to the left and throw your best strike ball. If you're a lefty trying to convert the 7-8 split, move your feet six boards to the right and throw your strike shot. To knock down the 9-10 split, move eight boards to the left and throw your strike ball.

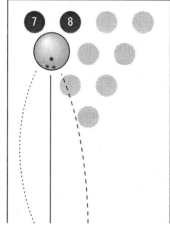

Figure 12-6:
Converting
the 7-8 split.

Key:
——— Straight ball
- - - - Right-handed hook ball
······· Left-handed hook ball

Picking up the more difficult splits

Converting one of the not-so-easy splits (presented in the earlier related section) requires a bit more effort than converting one of the easy splits. For example, instead of hitting a particular pin straight on, you may need to angle the ball so that it lightly taps one side of a pin, sending it (ideally) into the other pin(s).

The 4-9 and 6-8 splits

A right-handed bowler is more likely to see a 4-9 split, and a lefty is more likely to see a 6-8 split, but remember that a good bowler is ready for anything. To get rid of a 4-9 split, the ball has to barely hit the left side of the 4 pin and send it sliding across the pin deck to take out the 9 pin (see Figure 12-7). A similar scenario must occur to convert the 6-8 split: The ball must lightly tap the right side of the 6 pin so that it slides over and takes out the 8 pin.

Here are some tips for converting the 4-9 or the 6-8 split if you're a

- ✔ **Right-handed hook bowler:** Imagine that you're trying to pick up your 7-pin spare when you want to convert the 4-9 split. Go for the 10-pin spare to knock out the 6-8 split.

- ✔ **Left-handed hook bowler:** When you're converting the 4-9 spare, pretend that you're going for your 7-pin spare, the hardest single-pin spare for a lefty. Move to the right of your starting spot by a board or two and aim at an arrow that's farther out on the left to increase your chances of picking up this spare. Go for the imaginary 10-pin to knock out the 6-8 split.

- ✔ **Right- or left-handed straight bowler:** To convert the 4-9 split, use your 7-pin spare shot. Act like you're picking up the 10-pin spare to convert the 6-8 split.

Dealing with "the washout"

You have a washout on your hands whenever you leave the headpin and a split. Examples include the 1-2-10 split and the 1-3-7 split. (Although *technically* a washout isn't considered a split in the bowling world because the headpin's still standing.) To get the 1-2-10 split, throw your ball so that it slides the 1 pin into the 10 pin. To convert the 1-3-7 split, throw your ball so that it slides the 1 pin into the 7 pin. Whether you throw with a hook or a straight ball doesn't really matter as long as you're targeting the correct side of the headpin.

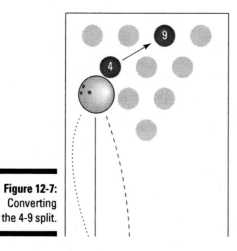

Figure 12-7:
Converting
the 4-9 split.

Key:
——— Straight ball
- - - Right-handed hook ball
······· Left-handed hook ball

The 5-10 split

The 5-10 split, which also goes by the name "the five-and-dime" in honor of the old retailer Woolworth's and is shown in Figure 12-8, is a common split that any bowler can get, whether you're right-handed or left-handed. The basic strategy for converting this split is to barely hit the 5 pin on its left side. If you can achieve this, the 5 pin should slide over to the 10 pin and knock it down.

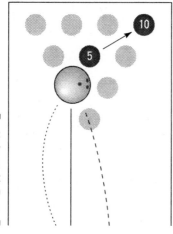

Figure 12-8:
Try to barely
hit the 5 pin
to convert
the 5-10
split.

Key:
——— Straight ball
- - - Right-handed hook ball
······· Left-handed hook ball

Following are our tips for picking up the 5-10 split if you're a

- ✔ **Right- or left-handed hook bowler:** Righties should move four boards to the right, aim for the 1-2 pocket, and throw their strike ball. Lefties should move three boards to the right and throw their strike shot.

- ✔ **Right- or left-handed straight bowler:** Aim for the left side of the 5 pin. To do this, a right-handed bowler should move four boards to the left, and a left-handed bowler should shift three boards to the right.

The 2-4-10 split

If you're a righty, you'll see the 2-4-10 split (see Figure 12-9) more often than left-handed bowlers will. To convert this split, you want to hit the left side of the 2 pin so that the 2 pin then slides into the 10 pin. While that's happening, the ball should take out the 4 pin.

Here's how to master this split if you're a

- ✔ **Right-handed hook bowler:** Move six boards to the left and throw your strike ball.

- ✔ **Left-handed hook bowler:** Move five boards to your right and throw your strike ball, using the 2-4 as the pocket and focusing on hitting the 2 pin.

- ✔ **Right- or left-handed straight bowler:** A left-handed bowler should move six boards to the right; a right-handed bowler should move four boards to the right. After shifting your starting spot, go ahead and throw your strike ball.

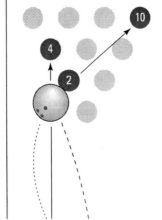

Figure 12-9:
Picking up
the 2-4-10
split.

Key:
—— Straight ball
- - - Right-handed hook ball
······ Left-handed hook ball

The 3-6-7 and 4-7-10 splits

Right-handed and left-handed bowlers have an equal chance of facing a 3-6-7 or 4-7-10 split at some point or another. With the 3-6-7 split (see Figure 12-10), you want to position your shot so you can slide the 3 pin into the 7 pin (the ball should take out the 6 pin as it does this). For the 4-7-10 split, you need to aim the ball to the left of the 4 pin so it can slide into the 10 pin (the ball should then fall back off the lane, taking the 7 pin with it).

Following are some tricks for converting either the 3-6-7 split or the 4-7-10 split if you're a

- ✔ **Right-handed hook bowler:** Move five boards to the left and throw the ball at your strike target in order to convert the 3-6-7 split. Rid yourself of the 4-7-10 split by aiming for the 4 pin and throwing as you would to pick up the 7-pin spare (see Chapter 11 for how to get this spare).

- ✔ **Left-handed hook bowler:** To convert a 3-6-7 split, move eight boards to the left and then throw your strike ball. To convert the 4-7-10 split, pretend you're just picking up the 7-pin spare; make sure to aim for the left of the 4 pin, though.

- ✔ **Right- or left-handed straight bowler:** Righties hoping to conquer the 3-6-7 split should move four boards to the left and aim at their strike target; lefties should move eight boards to the left and let loose with their strike ball. As for the 4-7-10 split, righties and lefties should make like they're picking up the 7-pin spare (refer to Chapter 11).

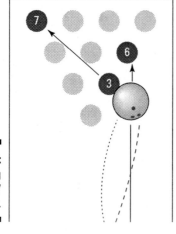

Figure 12-10: Converting the 3-6-7 split.

Key:

——— Straight ball

- - - - Right-handed hook ball

······· Left-handed hook ball

Picking up the toughest splits of all

Some splits, especially the 7-10, are more about luck than skill. But that doesn't mean you can't apply a little strategy to your throw when you're facing one of the almost-impossible splits that we talk about in the following sections.

The 7-10 split

If you ask any experienced bowler which split she dislikes or fears the most, she'll undoubtedly respond with the 7-10 split (which is shown in Figure 12-11; it's also called the *fence post, goal posts, mule ears,* and *snake eyes*). That's because the 7-10 split is the hardest split for any bowler to make. The 7 and 10 pins are located as far away from each other as possible, so the chances of knocking both down with one shot are pretty slim. It has been done, though not without a little luck in the way the pins fell and hit off the back or side of the pin deck or bounced out of the gutter to take out the other pin.

Whether you're a righty or a lefty, a hook bowler or a straight bowler, our advice for converting the 7-10 split is the same: Just pick one of the pins to aim at, preferably the one that you feel most comfortable with. So if you can hit the 7 pin easily, go for that one. If tapping the 10 pin seems easier for you, aim for it.

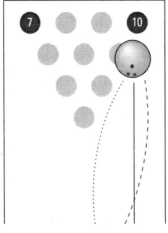

Figure 12-11:
Get rid of the 7-10 split by aiming for whichever pin is easiest for you to hit.

Key:
——— Straight ball
- - - Right-handed hook ball
········· Left-handed hook ball

Note: If you'd rather try to take them both out, add a little more power to your throw, taking care not to lose control of your shot. Then let the ball go and hope for the best.

The 4-6 and 7-9 splits

The 4-6 split and the 7-9 split look less scary than the 7-10 split (covered in the preceding section), but they're still tough little buggers to pick up. You can try to tap the outside of one pin so that it slides into the other one, but converting these splits is really about luck.

If the 4-6 or the 7-9 split is taunting you, simply pick a pin to aim for and try to knock that one down so you can get at least one extra point out of the frame.

Part IV
Staying on Your Game

The 5th Wave   By Rich Tennant

"Of course there is nothing wrong with your arm, but it will keep people from focusing on your bowling average."

In this part . . .

To the average bowler, the lanes look the same each time you bowl, but in reality they're always changing. Why? Because they're oiled and, at times, oiled with a different pattern. The oil pattern and amount of oil on a lane can change the way your ball rolls and force you to adjust how you bowl. Never fear, though. We review what the patterns are and how you can make adjustments to compensate.

Of course, it's not just the condition of the lanes that affects your game. Bowling is just as much a mental game as it is a physical game. This part provides exercises for keeping your body healthy, explains what to do if you get injured, offers drills you can do to improve, and reveals how to maintain a positive attitude. It also shares the benefits of working with a bowling coach when you're looking to improve even more or get some one-on-one support and advice. Last, but not least, this part explains how bowling can still be a part of your life no matter what your circumstances.

Chapter 13

Understanding the Ins and Outs of Oil on the Lanes

In This Chapter

▶ Discovering more about the lanes you bowl on

▶ Understanding why oil is used and how it affects your bowling

▶ Scoping out the specifics of oil patterns

▶ Adjusting your throw for too much or too little oil

*W*hen you bowl, you may notice that the lane seems a bit shiny or wet. That shine is caused by special oil that all bowling centers apply to protect the lanes and to help you bowl. If you're bowling noncompetitively, you probably aren't focusing on what the oil is doing to your ball, but if you want to become a better bowler, you should be.

This chapter is devoted to everything you need to know about oil, from how it affects your score to how you can make adjustments so it doesn't throw off your game.

Flooring Basics

Bowlers used to always bowl on hardwood lanes, but hardwood lanes are expensive to install, maintain, and replace. Consequently, very few centers still use them. Nowadays, most centers use synthetic lanes that are made to resemble the traditional hardwood lanes. Synthetic lanes are typically more durable than their hardwood predecessors, so they can withstand more bowling.

No matter what the lanes are made of, they need to be kept in tiptop shape, so centers apply a thin coat of oil conditioner in a special pattern (we tell you about the different oil patterns in the later "Looking at Oil Patterns" section). Oil conditioner protects the lanes and keeps them shiny, much like hair conditioner does for your hair.

Recycled bowling lanes

If you're bowling on a hardwood lane, you're either in a center that has original hardwood lanes or in one that uses recycled lanes. Recycled bowling lanes are hardwood lanes that have been taken from a closed center and moved to a new center. They're an affordable solution to the problem of installing new hardwood floors and a great way to recycle.

No two bowling centers are completely alike, largely due to the different oil patterns that they choose to apply. Some patterns place more oil in the middle of a lane, whereas others place more oil on the outside of a lane. Even if one lane is oiled with the same pattern as another, that lane may have a slight divot because a bowler's ball once hit the lane too hard. Also, lanes can have different amounts of oil on them at different times of day. If you bowl in the morning right after a center has oiled its lanes, the lanes will be oilier than if you bowl at that center in the afternoon or evening because fewer bowling balls have rolled on the lane, redistributing the oil as they go. (When oil is moved around the lane by a bowling ball, this is referred to as *carry down.*)

Should you ever find yourself bowling on a traditional hardwood lane, keep in mind that the oil dries up faster because the wood absorbs it. (With a synthetic lane, the oil sits on top of the lane.) You must be prepared to adjust your shot to account for the oil on the lane; see the later "Compensating for Oil" section for help.

Oil, a Slippery Topic

Oil does more than just protect the lanes and keep them looking shiny. It also prevents your ball from hooking too much. In the following sections, we explain in more detail what happens to a bowling ball when it hits the oil and what else affects the oil (calling Mother Nature!).

Recognizing how oil affects your bowling

After you know how oil affects your game, you might see it as a necessary evil or a boon to your game. As we explain in Chapter 9, hook shots are good for throwing strikes, but in order to throw a great hook, you need some friction between your ball and the lane. The more oil there is on a lane, the more your ball, which is supposed to hook, is going to go straight. Therefore, too much oil means not enough hook.

On the flip side, you don't want the lanes to be bone-dry either. If they are, your hook shot has too much friction to grab onto, and it can hook way out of control. So the idea is that you want *some* oil on the lane but not too much. That's why it's important to know what pattern you're bowling on, as well as how much oil has been applied, where it's been applied, and when. After you have this information, you can make any necessary adjustments to your throw. For example, if you find out that the pattern has a lot of oil in the middle of the lane but not as much on the outside, you can throw your ball toward the outer portion of the lane so you don't pick up as much oil (which could send your ball off course).

Knowing the oil pattern of your lane has nothing to do with becoming a professional bowler. It has everything to do with recognizing how to adapt your shot to the oil that's on the lanes.

Factoring in the weather

Believe it or not, you may have every right to blame Mother Nature if you don't bowl well. Outdoor weather really can affect your bowling scores. The colder the temperature is outside, the longer it takes the oil to break down (dry up) on the lane inside the center. As a result, your ball may hook less because it's dragging the oil all around the lane. As temperatures rise in the summer, that outdoor heat and humidity can warm up the center and cause the oil to break down faster than normal, causing the lanes to dry out and making your ball hook more.

Note: If the center can maintain a fairly consistent indoor temperature year-round, you shouldn't have to add the weather to the list of things you need to think about when throwing your ball.

Looking at Oil Patterns

Bowling center owners have hundreds of patterns that they can choose from when it's time to oil the lanes. Lanes used for open bowling may feature one pattern, and lanes used for league or tournament play may use a different pattern that has been specified by the league or the tournament's organizers.

The lanes can be oiled multiple times during the day; the frequency of application depends on the center and on what events are going on (such as league play and tournaments).

The sections that follow not only give you the inside scoop as to who creates the different patterns but they also give you a peek at some specific patterns.

Knowing where oil patterns come from

Bowling lanes are 60 feet long, but not all of the lane gets oiled. Typically, oil patterns are only applied 35 to 45 feet down the lane, starting at the foul line. Following are the three common types of patterns:

- **House patterns:** House patterns are the patterns that your bowling center chooses to use, usually for open bowling and leagues. According to the United States Bowling Congress (USBC), house patterns call for more oil to be applied in the middle of the lane than the outside of the lane. Centers can select from hundreds of combinations and change the pattern each time they oil the lanes, although most centers use only a few standard, preferred patterns.

   When a center hosts league play, it oils the lanes with a special pattern that's just for that league. Tournaments also call for special oil patterns that are dictated by the tournament's organizing body. Regardless of whether a special pattern is applied for a league or a tournament, that pattern is typically applied only on the lanes that are being used for the event.

   If you bowl after a league has finished playing, you're bowling on the pattern it was using, and that pattern may or may not be a house pattern. If you want to know about the pattern the league was using, ask the staff person at the front desk.

- **The USBC pattern:** The USBC has its own bowling pattern, called the Red, White, and Blue pattern. The Red pattern is similar to the typical house pattern, with a larger volume of oil in the middle of the lane. The White pattern is a bit tougher to bowl on, with less oil from the inside to the outside of the lane; the Blue pattern is more challenging than the White pattern. Consider the USBC's Red, White, and Blue pattern a stepping stone from house patterns to the various Professional Bowlers Association (PBA) patterns.

- **PBA patterns:** Leagues and tournaments operated by the PBA must use one of several patterns, which include the Chameleon, Cheetah, Scorpion, Shark, and Viper (see the later related sections for more on these patterns). These and other PBA patterns are considered the toughest of them all.

Zooming in on PBA patterns

Because we want you to be able to see a few patterns and understand how to read them, we asked the PBA for permission to show you what a few of its patterns look like and explain what it means to bowl on them. ***Note:*** Understanding oil patterns helps you become a better bowler, so please don't skip over this information because you think it's meant solely for the professional bowler. Anything you discover about patterns in the following list can help you, no matter what pattern you're bowling on.

The most important thing to keep in mind when looking at the following patterns is that the darker a part of the pattern is, the more oil there is on that part of the lane. The lighter-colored areas have less oil.

- ✔ **The Chameleon pattern:** In order to bowl on the Chameleon pattern (see Figure 13-1a), you must be as versatile as a chameleon and be able to adapt to various angles. That's because the oil in this pattern is placed in different sections, or zones, of the lane, so you have different options for how to bowl. Consequently, this pattern is difficult, and scoring can be low, especially because you have to adjust so much (the PBA says that moving more than five boards at a time is common with this pattern).

- ✔ **The Cheetah pattern:** According to the PBA, the Cheetah pattern (see Figure 13-1b) is the highest scoring of its five animal patterns. It has more oil in the middle of the lane, so it forces you to bowl near the gutter. This actually allows you to create the best angle toward your pocket and the pins.

- ✔ **The Scorpion pattern:** The Scorpion pattern (see Figure 13-2a) is one of the more challenging of the PBA's five animal patterns. It places a lot of oil at the front part of the lane, making it very slick, and is considered a medium-scoring pattern because it can be confusing to bowl well on until you find the right spot for you. Just like the Chameleon pattern, you can try different angles on this pattern to find your pocket.

- ✔ **The Shark pattern:** When dealing with the Shark pattern (see Figure 13-2b), think of the middle of the lane — where most of the oil is — as where the sharks are. To avoid the shark, you must bowl so far out that you risk having the ball fall into the gutter. This pattern also makes your ball hook sooner.

- ✔ **The Viper pattern:** The Viper pattern (see Figure 13-3) is a very difficult pattern to bowl on, but if you can adapt quickly and bowl from multiple angles, you can succeed. When a lane is freshly oiled with a Viper pattern, you have to bowl straight through it until the oil has broken down. After that happens, you can try bowling at different angles to work around any large deposits of oil.

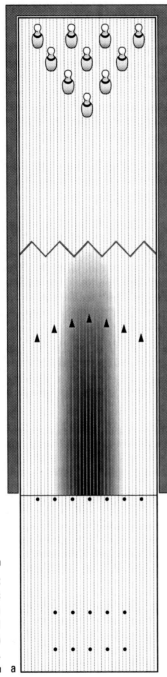

Figure 13-1:
The PBA's
Chameleon
(a) and
Cheetah
patterns (b).

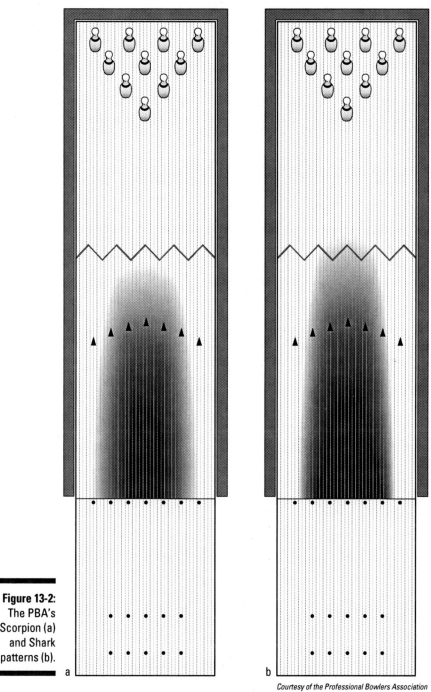

Figure 13-2:
The PBA's
Scorpion (a)
and Shark
patterns (b).

a

b

Courtesy of the Professional Bowlers Association

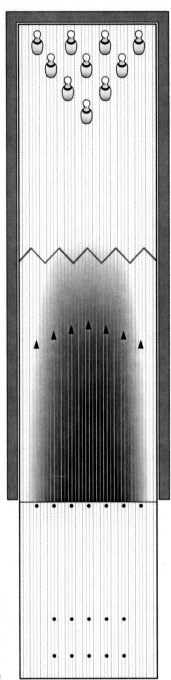

Courtesy of the Professional Bowlers Association

Figure 13-3:
The PBA's
Viper
pattern.

Compensating for Oil

When it's you versus the oil pattern, you want to come out on top. The following sections reveal what you can do to adjust your approach and throw to have a high-scoring game.

To figure out approximately how much oil is on the lane, take a good look at your ball after you've bowled. Is there a lot of oil on it or none at all? You can also ask other bowlers what they think. Finally, use your practice time to see how your ball reacts to the lane. Doing so gives you an idea of how much oil is on the lane and how you need to adjust.

Cleaning your bowling ball is one way to compensate for the oil on the lanes. Whether you clean yours, and how often you do, is up to you. We know bowlers who clean their bowling balls after every shot and some who never clean them. If you do decide to clean your ball, you can use a microfiber towel and ball cleaner or have your pro shop do a professional cleaning. If you want to clean the ball during a game, consider investing in a seesaw towel (see Chapter 4 to get an idea of what one looks like). Pulling the handles up and down forces the ball to rotate, wiping off the oil. You can purchase one at your local pro shop or through an online bowling store.

Adjusting your approach

You may not always need to adjust your approach based on the oil pattern. Try practicing on the lane first, making sure you're not bowling any differently than you normally would. After several practice throws, you may find that the pattern is perfect for your particular form and style. If, however, you need to make some adjustments, follow these tips:

- **Decrease your ball speed.** If there's too much oil on the lane, slow down your ball speed a little. To do that, shorten up your arm swing by holding the ball lower at the start of your approach.

- **Move your feet.** If the ball isn't hitting your desired pocket, you may have to stand a little more to the left or right of your starting position. For example, if there isn't enough oil on the lane, you may need to move your feet to throw the ball in the middle of the lane, where all the oil is. Use your practice time to figure out what the best starting position is for you based on the particular oil pattern you're dealing with.

✔ **Use a different ball.** If you're bowling on a pattern that has a lot of oil on a regular basis and your ball just isn't cutting it, you may need a more aggressive ball. Talk to the staff at your local pro shop for recommendations.

✔ **Straighten out your hand.** Got a drier lane and a ball that's hooking too much? Straighten out your hand when you're bowling and move your pointer and pinkie fingers out on the ball to create a straighter shot.

✔ **Increase your arm swing.** Hold the ball higher in order to create a bigger arm swing if your ball is hooking too much because the lane is a little dry.

If you're really struggling on one lane and you're at the center during open bowling, ask to switch to another lane. If the center has the space, the staff may be able to accommodate you. However, a challenge is a challenge, and sticking it out helps you become a better bowler in the long run.

Bowling around the pattern

After you have an idea of how much oil is on the lane, you have a better idea of where you should be bowling. Too much oil in the middle? Throw more toward the outside. Too much oil on the outside? Throw a little straighter down the middle of the lane. Always strive to find the right angle that will allow your ball to hit the pins. Because that angle has to get through the oil on the lane, you need to adjust your angles accordingly.

Aiming for the pro experience

Do you ever watch the pros on television and wish that you could bowl the way they do? If so, then why not see what it's like to bowl with the same lane conditions as the pros? The USBC PBA Experience League gives you that opportunity (for more on leagues, see Chapter 18). In this league, which combines the PBA and the USBC Sport Bowling program, you bowl on the same lane conditions of the Lumber Liquidators PBA Tour.

When you join a USBC PBA Experience League, your goal is to tame the five oil patterns known as "the beasts": Chameleon, Cheetah,

Scorpion, Shark, and Viper. These wild animals are the same patterns that pro bowlers Walter Ray Williams, Jr.; Chris Barnes; Wes Malott; Pete Weber; Patrick Allen; Tommy Jones; and others try to subdue in the regular events of the Lumber Liquidators PBA Tour.

Note: You don't need to be an advanced bowler to join a USBC PBA Experience League. (Some centers even offer this league to their youth bowlers!) It's really just an opportunity to challenge yourself and see what professional-style bowling is like.

Bowling isn't a stagnant sport. You have the capability of changing your throw so you can feel comfortable with it and have the best possible chance of getting a strike. Practice on different patterns or even at different centers if more than one is available in your area.

If a particular pattern is like a thorn in your side, ask a coach who's familiar with that pattern for tips on how to adjust so you can conquer it.

Chapter 14

Staying in the Game, Physically and Mentally

*I*t's time to get your head, and body, into the game. We're not saying you have to be a muscle-bound athlete to bowl. Nor do you have to be able to run miles or live your life in the gym, training for hours at a time. However, a healthy body leads to better bowling, plain and simple. That's why we suggest you take some measures to help yourself stay flexible and prevent injuries.

This chapter focuses on keeping your body fit and your mind focused to bowl your best. We share specific stretching exercises that you can do before you bowl (believe it or not, these stretches are good exercise for everyone — even if you claim you're allergic to exercise). We also explain what to do if you sustain a bowling-related injury and how to stay positive and visualize a great game. The basics of the game and the techniques are important, but the information in this chapter is essential too because it keeps you healthy and mentally focused so you don't get psyched out by a few bad frames.

Bowling as Exercise? You'd Better Believe It!

When we hear someone who hasn't bowled before say, "Bowling isn't exercise; you only use one arm," we chuckle. These folks don't realize that bowling uses just about every muscle in your body, including your brain (more about that at the end of this chapter), making it a bona-fide form of exercise.

Just think about it. When it's your turn to bowl, you stand up, walk over to the ball return, and bend over to pick up your, say, 14-pound ball. You carry the ball, position yourself, make your approach (which includes swinging your arm, walking, and supporting your upper back), and release the ball. Depending on how many games you complete, you can wind up performing this routine almost 100 times in one night at the center.

Bowling is a better strength-training activity than a cardiovascular one, so make sure you include a 30- to 60-minute cardiovascular routine to round out your daily exercise program. Go for a walk, take a fitness class, or get moving in some other way that you enjoy. Doing so gives you the endurance to bowl multiple games without tiring so easily.

Of course, you don't just have to take our word for it that bowling is exercise. A couple respected, health-related organizations think so too:

✔ The National Heart, Lung, and Blood Institute lists bowling as a moderate-intensity exercise that's helpful in lowering high blood pressure.

✔ The President's Council on Physical Fitness and Sports, operator of the President's Challenge program, recommends bowling as one of the activities you can do to win exercise-related presidential awards.

Staying Flexible for Better Bowling Form

The more flexible you are, the easier it is to improve your bowling form. Your arm swing will be more fluid, and you'll be able to get lower to the lane for your release and follow-through. Flexibility also reduces the risk of muscle aches, pains, and strains.

To stay flexible, we strongly encourage you to do a few stretching exercises before you bowl. The following sections outline some stretches you can do at home or at the center. They don't require any special equipment, and you can perform them in less than ten minutes right at your lane or in your chair. (You can even repeat them while you wait for your turn to bowl; just don't hold anyone up because you're stretching.) We list the stretches in top-down order, so to speak, so you can start with your neck and work your way down to your toes. That way you won't forget to loosen up any body parts.

Check with your doctor before performing these stretches. She knows your medical issues best and can confirm whether these stretches are a good idea for you. Also, if you're cleared to perform these stretches and you feel any pain while doing them, stop stretching immediately and call your doctor.

The following stretches are only some of the ones you can do before you start to bowl. For more ideas, check out *Stretching For Dummies* by LaReine Chabut (Wiley), visit mayoclinic.com and search for "stretches," ask your doctor or personal trainer, or visit a local gym.

Loosening up your neck

When you release the ball, your neck muscles can feel tugged. To avoid this unpleasant experience, loosen up your neck with the following exercise:

1. **Bend your head forward and slightly to the right.**
2. **With your right hand, gently pull your head down toward your right shoulder, as in Figure 14-1.**
3. **Hold for 30 seconds and release.**
4. **Repeat on the opposite side.**

Repeat this exercise a total of five times on each side.

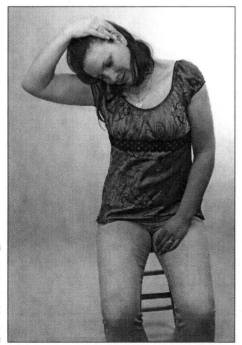

Figure 14-1: Stretching your neck helps keep it flexible.

Crossing over to stretch your shoulders

Your shoulders help you carry the weight of the ball and support your throw, so they do a lot of work when you bowl. Get them ready for the task by stretching them out beforehand. Here's how:

1. **Take your right arm and reach across your chest as if you're touching your other shoulder.**

2. **With your left hand, apply slight pressure beneath your right elbow and push your right arm slightly to really help your shoulder stretch (see Figure 14-2).**

3. **Hold for a few seconds before repeating with your opposite arm.**

To get the most from this stretch, repeat it for a total of three to five times on each side.

Figure 14-2:
A gentle stretch for your shoulders.

Stretching to avoid the "Oh, my aching back" scenario

Bowlers who don't stretch before a game often complain about backaches from all the bending and throwing. Don't be one of 'em. Perform this stretch to keep your back muscles loose and reduce the risk of bowling backaches:

1. **With your bowling arm, reach behind your head and put your hand on your upper back, as if you're patting your back.**

2. **Keep your elbow close to your head and hold it in place with your opposite hand.**

3. **Now push your elbow toward your back, as shown in Figure 14-3.**

   Your bowling arm should be reaching toward the middle of your back, and you should feel a stretch in your upper back muscles.

4. **Hold for a few seconds and release.**

5. **Repeat on the other side.**

Repeat this exercise a total of five times on each side.

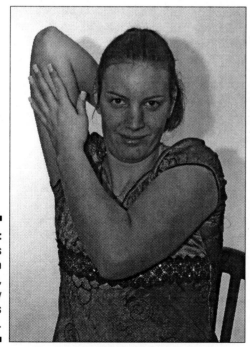

Figure 14-3:
This looks like an arm stretch, but it really stretches your back.

If you suffer from a chronic bad back, check out Chapter 16 for some additional precautions you can take and stretches you can do to stay in the game without making your situation worse.

Keeping your hands and fingers limber

Keeping your fingers limber and strong allows you to maintain a better grip on the ball. If you want to, you can purchase a hand grip or exercise ball that you squeeze to help strengthen your hand. Or you can just practice this exercise (Figure 14-4 gives you the visual):

1. **Put your bowling arm straight out in front of you with the palm up and fingers pointed down.**

2. **With your other hand, gently pull the fingers of your bowling hand back for a few seconds, keeping your bowling arm straight.**

   You don't want to yank your hand. A gentle pull is sufficient.

3. **Release and repeat the stretch on your other hand.**

   Although you only bowl with one hand, your other hand supports the ball and can therefore also benefit from this exercise.

After you've completed this stretch a couple times on both hands, place your bowling arm straight out in front of you and pull your hand down for just a few seconds. Repeat on the other arm.

Figure 14-4: This exercise is great for stretching hands and fingers.

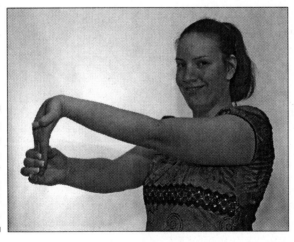

Being nice to your knees

Your knees keep you stable while you're bowling, and your quadricep muscles (found in your thighs) support your knees. Help them stay strong by stretching them out in the following manner:

1. **Hold on to a table or chair for balance and stand on one leg.**

2. **Bring your knee up to your chest.**

3. **Reach down and grab the ankle of your raised leg.**

4. **Slowly lower your knee toward the floor, but don't let go of your ankle.**

   Check out Figure 14-5 for the proper form. Also, note that you should be feeling a stretch along your thigh muscle.

5. **Hold for a second or two before bringing your knee back up, putting your foot back on the floor, and repeating the stretch on the other leg.**

Perform this stretch a total of three to five times on each leg for the best results.

Figure 14-5: Stretch your quads to keep your knees strong.

Moo-ving on to the calf stretch

Calf muscles support your release, which includes the long slide you do before letting the ball go. How so, you ask? Your calves help your legs come to a complete stop. If you don't stretch them out, you can develop muscle cramps. Here's how to stretch your calf muscles:

1. **Sit down on a chair.**
2. **Straigthen out you right leg.**
3. **Grab the toes of your right foot and pull your foot toward your body, keeping your heel on the ground (see Figure 14-6).**
4. **Hold for a few seconds before repeating on the other leg.**

Repeat this exercise for a total of three to five times on each leg.

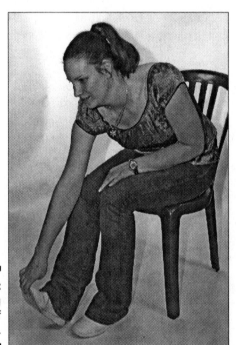

Figure 14-6:
Stretching out your calf muscle.

Common Injuries: How to Avoid Them (And How to Treat Them If You Can't)

Bowling is a fun sport, but you can get injured while doing it. The most common injuries result from trying to overthrow the ball, throwing improperly, or bowling too much. Of course, there's also the occasional I-can't-believe-I-just-dropped-the-ball-on-my-foot injury as well as other types of bumps and bruises.

Bowling centers typically have first-aid kits on hand for any minor emergencies, such as cuts and scrapes. However, centers aren't required to train employees in first aid or CPR. Instead, the staff is aware of how to notify local emergency personnel should something go wrong. If an emergency occurs while you're at the center, notify a staff member right away so she can help you.

The following sections tell you how to avoid the most common bowling-related injuries. They also clue you in to what you should do to speed healing if by chance you get injured anyway. *Note:* If you have a bad back and are worried about injuring it further, flip to Chapter 16. There we provide information about keeping this important body part strong and healthy.

The number one thing you should do if you get hurt is take care of the injury immediately and in the right manner. If you do, you'll likely be back at the lanes in no time.

Bumps and bruises

If you bowl fairly regularly, you're inevitably going to acquire a bump or bruise. To make sure you don't get them too often, always take the following basic precautions:

- ✔ **Watch your form.** If you're occasionally hitting your leg or knee with the ball, your form is off. Chapter 7 offers advice on throwing properly; use it to evaluate what you're doing wrong. If that doesn't help, ask an experienced bowler to watch you bowl a few frames and suggest ways to correct your throw.

- ✔ **Keep your hands out of the ball return.** Getting your fingers caught between bowling balls or in the return itself can be painful and cause serious injury to your hand or fingers. Pay attention to what you're doing when you grab the ball, and the odds of that happening to you will be pretty slim.

✔ **Watch where you're walking.** If you don't pay attention to where you're walking, you can easily slip and fall by stepping in someone's baby powder, in the water someone spilled on the approach, or in other debris.

For those occasions when you wind up with a nasty bump or bruise, ask the center's staffers for ice from the concession stand or an ice pack from the first-aid kit.

Cuts, scrapes, and blisters

Finger cuts, scrapes, and blisters are possible boo-boos when bowling. Most of the time they occur because your form isn't correct and the ball is being released at the wrong time, causing it to press on a part of your finger that it shouldn't. You can avoid cuts, scrapes, and blisters by double-checking your form.

Fingertip injuries may also be caused by an improperly fitting ball. If you're retaining water or have had an injury that could cause swelling in your fingers or hand, your grip may change, resulting in pressure on your fingers. You can solve this problem in one of two ways:

✔ If you own the ball and the problem is chronic, have the fit adjusted (which means having the pro shop redrill the holes).

✔ If you're using a house ball, simply find one with bigger finger holes.

If you have a cut on one of your bowling fingers, don't be afraid to put a bandage on it and continue bowling (don't worry about the bandage damaging the ball; it won't). Bowling this way isn't easy, but it's not impossible either.

Can't find a bandage? Use bowling tape! Cut off a strip and put it on your scraped finger. Or you can use a product that you brush over the cut or scrape to seal it off from bacteria and protect it. Be careful, though, because these products can sting a little.

You shouldn't get blisters on your fingers when you bowl, but if you do, stop bowling immediately. Check with the center's pro shop to see whether your bowling ball is fitted properly. By taking care of the problem immediately, you can prevent the blister from becoming worse.

Wrist and knee sprains

Because you use so many muscles when you bowl, sprains and twists are a possibility. Wrist sprains occur when you twist your wrist incorrectly while holding or throwing a heavy bowling ball; knee sprains are the result of a leg that has twisted wrong or stopped short. Symptoms of either sprain include swelling, pain during movement, bruising, tenderness, popping or tearing, and a warm feeling to the skin.

To reduce the risk of sprains, consider using a splint for extra support when you're bowling. Also, don't overthrow the ball or use one that's too heavy for you.

If you do happen to suffer a sprint, follow the RICE treatment: rest, ice, compress, and elevate. Take at least a few days off from bowling, making sure to ice the sprain to reduce swelling. Compress any swelling with an elastic bandage and elevate the joint above the level of the heart. Don't return to bowling until you feel like you can throw the ball comfortably.

Shoulder injuries

According to the American Academy of Orthopaedic Surgeons, millions of people visit their doctor each year complaining of shoulder pain. More than half of these complaints turn out to be rotator cuff problems (the *rotator cuff* is made up of the muscles and tendons that hold the arm and shoulder bones together). Shoulder injuries are often caused by athletic activities that involve excessive, repetitive, overhead motion — sounds a bit like what you do in bowling, huh?

To prevent shoulder injuries, don't use an exaggerated high backswing or overthrow the ball. Your backswing and throw should be comfortable. Also, avoid swinging the ball too far behind you or sending it down the lane like it's the Space Shuttle and you're the rocket launcher. (See Chapter 7 for the scoop on proper throwing techniques.)

Don't try to keep bowling if you're feeling pain in your shoulder (or any part of your body, for that matter); you can make the injury much worse if you do. Also, be aware of the other signs of a shoulder injury, which include stiffness, lack of rotation, a popping or sliding feeling, and lack of strength.

If you injure your shoulder while bowling, rest it and apply ice for a few days. Also make sure to contact your doctor to rule out serious injury. Depending on the extent of the injury, your doctor will prescribe exercises for you to do and possibly physical therapy. She may also prescribe an over-the-counter anti-inflammatory medication to reduce pain and swelling. Regardless of the prescribed treatment, return to bowling only when you can comfortably move your arm and release the ball.

Repetitive stress injuries

Bowling requires you to make the same movements over and over again, which can lead to a *repetitive stress injury,* which is when a joint becomes injured as a result of making the same movement over and over. The most common repetitive stress injuries among bowlers are *tendonitis* (inflammation of the tendons that attach your muscles to your bones) and *bursitis* (inflammation of the bursa sac that acts as a cushion between bones, muscles, or tendons). These conditions can occur in your shoulder, elbow, wrist, knee, hip, or ankle joints.

The best way to prevent a repetitive stress injury is to keep your joints flexible and strong. Spend some time warming up before you bowl by doing some mild stretching exercises. (We present several helpful stretches in the earlier "Staying Flexible for Better Bowling Form" section. ***Note:*** If your problem is more severe, consider doing these stretches several times per day.) Also build in some break times to keep your ligaments flexible; grab a snack, walk around the center, stretch . . . do whatever you need to do to give your joints a rest from the repetitive motions they make during a game.

The first sign of tendonitis or bursitis is a gradual pain, which can get more severe over time and is usually made worse by movement. You need to treat either condition early so it doesn't become worse.

Here's what to do when you start feeling bowling-related aches in your joints, muscles, or tendons:

- ✔ **See your doctor.** Only doctors can diagnosis tendonitis or bursitis, and they usually try to rule out other medical conditions (such as a bone problem) before treating you for a repetitive stress injury.

- ✔ **Rest the inflamed joint.** This may mean taking a week, or even a few weeks, off from bowling, but don't worry. The center will always be there. Your health is the more important thing.

- ✔ **Ice the affected area.** Do this for 10 to 15 minutes once or twice a day to reduce inflammation.

- ✔ **Use a brace.** Consider using a bowling brace on your elbow, wrist, or knee to ease the pain in your joints. Keep in mind that you may have to try a few before you find the one that works best for you.

- ✔ **Take a break during a game.** If you're open bowling with friends, stop and grab something to eat or take a rest. If you're bowling in a league, rest between games. Let the teams know you're having some difficulty and need a short break; most bowlers will understand.

✔ **Consider investing in (new) bowling shoes.** If your shoes aren't comfortable or they're wearing down, it may be time to buy new bowling shoes (or your first-ever pair). New bowling shoes that fit well give you the support you need and decrease the stress on the tendons in your ankle.

Having a Good Mental Game

When you want to succeed in something, whether that's a sport, a career, a relationship, or a hobby, you need to concentrate on your goal and stay positive. Successful businesspeople, celebrities, and athletes operate this way; you can too when you bowl. After all, you can't bowl a good game without the right concentration and attitude. The next sections offer ways to keep your head in the game (and keep from psyching yourself out).

Visualizing success

It may sound cliché, but you *can* visualize your success. *Visualization* involves imagining the outcome you want and the steps you must take to achieve it. Have you ever noticed how advanced bowlers take a second before they bowl to look down the lane? Chances are they're visualizing themselves throwing a strike. If they don't get the strike, they visualize throwing a spare on the next frame.

Say you want to throw a strike. First, picture yourself making a perfect release of the ball. Then imagine the ball heading straight into the pocket. Finally, picture all the pins falling down. Strike!

Visualization also helps you block out distractions, like those bowlers a few lanes down who are laughing hysterically or the child in your pit who's screaming because she doesn't want to leave. Visualizing your goal and each step it takes to get there helps keep you focused.

Visualization also helps you relax. Before you visualize, take a deep breath. You'll feel your body start to de-stress, enabling you to better focus on your target.

Staying positive

The number one rule in bowling is this: Have fun! Getting upset over not throwing a strike, not picking up a spare, having poor form, or throwing a gutterball just isn't worth it. In fact, becoming tense and frustrated may actually make your next throw worse. Instead of getting angry and down on yourself, think positively.

Every bowler throws a bad shot from time to time. The trick is to remember that you're going to bowl again (unless of course it's the tenth frame, but even then you know that sometime in your life you're going to bowl another game). That next frame (or game) is a new chance to throw better, and even one strike or spare can turn your game around. Focus on that concept and don't let one bad throw ruin your entire game.

Following are some additional suggestions for keeping a positive mindset. Try them and watch your game (and attitude) improve.

- ✔ **Encourage other bowlers.** Give them high-fives, clap when they do well, and encourage them on difficult shots (but not, of course, when they're actually bowling). We bet you soon find that it's hard to be negative about your own bowling when you're trying to encourage your fellow bowlers. And what goes around comes around. When you encourage others, they'll encourage you too.

- ✔ **Bowl with other positive bowlers.** Bowling with friends who are always negative isn't much fun. You wind up all tense, and your game goes down the tubes. Instead of bowling with Negative Nellies, bring along friends or family members who know how to have a good time. When you're having fun, you're relaxed, and when you're relaxed, you have a better game.

- ✔ **Read about successful pro bowlers.** Checking out the stories of successful and positive pro bowlers can inspire you to stay focused and positive in your own game. You can find these stories on the Web sites of the United States Bowling Congress (bowl.com) and the Professional Bowlers Association (www.pba.com).

- ✔ **Fill a poster board with positive reinforcements.** These reinforcements can be anything: your highest score to date, quotes from positive influences in your life, you name it. As long as they're inspiring to you, that's what counts. Add all the positive reinforcements you can think of to your board and refer to them before you head to the center. (*Note:* This positive-thinking tactic is especially helpful for children.)

Chapter 15

Improving Your Game on Your Own or with a Coach's Help

In This Chapter

▶ Bettering your bowling all by yourself

▶ Determining whether your game needs a coach's touch

▶ Finding and teaming up with the right coach

After you've been bowling for a while, you're bound to want to take your game to the next level, improve your approach, or even change your style. In some instances, you can do all of this on your own, but the best and fastest way to become a better bowler is to work with a bowling coach. Why? Because a coach watches you bowl, evaluates your technique, and makes suggestions for improvement — all of which are a little tough to do on your own.

This chapter focuses on ways to improve your game, including some drills you can perform solo. It also helps you figure out when the time is right to work with a coach, how to find the right one for you, and how to work with him to set attainable goals.

Achieving that perfect 300 game takes practice, practice, and more practice. Regardless of whether you work on improving your game with a coach or by yourself, getting better requires equal parts dedication and practice. So get out there and bowl already!

Doing as Much as You Can on Your Own

Sometimes working with a bowling coach is the only real way to improve your game, but first you should spend some time working to better your bowling on your own. You can start improving your game on your own by working on any common problems you may have (we help you fix those in Chapter 8) and by trying one or more of the following drills:

✔ **Tape yourself in action.** Have a family member or friend accompany you to the center to tape you in action. He should set up the camera to get a side view of your bowling (if at all possible) and then a back view, making sure your entire body, including your feet, is captured on the screen. Your job is to forget you're being recorded and just bowl. When you watch the tape later, follow your approach, throw, and follow-through and look for areas you need to improve. You can even slow the video down or freeze it to focus on certain aspects of your game to get a closer look.

If you're going to film yourself, go to the center at a slower time of day when the place isn't filled with bowlers. Also, be sure to get a staff member's permission before setting up the camera.

When you have the all-clear to proceed with taping, ask to be placed on the lane that'll give you the best angle for viewing the playback of your throw. A right-handed bowler should be videotaped on an even-numbered lane and a left-handed bowler on an odd-numbered lane in order to keep the ball return from getting in the way of the camera.

✔ **Try the "no-score" technique.** The higher your score goes each frame, the happier you get. But when you're not doing well, watching your score may make you angry or frustrated, both of which can affect your game. Stop focusing on the score and focus on your form instead. We know that's easier said than done because watching your score climb higher and higher is exciting, but when you don't focus on the numbers, you start to zero in on your throw. Try this technique during games and practice sessions to improve your mental game.

✔ **Use a speed detector.** A radar gun — similar to the ones policemen use to catch speed demons — can clock how fast your bowling ball is going down the lane (the ideal speed is 16 miles per hour). The ball needs the right amount of power and speed to knock down all the pins. Without this combination, the ball just isn't going to do its job. A speed detector can help you figure out how fast you're throwing so you can determine whether you need to speed up or slow down.

Some centers have automatic speed detectors in their computers (you can find out your speed by watching the monitor), but if your center doesn't have a speed detector, you can invest in one of your own. Otherwise you're just going to have to judge the "right" speed of the ball by the success of your shot.

After you've improved as much as you can on your own, the only way to step your game up to the next level is with the aid of a coach, which is the focus of the rest of this chapter.

Bowling superstitions

Bowlers are like many other athletes. They work hard and love what they do, and some even believe in *superstitions,* beliefs that something they do affects how they bowl. Some common bowling superstitions include the following:

✔ **300 game jinx:** If you see someone starting out a game with several strikes, don't mention that he's on his way to a perfect game of 300! That's considered a jinx and can make the bowler nervous. Instead, just keep high-fiving and encouraging him.

✔ **Good-luck charms:** Some bowlers pull a stuffed animal out of their bowling bag and set it where they can see it; others wear the same shirt or the same charm around their neck each week. Either way, they're hoping that talisman will bring them lots of strikes and spares!

✔ **Doing things the same way:** Professional bowler Pete Weber has been known to sit in the same spot the same way whenever he bowls well; he also likes to fold his towel the same way. Other bowlers make sure they repeat certain mannerisms while making their approach. The idea? If it worked, keep doing it.

✔ **Cleaning the bowling ball before every frame:** Some bowlers believe that cleaning their ball before each frame helps them bowl better.

Deciding Whether You Need a Coach

If you're experiencing any of the following situations, odds are good you can benefit from the instruction of the right bowling coach:

✔ You can't get your score to go any higher, no matter how hard you try. For example, you're bowling in the 150s, which is good, but you want to bowl in the 160s or even the 170s.

✔ You're looking to take your game to the next level. For instance, you want to bowl your first 200 game.

✔ You want to improve your form, approach, or technique. Maybe you want to perfect your hook so that it looks like that of the advanced bowlers at your center.

✔ Your mental game just isn't there. Perhaps there's too much negative self-talk going on and you need someone to help focus your mind and create some goals for you to achieve.

 Not sure whether you can make the financial and time commitment of hiring a coach? Take the intermediate step of asking an advanced bowler whose style and form you admire for some tips and suggestions on improving your game. If his tips don't help, then you can consider talking to a coach who can give you personalized instruction.

Wanted: A Personal Bowling Coach

Before you start the search for a bowling coach, you need to know what you want out of your coaching sessions and what kind of commitment (of both time and money) you can make to improve your skills. The following sections help you figure that out so you can start the search for a coach.

Working with a bowling coach helps kids get on the right track to good habits, so consider finding a youth coach while you're looking into a coach for yourself.

Considering your goals and commitment level

First things first: Decide exactly what you want from a bowling coach. Whether that's a higher average, better technique for converting splits and picking up spares, the ability to bowl with your opposite hand, or any combination of goals, write it down. Knowing what you want to achieve ahead of time helps you find the coach who can best help you realize those goals and maximize your lesson time.

Speaking of time, another big point to consider is how often and when you can meet. Some certified coaches require a three-lesson minimum, but maybe you only need one lesson to review and correct a few technique problems and get some tips. As for when you can meet, is your schedule flexible? Can you meet in the evening or only on Monday mornings? Look at your schedule ahead of time. Most coaches hold regular jobs in addition to coaching and may only be available at certain times of the day. Is one of those times compatible with the time you're available?

Finally, you should think about how much of a financial commitment you're willing to make. Your lessons should fit your budget. On average, most bowling coaches charge $35 per hour and require a minimum of three lessons, although some may offer a discount if you pay for all three lessons upfront. In areas with a higher cost of living, such as New York City or Los Angeles, the hourly coaching fees may be pricier than those in a small town in Pennsylvania or Kansas. But you also have to consider the payoff of working with a certified bowling coach: For example, if after your lessons you win prize money in a tournament, your coaching sessions have paid for themselves.

Finding a coach

When you're ready to acquire the names and contact information of bowling coaches near you, start

- ✔ **Talking to other bowlers:** Some of your fellow bowlers may be working with a coach; you'll never know if you don't ask. If they are, ask whether they can recommend someone and share what they liked and didn't like about him.

- ✔ **Asking around at the bowling center or pro shop:** The staff members at centers and pro shops are familiar with the coaches in the area and can give you some names and contact information. If you're lucky, they may even share some inside information about them, such as personality and coaching style.

- ✔ **Checking out the United States Bowling Congress's Web site:** The USBC Web site (bowl.com) allows you to look up coaches by state. Just go to the Find a . . . box on the upper-right-hand side of the page and click on Find a Coach to access the state-by-state search function.

The USBC Web site is a great way to find a coach in another area when you travel to participate in a tournament. Contact a coach in that area before you go and schedule some practice time with him (on the tournament lanes, if at all possible). Doing so gives you an opportunity for last-minute tips as well as time to get used to the lanes before the tournament begins.

- ✔ **Contacting local colleges that have a bowling program:** Collegiate bowling coaches may want to make extra money by coaching off-season or on days their team isn't practicing. However, they may or may not be certified (we fill you in on the value of certification in the next section).

Knowing what to look for

We strongly advise against handing your money over to a bowling coach without doing a little background research on him. The goals are to make sure that the coach you decide to work with is who he says he is and to know that he's going to be a good fit for you.

Following are some characteristics to look for when deciding on a bowling coach. Note that the first one, training or certification, is the only thing you can verify without ever speaking to the coach. For the other three characteristics, you'll need to chat with the coach on the phone, meet in person, or set up a trial lesson.

✔ **Training or certification:** The USBC runs a certification program for coaches and maintains a database on its Web site of those individuals who've completed the program. USBC coaches take courses and pass tests in order to achieve various levels of certification (Level One, Bronze, Silver, and Gold). The higher the level, the more experience the coach has.

✔ **A good personality:** Nothing will turn your experience sour faster than working with a bowling coach who has a horrible personality. Ask yourself whether the coach seems likeable and willing to help. Also gauge whether you feel comfortable asking him for advice.

✔ **A positive attitude:** A good coach helps you feel positive about your bowling and shows you techniques to stay focused and handle the difficult shots. A bad coach puts you down and makes you feel like you can't get any better.

✔ **A good style:** We're talking about coaching style here, not whether your prospective coach has a stylish wardrobe. Is the coach a hands-on person who gets up on the approach with you and helps correct your style, or does he stay back and talk you through it? Does he use any training aids, such as videotape or diagrams? Does he support his student or not say much? After you decide what kind of coaching style you like best, you can narrow down your coaching selections.

A coach should never verbally or physically abuse his students. If something about your lessons doesn't feel right, change coaches immediately and report the offending coach to the bowling center and to the organization that issued his certification.

Taking advantage of group lessons

Group lessons are sometimes a more affordable alternative to private bowling lessons. The best ways to find group bowling lessons in your area are to ask around at the center and contact someone at your local Parks and Recreation Department or community college. You can also contact your school district's Continuing Education Department.

At one of the bowling centers that coauthor A.J. manages, coaches have teamed up with the local school district and offered a weekly bowling course for beginning and advanced bowlers. The coaches keep a watchful eye on the bowlers as they practice and visit with each one, personalizing tips and suggestions and helping set weekly goals.

If you feel like maybe taking a trip to participate in a group bowling lesson, you may want to check out a bowling clinic or camp, such as Dick Ritger's Bowling Camps (`ritgerbowling camp.com/General_Info.htm`). Be sure to research any camp or clinic and its methods before you sign up.

Working with a Coach

After you find the perfect bowling coach for you, your success at the sport becomes a team effort. You must listen to the coach and practice what he has taught you (drills come in handy for this; we give you some drills in the earlier "Doing as Much as You Can on Your Own" section); you must also set goals for yourself. We help you with goal-setting and give you a preview of common coaching tools in the next sections.

Setting goals together

Goal-setting is an important part of improving yourself as a bowler. When you first start working with a coach, he'll either ask you what you want your goals to be or watch you throw the ball a few times and get an idea of where you need improvement. Then he'll turn these areas of improvement into goals for you.

For example, perhaps after watching you throw the ball a few times, your coach notices that the ball loses steam before it reaches the pins. In this case, you and he may decide that your goal should be to figure out how to increase your power and speed.

Here are some other goals you can set:

- ✔ Picking up the 7- or 10-pin spare.
- ✔ Hitting the pocket.
- ✔ Converting splits into spares.
- ✔ Adding 10 points to your average.
- ✔ Hooking the ball more or less.
- ✔ Releasing the ball earlier or later.

Setting goals allows you to see progress in your lessons. If you meet your first goal, set another one. Always keep looking for ways to improve your bowling skills, and you won't be disappointed in the results.

Setting SMART goals

Goals aren't just something you write on a piece of paper. You need to give them some thought. Many people follow the SMART style of goal-setting, which means the goals should be:

- **Specific:** What exactly does being a better bowler mean to you? Someone with a 200 or higher average? Someone who wins tournaments? Be specific when you write down your goal. Saying "I want to increase my average by 5 points in two months" is better than saying "I want to be a better bowler."

- **Measurable:** After setting your specific goal — in this case, increasing your average by 5 points in two months — consider ways you can measure your progress. List steps that you can not only take to achieve your goal but also measure along the way. Some measurable action steps for our example goal are "call a bowling coach," "take a few lessons," and "practice twice a week."

- **Achievable:** Is your goal achievable? Yes, a goal of increasing your average by 5 points is attainable, but bowling a 250 game when you're a 120-average bowler may not be. We've seen bowlers with low averages have a wonderful game, but we're not talking about the once-in-a-while good game here. We're talking about achieving truly attainable goals on a regular basis. If you want to achieve a 250 score regularly, you have to be prepared to put in a lot of practice and hard work. Can you do that right now?

- **Realistic:** Small, realistic goals set the groundwork for success. You can win lots of tournaments, but the odds that you'll win every bowling tournament your center has or bowl multiple 300 games is a shot in the dark. Stay focused on what's realistic — in this case, shooting for a 5-point increase is completely realistic.

- **Timely:** Your goals should always be timely. So you want to raise your average 5 points. Do you have time to practice? Is it important that you raise your average now? Or should you be focusing on throwing a better hook or picking up the 5 pin that you keep missing?

Looking at commonly used coaching techniques and drills

Your coach may use a combination of various coaching techniques and drills to help you achieve your goals. Following are a few of the most common ones:

- **Bowling on paper:** Watching the ball roll down the lane is easy; telling whether or not it has rolled over the intended target isn't. Your coach may choose to use *tracking paper*, a special paper that's put on the lane (with permission, of course). You bowl onto the paper, and your oil track tells you whether you're hitting your target.

✔ **Throwing around a cone:** Sometimes coaches use a cone as a way of helping students learn how to throw a hook. When a cone is placed on the lane, you have to figure out how to throw so your ball hooks around it. This may require you to reposition your feet, but it's still a great exercise.

Never place a cone on the lane without the center's permission because you might damage the lane.

✔ **Shadow bowling:** This technique is for the coach who prefers to show you what to do and have you copy him. It's beneficial because you get to see someone actually doing the approach instead of just having it explained to you.

Chapter 16

Bowling When You Have Special Health Conditions

In This Chapter

▶ Having fun at the center whether you're pregnant, a senior, or have special needs

▶ Bowling safely after surgery or when you have back pain

*L*ife circumstances don't always make it possible for you to bowl the regular way. Maybe you're wondering whether you can bowl while you're pregnant or after you've had surgery. Perhaps you feel your age creeping up on you and wonder whether you need to make any adjustments based on aches and pains or other changes in your body. Maybe you have a disability and wonder whether accommodations can be made for you to participate in the sport.

The good news is that, yes, it's possible to bowl when you're pregnant, when you're into your senior years and your body has changed, when you live with a disability, after you've had surgery, and when you have various aches and pains. Whatever your situation, this chapter gives you points to keep in mind so you can safely enjoy bowling with your friends and family.

The information you receive in this chapter is purely guidance. Discuss your individual situation with your doctor. After all, she knows your personal health background — and whether you should be bowling in the first place. Sure, we want you bowling, but we also want you at the center safe and healthy.

Staying Safe with Baby on Board

First off, congratulations on your future little bowler! While you wait for his or her arrival, you'll be glad to know that you can probably still enjoy your Friday bowling nights with friends or your weekly bowling league. That's right. In most cases, bowling is an activity that all pregnant women can enjoy. We've even seen pregnant woman at the center who are only days away from their due date.

Double-check with your obstetrician to make sure you're cleared to bowl and to find out whether she wants you to adjust how you're bowling or avoid doing anything specific.

In most cases, you're not likely to injure yourself when you bowl while pregnant, but we recommend you take the following precautions just to be safe:

- ✔ **Use the right bowling ball.** The weight of the ball should always be comfortable to you, but as your pregnancy progresses, you may find that your current ball begins to feel a little heavier due to your weight gain, changing muscle tone, and personal comfort level. When the ball feels heavier, you tire out faster and tend to drop the ball onto the lane instead of rolling it. The solution? Switch to a lighter-weight ball, no matter how early or late it is in the pregnancy. For example, if you normally use a 12-pound ball, start using a 10- or even an 8-pound ball to cut your back and abdominal muscles some slack. Whatever weight of ball you're using, make sure you lift it properly. Bending your knees a little and using two hands helps prevent muscle strain.

- ✔ **Watch the oil.** This advice is really for every bowler, but it bears repeating, especially for pregnant women. Oil on the lanes means it's pretty slippery out there. If you normally slide your foot really close to the foul line, you may want to take a step or two back from the beginning of your approach so that you release the ball a little farther from the line. This precaution reduces the chance that your foot will accidentally slide onto the lane and you'll slip and fall.

- ✔ **Ease up on your throw.** Bowling is meant to be fun, so as you get closer to your due date, you may feel more comfortable if you ease up on your throw a little. That could mean not powering the ball as much as you typically do, not bringing your backswing up so high, or not bending so low. Also, you may need to make some adjustments as your belly expands. Your score may suffer, but you'll still be having fun, as well as exercising. And don't worry — pretty soon you'll be back to bowling with your proper form.

- ✔ **Stand up for a while.** For some pregnant women, the hardest part about bowling is the getting up and down when it's their turn. You may want to stand for a while just to give yourself a bit of a break from the up-down-up-down flow of the game. We also suggest sitting down and taking a break between games.

If you feel any contractions starting or that something isn't quite right when you're bowling, stop immediately and contact your doctor.

Heading to the Lanes in Your Senior Years

Bowling has no age limit. In fact, the oldest bowler known to date was a 106-year-old Georgia man named Bill Hargrove. Of course, just because you can bowl at any age doesn't mean your body always wants to cooperate. In the following sections, we take a look at the advantages of continuing to bowl (or picking up bowling as a hobby) as you grow older.

Adding some sparkle to your golden years

Bowling is a perfect activity for seniors for a host of reasons. First, you're never too old to bowl, which means you can enjoy bowling way past your retirement years. Second, studies have shown that seniors can improve — and even extend — their lives by participating in social activities.

Seniors also reap many health benefits from bowling. As people age, joint problems such as arthritis can set in and make activity difficult. A lightweight bowling ball plus the motion that occurs in the joints while you throw the ball help keep your body active. Even seniors who have joint problems can still bowl with the assistance of wrist supports and back supports. As for mental health, bowling helps boost self-confidence. Some days few things feel better than throwing strikes and spares.

Bowling is also an affordable retirement activity. Many centers provide special perks for seniors, including discounted rates and free coffee. Ask your center what seniors-only specials are available.

A lifelong pursuit

At 106 years of age, Bill Hargrove of Atlanta, Georgia, was believed to be the world's oldest bowler. He passed away in 2008, and *The Washington Post* reported on his death, saying that Hargrove began bowling in 1924 by playing duckpin bowling. He later moved on to ten-pin bowling, asserting that it helped him cope with the death of his wife in 1973 and gave him something to look forward to after he retired. In May 2007, the United States Bowling Congress dubbed him the "World's Oldest Bowler." Even though his eyesight had deteriorated over time, Hargrove was still able to imagine the pins and keep on bowling.

Accommodating special senior circumstances

If you've made it to your golden years and you want to continue (or start) bowling, here's what you need to know about age-related conditions before stepping out on the lanes:

✔ **Arthritis:** Bowling with arthritis in any of your joints isn't easy. Sometimes bowling can help keep your joints limber; other times it can make you stiff and sore. Chat with your doctor about using an anti-inflammatory medication, ice, heat, or rest on the nights you bowl (the treatment depends on the severity of your arthritis).

At the bowling center, you may also want use a lighter ball that isn't so stressful on your joints. If you have arthritis in your hands, you may find it easier to start at the foul line and roll the ball instead of creating a full backswing (see Figure 16-1). Whatever you decide to do, always make sure you're warming up and cooling down (see Chapter 14 for specific exercises you can do). You can also try wearing a bowling brace to help alleviate the pain.

Figure 16-1: If you suffer from arthritis, you can start at the foul line and roll the ball instead of using the traditional backswing.

✔ **Loss of strength:** As you age, you lose some of your muscle mass, which reduces your strength. You may find that bowling with a lighter-weight ball helps make up for this decrease in strength. Of course, after you switch to a lighter ball, you may have to adjust your speed or power in order to reach the pocket.

✔ **Pacemaker:** A *pacemaker* is a small device that's placed in the chest or abdomen to help control abnormal heart rhythms. It uses electrical pulses to prompt the heart to beat at a normal rate. As long as your physician gives you the go-ahead, we know of no other bowling-related limitations for folks with pacemakers other than that bowling isn't recommended within the first month after having a pacemaker put in.

Bowling with Special Needs

Living with a disability doesn't mean you can't have as much fun at the local bowling center as the next person. If you need it, you can use special equipment to help you bowl, and you can even get involved with different organizations that promote bowling among people with special needs. We cover what you need to know in the sections that follow.

To find a special needs bowling group in your area, ask the staff members at your local bowling center whether they know of any local ones.

Adjusting for physical limitations

Some people with disabilities can bowl without any assistance; others may need to modify how the ball is sent down the lane based on their physical limitations. If you

✔ **Are restricted to a wheelchair:** Bowling in a wheelchair takes some practice, but it can be done. To give yourself as much range of motion as possible for your throw, try stretching out as far as you can. Having trouble getting the ball down the lane? Consider using a ramp or ball pusher to get the ball moving toward the pins.

Wheelchairs are welcome on the approach, but please make sure the wheels are dry and clean to help prevent damage to the lanes and prevent injury to other bowlers.

✔ **Have vision loss:** You can still bowl even if your eyesight is deteriorating or completely gone. Some visually impaired bowlers prefer to have a "spotter" with them to tell them what pins are left for their second shot so that they know where to aim for their spares. Another option is to use a ramp as a guide to position yourself correctly before the foul line so you can swing the ball back and roll it onto the lane (we describe ramps in the next section).

If you have only partial vision loss, try bowling with a brightly colored ball that's easier to see in the ball return and on the lane.

Taking advantage of special equipment

Bowling centers offer several special devices that can help you bowl if you can't throw the ball down the lane on your own:

- **Ramps:** A *ramp* helps the ball gain momentum so it can speed down the lane and hit the pins. To use it, simply have a friend or family member set the ramp up at the foul line. Put the ball at the top of the ramp and then give it a push. Ask your local center whether it has a ramp. Even if you've never seen one there, that doesn't mean the center doesn't own one. It may just be stored away until a bowler needs it.

- **Ball pushers:** A *ball pusher* (also called a *bowling stick*) lets you push the ball on the ground. You can use one from either a standing or sitting position.

- **Bumpers:** *Bumpers* are rails that can be pulled out of the sides of a lane to cover the gutters. They're useful because they prevent gutterballs. You may need special permission from the center to use the bumpers because they may have to be opened for you. Other centers have bumpers with a handle that's easily reachable and can be pulled out by the customer (just don't step on the lane to do so because it's slick and you might fall).

Finding bowling opportunities through special organizations

Over the years, several organizations for people with disabilities have created bowling opportunities, including leagues and tournaments. Some of these organizations are recognized nationally and have local chapters; others are operated by local community groups. Following are a couple of the nationally recognized organizations that you may recognize:

- **American Wheelchair Bowling Association:** Founded in 1962, the American Wheelchair Bowling Association (AWBA) has grown to include more than 500 members throughout the continental United States. It works with the Veterans Administration, Paralyzed Veterans of America, and various youth organizations to promote wheelchair bowling. Bowlers of all skill levels can participate in the AWBA's tournaments; you can find out more at www.awba.org.

✔ **Special Olympics:** Special Olympics teaches sports, including bowling, to anyone age 8 or older who has an intellectual disability. Check the Web site (www.specialolympics.org) for more information or to find a group near you.

Post-Surgery Bowling, Your Doctor's Decision

Whether you've had a hip replacement, heart surgery, or an appendectomy, returning to bowling after surgery is up to your doctor, not us. Each medical procedure comes with its own healing time as well as certain precautions and activities you have to avoid. That's why you should never return to bowling without obtaining clearance from your doctor. (*Note:* Low-impact sports such as bowling are often actually recommended after surgery; high-impact sports such as running and basketball typically aren't.)

After you have your doctor's permission to bowl, you may find that you need to work your way back gradually, especially if you've been sidelined for a while. Your strength may not be the same, and depending on what type of surgery you had, you may find that throwing a bowling ball isn't as easy as it was before. If that's the case, head to Chapter 6 for a refresher course on your approach (you may need to tweak your approach to compensate for your current condition).

Bowling with a Bad Back

We see many bowlers who have a bad back and want to bowl because they want to get a little bit of exercise that isn't as hard on the back as other activities, such as jogging or weight lifting. Remember, though, that bowling uses just about all the muscles in your body, not just your arm. It especially uses your back muscles, so if you don't throw the ball properly, you can wind up doing more damage to your back. The next sections explain why bowling may aggravate your back and what you can do to minimize the amount of discomfort you experience.

Talk to your doctor about how you can continue bowling without injuring your back any further. Among other suggestions, she may encourage you to wear a brace while you bowl to provide extra support.

Understanding how bowling affects your back

Bowling is a one-sided sport, meaning you bowl either right-handed or left-handed. Your body automatically reacts to holding the bowling ball on one side of your body by shifting the extra weight of the ball so that your center of gravity remains in the center of your body. You may not feel this adjustment, but it happens. When your body repeatedly adjusts itself in response to the extra weight of a bowling ball or shifts your center of gravity for hours at a time, that takes a toll on your muscles. Add the act of throwing a 10-, 12-, or 16-pound ball to the mix, and you can see why your back may hurt after a long night of bowling.

Your back will speak to you — listen to it. Perhaps you're leaning over too far at the line, putting your body weight more on your back than on your legs. Or maybe you're throwing the ball really hard and feeling a twinge of pain. That pain is your back screaming out to you to ease up a little. Don't throw the ball so hard, consider using a lighter ball, and try not to twist your body when you throw. If the pain doesn't go away, stop bowling and see your doctor.

Taking care of your spine

Because we want to give you the most accurate information possible about caring for your spine so bowling doesn't make your bad back worse, we spoke with Dr. Dolly Garnecki, the founder, president, and director of Spinal Health & Wellness in Charlottesville, Virginia.

Dr. Garnecki explains that the *spinal discs* — the cushiony, gelatin-like spacers found between the protective bones of the spine — need to be warmed up and cooled down appropriately before any type of physical activity, including bowling. She likens it to adding water to gelatin: "What happens when you add hot water to gelatin? It warms up, softens, and is malleable. When you chill the gelatin, it hardens in whatever mold or position you last left it. The same holds true for the gelatinous matrix of spinal discs." So when you warm up your body's spinal discs during bowling, the last thing you want to do is let those discs mold into a poor position by resorting to bad posture as soon as the game is over.

To make sure your spine stays healthy and to minimize stress on your back, Dr. Garnecki recommends performing the exercises described in the following sections.

Try treating any bowling-related back pain with ice. Ice can help suppress muscle soreness if you leave it on for 20 minutes and take it off for 40 minutes.

Do warm-up spinal twists

Warming up your spine by doing some spinal twists loosens tight muscles. Perform this exercise first thing in the morning, before bowling, and before bedtime. Here's how:

1. **Sit on the edge of a chair with both feet flat on the floor.**

2. **Hold your arms up level with your collarbone (so that your elbows stick out), arch your lower back, and stick out your chest.**

3. **Twist as far as you can to the right.**

4. **Keep your eyes looking up and turn your head to the right (see Figure 16-2).**

5. **Repeat to the left to complete one full repetition.**

6. **Speed up your twist a little and repeat 25 times.**

If you get dizzy during the twist, remember to keep your chin up and eyes looking upward.

Figure 16-2:
A warm-up
spinal twist.

Practice with your nonbowling hand

When you're warming up before a game, take some practice shots with the hand that doesn't normally throw the bowling ball (also known as your non-bowling hand). Doing so strengthens the muscles on that side of your body in order to prevent injury. Basically, if you typically warm up by throwing ten shots with your right hand, instead do five or so easy throws with your left hand. The movement will be awkward at first, but that's okay because you're doing this purely as a warm-up exercise.

After the game, throw a few cool-down throws with your nonbowling hand. The combination of warming up and cooling down with your nonbowling hand will ultimately improve your strength on both sides of your body and lead you to a better game.

Finish with spinal molding

Molding your spine gives the natural curves in your neck and lower back time to position into place, reducing lower back or neck pain and allowing the discs in your spine to rehydrate, renew, and restore themselves overnight.

To mold your spinal discs into a strong and stable position, you first need to create a couple spinal molds. Take two bath towels, fold each one lengthwise into thirds, roll each one up so it's a comfortable thickness, and secure the ends of the towels with rubber bands.

Do 25 spinal twists (as explained earlier in this chapter). When you finish your twists, place one of your spinal molds beneath your neck, just above your shoulders, and place the other one behind your lower back (see Figure 16-3). Then lie on the molds for 20 to 30 minutes. *Note:* You can do this on the floor or on your bed, but the surface should be flat and comfortable.

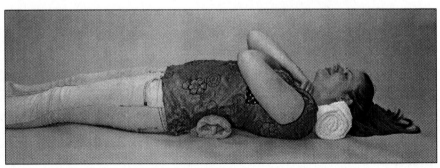

Figure 16-3:
Ease stress
on your
back with
spinal
molding.

Part V
Joining Others at the Center

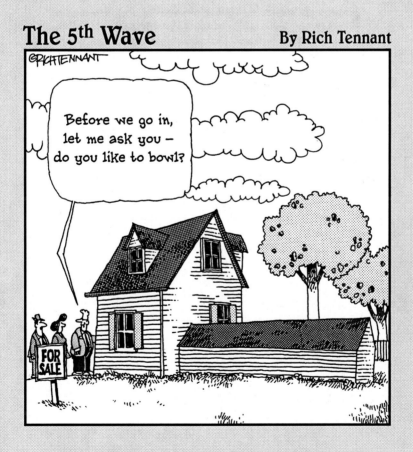

The 5th Wave   By Rich Tennant

Before we go in,
let me ask you —
do you like to bowl?

FOR SALE

In this part . . .

This part starts out with an entire chapter devoted to what you need to know when bowling with children. It shows you how to teach kids about the sport, how to sign them up for a youth league, and how to throw a fun bowling birthday party.

And because kids aren't the only ones who can have a great time bowling with others, this part also features a chapter on adult leagues and tournaments. By joining a league — and there's a league for everyone, we might add — you meet others who like to bowl and learn to play under some slightly different rules. When you're ready for a little more friendly competition, you can enter a bowling tournament. This part explains the nuts and bolts of tournaments, including the different types and how you can sign up.

Chapter 17

Taking the Kids Bowling

*W*hen deciding on an activity for your child, bowling should be first on the list! Okay, so we're a little biased, but kids of all ages (and skill levels) can enjoy bowling. Little ones can use ramps or bumpers, and older children can participate in youth leagues or on school teams.

This chapter has all the information you need to know to get your kid bowling. It fills you in on what life skills your child can pick up from bowling, explains how to choose the right-sized bowling ball and teach her the basics of the game, and covers how to sign him up for a league or tournament.

As your son or daughter grows and becomes even more interested in bowling, you can refer back to this chapter to discover how bowling can become a part of your child's school experience all the way through college and how it can open up great scholarship opportunities for him or her. And what better way to celebrate your child's birthday and keep the bowling fun going than to have a bowling birthday party? We help you figure out how to host one in this chapter as well.

Kids and Bowling, a Winning Combination

Kids and bowling go together like peanut butter and jelly. Kids can pick up the basics in no time, and whether they knock down one pin or all the pins, they get excited. Ultimately, kids like to bowl for the same reason adults do: They know it's just plain ol' fun!

The top ten reasons to encourage kids to start bowling

If your kids can't bear the thought of going with you to the bowling center for an afternoon or evening of family bowling, try using one of these arguments (or more if your kids are particularly stubborn) to persuade them that bowling is cool:

1. **It's fun!** When they get started, kids love bowling, and they have a lot of fun with it.

2. **Anyone can do it.** Sometimes children are discouraged from playing certain sports based on their size, but size doesn't matter in bowling. Anyone — short or tall, strong or weak — can bowl.

3. **You get to wear the coolest shoes.** Bowling shoes are pretty darn cool when you think about it. Everybody has to try on a pair of colorful house bowling shoes at least once.

4. **You can play against anybody.** Play against mom, dad, big brother or sister, Uncle Fred, or grandma. It doesn't matter. You can bowl against anyone.

5. **It gets you up and moving.** Bowling may not look like it takes much effort, but it does. Bowling keeps you active and gets you using all sorts of different muscles (see Chapter 14 for more details).

6. **You can be really good at it.** Even if you bowl gutterballs when you first hit the lanes, you can always improve with a little practice.

7. **You don't have to audition or try out.** Some children don't do well in a competitive environment of auditions or tryouts. Bowling (and youth bowling leagues) don't require tryouts; just sign up and you're in!

8. **You can meet cool new friends who like to bowl.** Joining a bowling league isn't just a fun thing to do — it's an opportunity to meet other boys and girls who enjoy bowling.

9. **You can win stuff.** Join a league or participate in a tournament and you can win cool prizes, including trophies, awards, and scholarships.

10. **You can bowl year-round.** Too cold outside? Bowling centers are open. Too hot? Go bowling. Rainy or snowy? Go bowling. You get the idea.

From a parental perspective, you should know that bowling is more than just fun — it's also a valuable tool for enabling your child's growth as a person. Without even trying, bowling teaches children social skills. Just think about it. When you're at the center, you can't just make up your own rules, play on someone else's lane, throw the ball whenever you feel like it, or pout when someone else bowls better than you. Instead, you have to follow the rules, stick to your own lane, wait your turn, and cheer on fellow bowlers who are doing well. What great behaviors for a child to learn!

The more your child bowls, the more her skills — both bowling and social — improve, and the more confidence she gains. She also develops discipline and concentration. All of these skills can be transferred into other aspects of your child's life, making bowling a good foundation for her personal development.

Choosing the Right Ball

If you want to encourage your child to love bowling, get him off to a stellar start with the right bowling ball. A ball that's too heavy can easily hurt your child when he drops it on his toes or falls over while holding it, and a ball that's way too light doesn't encourage your child to use proper bowling form because it's far too tempting to just fling a too-light ball down the lane as hard and as fast as possible.

So what exactly do we mean by "right"? Well, that all depends on your child's weight. And because children are still growing, you may want to consider whether it's more practical to use a house ball for a couple years instead of buying a new ball for your child every time he has a growth spurt. We cover each of these points in the following sections.

Finding a ball with the right weight and fit

The guideline for finding the right child-sized bowling ball is the same as the one for finding the right adult-sized bowling ball: The ball should weigh 10 percent of the bowler's body weight. So if Jimmy weighs 75 pounds, he should use a 7- or 8-pound ball. *Note:* A child who weighs less than 60 pounds should use a 4-, 5-, or 6-pound house ball (custom bowling balls start at 6 pounds).

After you know the weight that the ball should be, it's time to find one that your child can hold easily. Test a bowling ball he's interested in by having him put his thumb and middle and ring fingers into the respective holes to make sure he can hold the ball properly (see Chapter 4 for a picture of a proper grip). His fingers shouldn't be squeezed; if they are, the finger holes are too small. He shouldn't be dropping the ball either; if he is, the holes are too big.

If your child keeps dropping a ball even when his fingers fit in it properly, the ball is probably too heavy. Consider a lighter one.

Hunting down a house ball

Every center has a variety of house balls to choose from, which means you don't *have* to buy any equipment — not even bowling shoes (the center has those too) — to get a child started in bowling.

Children's bowling shoes: To buy or not to buy?

When your child bowls, he needs to wear bowling shoes to protect his feet and the approach. Because children's feet grow fast, sometimes two or three sizes in a year, we recommend that you rent shoes until Junior's physical growth slows down a bit. Shoe rental costs just a few dollars and can even be free if your child joins a league. When your child's feet have slowed or stopped growing, then you can invest in a good-quality pair of shoes. Head to Chapter 4 for pointers on buying bowling shoes.

The advantages of using a house ball are that

✔ It's free.

✔ You don't have to keep buying a heavier ball every time your child gains 10 pounds.

The drawbacks to using a house ball are that

✔ It takes time to find one that's the right weight and fit (you always want to make this search before heading to your lane, especially if you're paying by the hour).

✔ There's no guarantee that the ball that works for your child will always be available for him every time he's at the center because another bowler may be using it.

Bowling centers sometimes store the lighter house balls behind the counter, so if you don't find one on the ball rack, ask at the front desk.

Purchasing a child's bowling ball

Kids may beg for the cool-looking bowling ball in the pro shop window or the one with their favorite cartoon characters on it, but should you buy your child a bowling ball? If he bowls frequently, why not? His own bowling ball will be custom fit to his hand so he won't have to go searching through racks for one that fits but may also be full of dings and scratches. A new, smooth bowling ball fit to your child's hand starts him off right if bowling is going to be one of his regular activities.

Before you plunk down the money to buy a custom-drilled bowling ball, consider the following:

✔ **Your child's age:** A little one who doesn't put his fingers in the holes and instead uses a ramp (see Chapter 16 for more on this piece of equipment) to help power the ball down to the pins probably isn't ready for his own equipment just yet. However, if your child knows how to properly grip the ball and can throw it down the lane on his own, he can probably handle his own equipment.

✔ **Your child's weight and height:** Say little Baylee weighs 80 pounds. Following the guideline presented in the earlier "Finding a ball with the right weight and fit" section, the weight of Baylee's current bowling ball should be 10 percent of his body weight, or 8 pounds. But by next year, Baylee could hit a growth spurt and weigh in at 90 pounds. Consequently, he'd need a new 9-pound ball pretty soon. Instead of having to buy a new ball every time your child grows a bit, start your child on a ball that's slightly heavier so that he gets more use out of it and have it redrilled as your child's hands grow bigger. With this advice in mind, Baylee's parents should consider purchasing a 10-pound ball (of course, if Baylee can't hold a 10-pound ball yet, then the 9-pound ball is perfect for now).

Children grow fast, which means they can grow out of custom-drilled bowling balls before you know it. Also, their fingers get longer, and sometimes even thicker, so check the finger span and hole size every few months to see whether they need adjusting. If your child gets taller but his fingers thin out a little, the finger holes may need to be plugged so he can grip the ball properly.

✔ **Your child's level of interest:** Buying your child a brand-new bowling ball may spark his interest in bowling — or it may not. If your child's interest in activities waxes and wanes, let him use a house ball and check in with him when he gets a little older and has an easier time sticking with his interests.

✔ **Your budget:** Most kids start bowling with a plastic ball, which you can purchase for less than $80. Add a bag (about $20) and shoes (which average around $35 to $70) and you can give yourself a better idea of whether outfitting your child for a bowling hobby is really within your budget.

When your child outgrows a custom ball, your local pro shop may be willing to buy it back and give you credit toward a new one. If it doesn't, consider selling the ball online or at a garage sale, or just donate it to a local children's charity.

Teaching Kids the Basics of Bowling

Talk to your child before she begins bowling to make sure she knows the basics of the game and the rules, especially the ones regarding safety. (If you need a refresher on the rules yourself, see Chapter 2.) In the next section, we offer some ways to simplify the rules so youngsters can understand them.

Of course, explaining the game and the rules can go only so far. The best way to help kids see what bowling involves is to just let them bowl. In the later "Letting your child play the game" section, we give you suggestions for making your child's first games good ones. And because she's going to make mistakes, we also offer a few pointers to help you correct common kiddie bowling problems and get her back on track.

Explaining the game in kid-friendly terms

Kids understand basic concepts, so tailor your explanation to your audience. For instance, you can't explain the game to a 4-year-old the way you'd explain it to a 10-year-old. For example, a 4-year-old will understand, "roll the ball and hit the pins," whereas an older child can probably understand the rules of the game we present in Chapter 2 (although we encourage you to explain them in your own words).

Following are the basics of bowling that you can share with a younger child:

- ✔ You get two chances to knock down all the pins before your turn is over for that frame.
- ✔ If you knock down all the pins with your first ball, you got a strike (which is a great thing).
- ✔ If you knock down all the pins with your second ball, you got a spare (which is also pretty darn good).
- ✔ A strike is the best shot you can throw; it's worth more than a spare.
- ✔ Wait your turn. (If your child can read her name, tell her to keep an eye on the screen so she knows when it's her turn. If she can't, remind her when it's her turn and how many shots she has.)
- ✔ Don't run or shove while you're at the center, especially when you're about to bowl, because you might hurt yourself or someone else.

Keep an eye on the little ones and teach all children to steer clear of the ball return. It can seriously hurt them if they stick their hands, fingers, or heads inside it. Teach them to just take the ball and move away from the equipment.

Letting your child play the game

How you go about showing your child how to bowl really depends on her age. A toddler just wants to push the ball, whereas a 4- or 5-year-old is capable of putting her fingers into the ball and holding it properly. Here are some suggestions for teaching a child how to bowl:

✔ **Use a ramp.** Toddlers and some children with special needs can bowl with the help of a ramp placed at the foul line so that the ball rolls onto the lane when it's released. Either you or your child should place the bowling ball at the top of the ramp and then give it a push. The ramp provides the power and speed the ball needs to make it down to the pins. Even better? The ramp is movable so you can reposition it to help your child aim for specific pins. If you don't see a ramp sitting out at your center, ask a staff member at the front desk; the center may just store the ramp until a customer requests it.

✔ **Pull out the bumpers.** Without bumpers (shown in Figure 17-1), your child's ball can easily roll into the gutter, which can be an upsetting experience for her. To keep the game fun, use bumpers while she's still getting used to the sport and may not be able to power the ball all the way down the lane in a straight line.

Figure 17-1:
Bumpers can be placed over the gutters to keep a child's ball on the lane.

✔ **Show your child how to hold and release the ball properly.** Most young children, starting at 3- or 4-years-old, can hold a light ball with their fingers and thumb in the correct holes and learn how to swing their arm and release it down the lane. Teach them the right way to hold and throw the ball early on. If you don't, they may develop their own habits and become frustrated when you try to correct them. (For a refresher on how to properly hold and release a ball, see Chapter 7.)

✔ **Have your child watch you bowl.** Kids learn by watching. Take advantage of this fact by showing your child what to do. Get to the center early to throw a few slower-paced practice shots before the game starts so your child can see what you do.

✔ **Allow your child to stand at the foul line, swing her arm, and let the ball go.** Many kids start off this way. As your child gets older and more experienced, you can introduce the four-step approach to the foul line (see Chapter 6 for approach-related pointers).

✔ **Praise and encourage your child no matter what happens.** Congratulate her if she only knocks down a few pins and encourage her even when she doesn't hit any pins. Never, ever compare one child to another or say that one is a better bowler than the other.

✔ **Introduce new concepts as your child gets older.** As she understands more, teach her more. Add in additional rules she should know as well as ways she can aim her shot or improve her form. Keep adding to your child's knowledge of the sport as she masters each thing you teach her.

Avoiding common pint-sized bowling problems

Even though bowling is an easy sport to pick up, kids tend to make some common mistakes. Here's a list of 'em, along with how you can help your child avoid these issues:

✔ **They don't hold the ball right.** Young children typically put their pointer and middle fingers in the side-by-side holes on the ball rather than their middle and ring fingers. Check how your child is holding the ball before she throws. If she's using her pointer finger, gently correct her and show her the proper finger placement.

✔ **They throw the ball too early.** Kids are excited and impatient and may not wait for the *sweep* (the bar that moves the pins out of the way) to lift up before they throw either their first or second shot. As a result, the ball bangs into the sweep and starts to make a return trip down the lane. Encourage kids to wait a bit if they look like they're getting ready to throw the ball before the pins have been set.

✔ **They bounce or loft the ball.** When this happens, it's a surefire sign your child is releasing the ball too late. Remind her to let go of the ball a little earlier. Also look into whether the ball she's using is too light; see the earlier "Finding a ball with the right weight and fit" section for tips on selecting a ball that's the correct weight for your child.

Welcome to Bowlopolis

To keep the basics of bowling fresh in your child's mind, consider adding a little virtual bowling to her life. The United States Bowling Congress operates a fun Web site called Bowlopolis (www.bowlopolis.com) that serves as a virtual bowling center just for kids. At Bowlopolis, kids meet characters such as Layne, his dad Mr. Kegler, their dog Reset, and others (all the cute names are based on bowling terms). While at Bowlopolis, kids can do puzzles, bowl, send e-cards to friends, get coloring book pages, download wallpapers and ringtones, and more. Check it out!

Signing Your Child Up for a League or Tournament

If your child shows an interest in bowling on a regular basis, sign him up for a league. Youth bowling leagues meet once a week to give children the opportunity to bowl a few games, socialize with other kids, and compete against different teams.

Kids like league bowling because they enjoy being around other kids with shared interests. Don't put pressure on your child or yell at him when he's bowling. Make an effort to keep bowling fun, and there's a good chance your child will stick with it.

Youth tournaments are another bowling opportunity for children. Some are run by the local bowling center and have no requirements other than signing up and having fun. Others are operated by the United States Bowling Congress (USBC) Youth League and require that children be members of the USBC in order to participate.

In the sections that follow, we paint you a picture of the different types of leagues your child can get involved with and the different tournaments he can participate in.

Surveying your child's league options

All kinds of youth bowling leagues are out there these days, and you don't even have to try out to join one. The one you and your child choose depends mostly on your child's interests (skill level is a lesser concern in leagues with younger members). Following are some options (check with your center for exact age and other requirements):

- ✔ **Adult/child leagues:** If your son or daughter wants to bowl with mom, dad, grandma, grandpa, or Neighbor Joe, adult/child leagues are a great option. They're available to children of all ages.

- ✔ **Bumper leagues:** Kids who bowl in bumper leagues range in age from 3- to 6-years-old. They typically only bowl two games because many younger kids tire out by the third game.

- ✔ **Glow-bowl leagues:** Glow-bowl is open to all children, regardless of age. With their neon lights and upbeat music, these leagues are all about having fun.

- ✔ **Summer leagues:** Participating in a summer league is the perfect way to escape the heat. These leagues are shorter than a traditional September to April league and are appropriate for all ages.

All kinds of youth leagues keep track of standings, but they're relatively noncompetitive and more about having fun.

If your child is getting serious about bowling, encourage him to check out the local branch of the USBC Youth League (bowl.com/youth). Operated by the United States Bowling Congress, the USBC Youth League is the most popular youth league in the country. Many communities throughout the United States are home to a USBC Youth League that typically runs every week (most take place on a Saturday morning) from September to April. The USBC Youth League is open to bowlers age 20 and under as of August 1 of that bowling year.

The cost of youth leagues can vary, but the USBC Youth League at coauthor A.J.'s centers costs $8 per week; this fee includes three games (two for bumpers) and shoe rental but no snacks. The fees are paid weekly, and a reduced fee is available for weeks that the child is absent. The costs for other leagues may vary and include discounts for signing up more than one child. Before signing your child up for a league, find out what the payment rules are if he must miss a week and what the penalties are if he wants to leave the league at any time.

Before signing your child up for a league, make sure he actually wants to bowl in one. After all, a league is a time commitment for both you and your child; it's also a financial commitment for you. Be realistic. Consider your child's personality and stamina (some toddlers and preschoolers may not be able to bowl for a lengthy period of time week after week) and take your budget into account.

Bowl-crazy celebrities and athletes

Kids love celebrities and athletes, so why not drop the names of a few famous bowling-lovers the next time you're on your way to the center with your child? NBA player Chris Paul is a USBC spokesperson. Other celebrities who've bowled for fun or in tournaments include pro wrestler/actor Dwayne "The Rock" Johnson, former Pittsburgh Steeler Jerome Bettis, country music sensation Carrie Underwood, pop superstar Miley Cyrus, pop singer Justin Bieber, actor Nick Cannon, and rapper Ludacris.

Trying out a youth tournament

A youth bowling tournament is typically a one-day event (although sometimes tournaments last two days or over the course of a weekend or two). Bowlers pay an entry fee (the costs can vary) and compete against other bowlers for special awards, trophies, and scholarships. As long as a child is past the age of bumpers-only bowling, he can participate in a youth tournament. As for skill level, that depends on the tournament's specifications. You can find out about local youth bowling tournaments by contacting someone at your local center.

If your child belongs to a branch of the USBC Youth League, then USBC-operated youth tournaments become an option. USBC youth tournaments are a great way to meet other bowlers from different areas and, depending on the level your child has reached, bowl in different cities. Following are some examples of USBC youth tournaments:

- ✔ **USBC Youth Championships:** All USBC Youth League members are eligible to participate in this nationwide tournament. Qualifying takes place at local centers during the weekly league bowling time. If your child qualifies, you pay a one-time entry fee so he can advance to the state level. The tournament is scored as a handicap competition (see Chapter 18 for an explanation of handicap and scratch scoring), and winning bowlers have an opportunity to earn college scholarships.

- ✔ **USBC Youth Open:** In this national championship tournament, which doesn't require qualification rounds, USBC Youth League members compete against fellow members who are at the same skill level. The competitions include singles, doubles, teams, and all-events. Up for grabs are trophies and scholarships and the opportunity to be named a USBC Youth Open champion.

Before signing your child up for a tournament, ask for the information (think costs, days, and times) ahead of time, so you're not surprised about travel costs or pricing if your child advances.

Bowling in School

Many schools across the country incorporate bowling into their curriculums and athletic programs. Some even offer noncompetitive after-school bowling programs. School-sponsored bowling can take any of these forms:

- ✔ **Intramurals:** Considered a noncompetitive after-school bowling program, intramurals are open for students in elementary school through college so long as they pay the nominal fee required to participate. In elementary and high school, the school arranges for transportation from the school to the center for a couple hours of bowling fun.
- ✔ **Bowling lessons:** Some high schools rent portable equipment from local bowling centers to teach students how to bowl, and some colleges offer bowling classes for credit (check the physical education listings).
- ✔ **Bowling teams:** Some junior high schools, high schools, and colleges have bowling teams that compete with other teams across their region.

The following sections tell you what you need to know about preparing your student to bowl with her classmates.

Playing for the high school team

High school bowling offers students the chance to get involved on a high school athletic team and compete against other schools while improving their skills and potentially earning scholarships along the way. Not only that but bowling has earned the title of fastest-growing high school sport for the first decade of this century.

Some high school bowling teams hold tryouts because potential team members must have a certain average. Other high school teams accept anyone and everyone, regardless of average. The tryout requirements depend on the individual high school. As for practices, most are typically held after school. Competitions occur during the week and on the weekends.

Hitting the college circuit

College-level bowling isn't just an opportunity to break away from homework and studies — it's also an opportunity to compete. According to the USBC, more than 2,700 student-athletes on 180 college and university intercollegiate bowling teams compete in more than 80 certified tournaments each year. The country's top 64 men's and top 48 women's collegiate teams compete in regional events for the right to advance to the annual Intercollegiate Team Championships (ITC), a nationally televised tournament.

Like high school, the requirements for trying out for a college team depend on the individual college. For example, one of our local college teams doesn't have tryouts and takes any bowler who wants to participate, even if the bowler didn't belong to a high school team (not all bowlers bowl in each competition). The college bowling season typically runs through the academic year.

So what do college students get out of bowling at this level? Well, nearly 100 colleges and universities across the United States offer bowling scholarships. Collegiate bowlers can also receive All-American and Academic All-American recognition, Rookie of the Year honors, and Most Valuable Player honors.

Letting the Good Times Roll with a Bowling Party

A party is a great way to combine celebrating and bowling. Many centers have private rooms for parties, and most also offer bowling party packages for kids that can be used for birthdays, graduations, and other types of celebrations. Packages typically include a few hours of bowling, as well as food, soft drinks or juice, and decorations. Some centers may provide a cake if they have a connection with a local bakery (if yours doesn't, check to see whether you're allowed to bring your own cake into the center).

The great thing about throwing a child's bowling party is that you can manage it however you want. Guests can eat before or after they bowl. You can give awards to the best bowlers while guests are eating, or you can go ahead and give every guest an award, regardless of scores. We help you figure out how to host a bowling party that's fun for everyone in the next sections.

You can purchase bowling invitations, party favors, plates, cups, and other decorations through Web sites such as Birthday Express (www.birthday express.com), or you can make your own invitations and shape them like bowling pins, balls, or shirts.

Keeping things under control

Most centers have staff members who host the birthday parties and review the basic rules of the center with the partygoers, but if your center doesn't have a staff person dedicated to party duties, take time to remind the kids of how the game is played (we outline the basics in the earlier "Explaining the game in kid-friendly terms" section).

If you're the person throwing the party, it's ultimately your responsibility to make sure everyone stays safe. If the party is a large one, consider asking the parents of attending children to help chaperone.

Making sure everyone has fun

The best thing you can do to make sure everyone has fun at a bowling party is to keep things moving. Try to schedule a maximum of four partygoers per lane so kids don't have to wait too long to take their turn.

If you want to add some new twists and excitement to your child's bowling party, check out these fun ideas:

✔ **Give out awards for the highest and lowest scores, as well as the highest number of spares and strikes.** You can track the scores, strikes, and spares by asking for a printout of the score sheet at the front desk. As for the awards, you can buy Olympic-style medals from a party store or Web site.

✔ **Try bowling a different kind of game.** Have the partygoers bowl through their legs, with their opposite hand, standing on one leg or even sitting down.

✔ **Make the party glow-in-the-dark.** These glow-bowl parties are so much fun because the center pumps up the music and turns on special lights that make white clothing glow in the dark. If you're having a glow-bowl party, be sure to mention that in the invitation so partygoers remember to wear white.

✔ **Ask management to set the computerized scoring system for nine-pin tap tournament scoring.** In this game, bowlers who knock down nine pins get scored for a strike. Not only does nine-pin tap tournament scoring help move the games along a little faster, but kids always enjoy seeing strikes (especially those poor souls who often struggle to get any strikes at all).

✔ **Create special competitions.** Pit boys against girls, righties versus lefties . . . you name it!

Avoid suggesting rowdy games that may cause little bowlers to hurt themselves. Keep the party fun, and safe, and you should be fine.

Chapter 18

Playing in Leagues and Tournaments

. . . .

In This Chapter

▶ Navigating the world of league bowling

▶ Getting involved with a league

▶ Understanding league rules and scoring

▶ Competing tournament-style

. . . .

*B*owling by yourself is fine for practicing purposes, but you get the most enjoyment out of bowling when you bowl with others who like the sport as much as you do. You could just get your friends together every now and then to hit the lanes, but why not try joining a bowling league? Leagues provide weekly opportunities for socialization, a certain level of competition, the ability to develop your skills by bowling against others, and, most importantly, a ton of fun.

Tournaments are another way of sharing the bowling fun with others. They're one-day, weekend, or multiweekend events in which bowlers compete for various prizes and awards. These events really let you take your bowling to the next level of competition.

In this chapter, we review everything you need to know about leagues and tournaments, including how to find one that's right for you. We also explain the differences in league rules and scoring as compared to open bowling.

Introducing League Bowling

When you bowl in a league, you get to put your bowling skills to the test, watch other bowlers (and maybe even pick up some pointers from them), and socialize with folks who share your interest in the sport. But as with any sport, bowling in a competitive league environment still has the ultimate goal of winning.

In the following sections, we introduce you to leagues by providing an overview of their structure, listing the various types of leagues out there, and explaining the difference between those that are sanctioned and those that are nonsanctioned.

Most, but not all, league bowlers own their own bowling ball and bag, as well as other equipment, because they bowl on a regular basis. You don't need to own a ball, bag, or shoes to join a league, but if you don't want to hunt down a comfortable ball each week and you're looking to improve your score and do well, consider investing in your own equipment. See Chapter 4 for help buying a ball, bag, and more.

Discovering how a league works

A league has a slate of officers that can include a president, vice president, secretary, treasurer, and sometimes a sergeant-at-arms, all of whom share the responsibilities of dealing with paperwork, payments, bylaws, and issues that arise. A league can have any number of members, depending on its rules and the space available at the center, and those members are grouped into teams consisting of any number of bowlers. How the teams are formed depends on the league, but if you know a team you want to join and it has roster space for you, you can sign right up with that team. If you don't know any team members, you can ask the league officers to assign you to a team.

Most teams choose a name and meet a minimum of once a week throughout the season to bowl three games against another team (although some leagues bowl a different number of games each time they meet). Completing three games can take anywhere from two to three hours, depending on how slow or fast the other bowlers bowl, how many members are on each team, and how much socializing is going on.

Each week you bowl against a different team using two lanes and alternating your turns on each lane. (You alternate so that each team bowls on the same lane conditions.) After each game, your individual score is added to your teammates' scores for a team total. If you're playing in a scratch league (which means no additional handicapping points are added to your team's total; see the later section on scoring for more on this) and your team's total beats that of the opposing team, your team wins that game.

After all three games are bowled, all the scores for your team are added up. If your team's three-game total beats the other team's three-game total, your team earns an extra point. (This extra point is described as *taking wood*.) If your team wins all three individual games that week, you earn points for that too. These points determine your team's ranking as first, second, third, and so on. At the end of the season, the winning teams receive whatever prizes your league offers.

Note: How many points you earn depends on your league. For example, in one of coauthor A.J.'s Thursday night mixed leagues, teams earn 2 points for each game they win out of the three played and 1 extra point if they knock down more overall pins than the other team. That means 7 points are up for grabs each week.

The traditional bowling league season runs from September through April or May. If you can't or don't want to commit to that many weeks, look for a league that runs only 8, 12, or 16 weeks. Summer leagues are one such shorter-term option; they typically start in May and run through the end of August. Some centers also offer shorter seasons beyond the summer. Ask your center what it offers.

You do have to pay for the privilege of participating in a league. Fees can range from $8 to $30 (we've even seen some vacation leagues charge more) and are paid each week to your league's treasurer. They cover prizes, administrative costs, shoe rentals, banquets, and any applicable sanctioning fees (we fill you in on what a sanctioned league is later in this chapter).

Getting acquainted with the various kinds of leagues

More than 2 million people participate in bowling leagues each year, ranging from the ordinary (for example, a nighttime league made up of men and women) to the exclusive (a league made up solely of New York City freelance writers). The skill levels also vary, which means whether you're a beginner or a more advanced bowler, you can find a league that's a good fit for you.

Following is just a sampling of the most common types of leagues (you may have seen one or more of them in action at your local center):

- ✔ **Cash leagues:** The idea behind a cash league is that you earn money back at the end of the season depending on where you place in the standings individually and as a team, which means cash leagues can be a little more expensive than other leagues.

- ✔ **Men's and women's leagues:** These leagues are just like they sound. Membership in a women's league is restricted to women; membership in a men's league is limited to men.

- ✔ **Mixed leagues:** Some leagues mix up men and women on one team. In this case, each team is usually required to include at least one woman.

- ✔ **Saturday night leagues:** Some centers offer Saturday night leagues that tend to consist of younger adult bowlers.

✔ **Seasonal leagues:** Fall leagues usually start around September. Summer leagues are shorter leagues that start around May. Both fall and summer leagues can include any type of league. For example, you can have a fall cash league or a men's summer league.

✔ **Seniors leagues:** You can join some seniors leagues at age 50; others don't let you in until you're at least 65. Regardless of age limit, seniors leagues are held at any time of day, including the morning (which is convenient for retirees) and evening.

✔ **Singles leagues:** A singles league can be made up of men and women who are unattached and interested in mixing and mingling with other singles. Then again, it can also be made up of individuals who aren't socially single but who are just interested in bowling and don't have their own team.

If you're interested in an even more specialized league opportunity, consider joining one of the following less traditional leagues:

✔ **Charity leagues:** In charity leagues, a portion of your weekly fees is donated to a particular charity. For example, AMF Bowling (`amf.com`) has a Bowl for the Cure league that donates a portion of its weekly fees to the Susan G. Komen for the Cure charity.

✔ **Cruise or vacation leagues:** Basically, you bowl all season and use some of the money you've put toward your weekly fees (known as "prize money") for a cruise or other designated vacation. Cruise and vacation leagues can be a little pricier than other leagues, but they're a great way to have fun while saving up for some well-deserved time off.

✔ **Special needs leagues:** These leagues allow bowlers with disabilities to enjoy the fun, camaraderie, and competition of bowling.

✔ **Traveling leagues:** You can never get bored with your surroundings (or the oil patterns) in a traveling league because you travel to different centers each week to bowl.

If you can't find the kind of league you want to join, ask your center to start one up.

How long each type of league's season lasts, the fees, and so on all depend on the league and can vary from center to center. Check with your center for the particulars on any league you're interested in joining.

Deciding whether to go sanctioned or not

A league, no matter what type, is either sanctioned or nonsanctioned. A sanctioned league is protected by the United States Bowling Congress (USBC). The USBC is a governing body with an extensive set of league rules that all leagues under the auspices of the organization must follow. The USBC also protects the prize fund and keeps everyone's averages in a national database. Members of a sanctioned league pay an annual fee to the USBC in addition to their league's weekly fees. After you pay your sanctioning fee, you become a member of both the USBC and your state chapter of the organization (note that most state and local chapters have a modest sanctioning fee as well).

Nonsanctioned leagues aren't affiliated with the USBC and can create their own rules, awards, and prizes. Of course, because they aren't connected to the USBC, they're not eligible for USBC awards.

Which type of league should you choose? Like most things in bowling, it's really a personal decision. However, joining a league that's sanctioned by the USBC can give you a little peace of mind because you know that the league is protected and that its rules are consistent.

Joining a League

Making sure you join the league that's right for you requires a little thought. You first need to decide which type of league you want to join. Then you want to ask around for recommendations and visit the center when that league is bowling to see how the people interact and what the level of competitiveness is. In the sections that follow, we share everything you need to know to find, choose, and sign up for a league. We even fill you in on what to do when you can't make it one week.

Finding a league

The best way to find a league is to first visit your local center and ask the staff what leagues have openings. If you sign up before the season begins, you can attend a meeting and be added to a team at that time. Or you can join a league with a partner or other teammates and enter as a team if the league you're interested in has room.

Whether you can join a league depends in part on whether that league is open or closed (you can find this information out from the center). An *open league* lets anyone join as long as there's room on a team. For example, all that's required for joining a Saturday night men's league is that you're a man and that the league has an open spot. A *closed league* accepts only those individuals who belong to a particular organization, attend a particular school, work at a particular place, and so on. For example, a local school district may start a closed league that's only for its employees. To be allowed to join, you must show proof that you work for that school district.

If a league requires four bowlers per team and only two of your friends are willing to be on your team, don't worry about not having a fourth bowler. Your fourth person can be considered an *absentee bowler,* or what's called a *vacant-score bowler.* The absentee bowler typically has an average of 150 and is included in your team's scores and averages.

Making your choice

Bowling in a league is a commitment, and as with any commitment, you want to guarantee you're making the right decision for your time and money. So how do you know whether the women's league that bowls on Tuesday nights at 7 p.m. is right for you or whether you should join the mixed league that bowls on Thursday afternoons? Ask yourself these questions:

- ✔ **Does the league fit my schedule?** If you joined a league that bowls on Tuesday nights at 7 p.m., do you have enough time to get home from work, eat dinner, and get to the center? Keep in mind that you can eat dinner at the bowling center one day a week, but make sure you have enough time to get there in case you run late. Joining the Thursday afternoon league, when you're off from work, may be a better fit. On the other hand, it commits you to sticking around town on your day off.

- ✔ **Can I make the weekly commitment for the season?** Whether it's a 12-week-long league or a seven-month-long league, be realistic about your ability to make the commitment. If you have children, upcoming school events, not to mention illnesses, may force you to miss a week of bowling here and there. Look ahead in your calendar, and if you see that too many events may conflict with your bowling night, choose another league.

- ✔ **Does the league fit my budget?** Weekly league fees can range from $8 to $25, depending on the league (for example, a cruise league may cost even more). And if you miss a week, most leagues require you to still pay your full weekly fee, so if you commit to a league, make sure it's within your budget.

- ✔ **How do I like the people?** If you have the chance, watch a few leagues and take note of how the members interact. Can you see yourself as part of that group?

Leagues are competitive, but bowling is still supposed to be fun. If you're not having fun in your league, try another league out to see whether it's a better fit.

Signing yourself up

Wondering how to sign yourself up for a particular league? Just contact one of the league's officers; your local center can provide you with the correct contact information. The officer can explain in detail the league's sign-up procedures, but in most cases, you either attend a league meeting or show up to the first night of bowling and go from there.

If the league is sanctioned by the USBC, you'll have to fill out sanctioning paperwork and pay an annual sanctioning fee. After the paperwork is complete, you'll receive a temporary sanction card. The USBC will mail you a card that's good for the year.

After you take the plunge and join a league, give it a few weeks to see whether you're really happy and whether that league is in fact the one for you. If it's not, don't lose heart. Not all bowlers stick with the first league they join.

Before you join, be sure to ask the league you're interested in how flexible it is with new members. Some leagues allow you to bowl for a few weeks without any additional charges should you decide that the league isn't for you. Other leagues may require you to pay for the weeks you already bowled plus a few additional weeks if you decide to leave the league for any reason (after all, they don't want to lose money while they look for your replacement).

If your team doesn't already have one, choose a team captain. According to the USBC, the team captains in sanctioned leagues determine the order of the bowlers, collect dues, and give the dues to the league's treasurer. The team captain also enters the lineup into the computer each week, signs score sheets, distributes prize money, and has the authority to remove any player from the team for breaking rules.

Using a substitute when you can't bowl

Inevitably, you aren't going to be able to bowl every time your league meets. You may be sick, or you may just have other obligations. In a sanctioned league, you can try to find a substitute to bowl for you, although you'll still have to pay your weekly fee. Your substitute doesn't have to pay your league's fee, but she does have to belong to another sanctioned league.

To find a substitute, ask your league's officers whether they have any recommendations. Some leagues maintain lists of substitute bowlers to contact when they're needed.

If you don't use a substitute, your team enters you as an absentee bowler and subtracts points from your current average to arrive at your score for the week. The amount of points subtracted depends on your league's bylaws, but the typical amounts are 5 to 10. So, for example, if you have a 132 average but you can't make it to a night of league play, your score gets entered as 122 for each game.

If you're bowling in a nonsanctioned league, ask the league's president what the rules are for when you have to be absent. You may or may not have to find yourself a substitute.

Following League Rules for Bowling

If you're bowling in a USBC-sanctioned league, you need to be aware that sanctioned leagues have their own special rules that are different from and in addition to those that apply to open bowling. Honestly, we could write an entire book just explaining the rules of league play, but the USBC already took care of that. If you're interested in reading all the rules, visit the USBC's Web site at bowl.com and search for "rules."

Here, we review some of the important rules you should know about if you're in or planning to join a sanctioned league:

- ✔ **You must use a USBC-approved bowling ball.** To find one, check the USBC Web site, ask the local pro shop owner, or look for a ball with a USBC stamp and serial number.

- ✔ **You can't step over the foul line.** The *foul line* is the line at the start of the lane. Step over it while you're bowling in league or tournament play, and you'll hear a loud buzzing noise that tells you you've fouled (the foul line may or may not buzz in open bowling; that depends on the center). Whether or not you're penalized for that throw depends on whether you threw the ball. If you released the ball and it knocked down any pins, the sweep will reset the pins, you'll take your second shot with all ten pins standing, and you'll receive an "F" on your score sheet for that throw. However, if you accidentally step over the foul line and don't release the ball, then that's not considered a foul, and you can take your shot again. Have the center reset the frame to start over.

- ✔ **You can't rebound.** *Rebounding* is when you throw your ball down the lane, it goes into the gutter or the pit and rebounds back onto the lane, and then it knocks down some pins. The pins knocked down after the ball reenters the lane don't count, and your score must be adjusted by either league officials or the center's staff.

✔ **You can't make changes to the bowling order after play has started that day.** Make sure you and your teammates decide who's going first and who's going to be the *anchor* (the last bowler) before you commit to an order. If you're listed as the second bowler, for example, then you're the second bowler for that week. Typically a stronger bowler is put into the last position in case the game is close. If you want to change your order, you can do it before bowling starts that day.

✔ **You can't switch bowling hands.** If you're lucky or talented enough to be able to bowl with both hands, that's great, but you can't switch the hand you bowl with during the season. This rule helps with tracking averages and calculating handicaps (more on those in the next section). So if you joined the league as a right-handed bowler, you must bowl right-handed throughout the entire season. However, if you want to bowl in one league as a right-handed bowler and another as a lefty, that's a-okay.

✔ **You can't alter the surface of your bowling ball.** You can clean your ball during league play, but you can't polish or sand it until the week is over.

✔ **You must be courteous to others.** During open bowling, it's suggested, although not required, that you wait for bowlers on the left and right sides of your lane to bowl before you step onto the approach. In league bowling, one-lane courtesy (to each side of you) is required, not merely suggested. So if you're bowling on Lane 13 and bowlers on Lanes 12 and 14 are ready to bowl, you should step back and let them bowl first.

If you're in a nonsanctioned league, ask the league officers or persons who are monitoring the league for an explanation of the league rules.

Doing the Math for League Scoring

Scoring for league bowling, whether sanctioned or nonsanctioned, works the same as scoring for open bowling: You bowl ten frames, tally strikes and spares as per usual, and calculate your score along the way. Where league scoring differs from open bowling scoring is when league scores are handi-capped. Here are the two types of games you can have in league play, based on how you score the points:

✔ **Scratch game:** A *scratch game* (which is also used during open bowling) is when the team's individual scores are totaled and compared against the other team's total score with no extra points added in. Whoever has the highest team score wins the game. In the case of Mike's Monkeys versus the Cowboys, the four individual scores of Mike's Monkeys total

649 for one game, and the Cowboys' team total for the game is 751. The Cowboys' score is higher, so that team wins that game.

✔ **Handicapped game:** In a *handicapped game* (which is typically used in league play), teams receive additional points that put both teams on an even playing field before the game starts. Say the Cowboys are the stronger team; in a scratch game against Mike's Monkeys, the Cowboys almost always win. When the two teams play a handicapped game, each team is given a certain amount of points based on the individual averages of each team member. These points are added to the team scores at the end of each game. So Mike's Monkeys may be given a 75-point per-game handicap, and the Cowboys may be given a 15-point per-game handicap. With the handicap, Mike's Monkeys can beat the Cowboys. (It doesn't always work out that way, but handicap points certainly increase the chances that the Cowboys won't always win.) The handicap changes the following week based on how the teams bowled the prior week.

In the next sections, we explain how to calculate individual and team averages as well as handicaps.

Calculating your average

Bowling in a league allows you to establish an *average,* a number that measures your performance as the season goes on. To calculate your average, use this formula:

Total number of points scored ÷ Total number of games bowled = Your average

Say you bowl nine games, and the total of all of your scores is 1,800 points. Follow the formula and you get 1,800 ÷ 9 = 200. Your average score for those nine games is 200 (very good!).

The next week you bowl three more games for a total of 700 points. To calculate your new average, add the 700 points from this week to your total of 1,800 points from last week for a new total of 2,500 points. Then divide your total points by the 12 games you've now bowled. The math looks like this: 2,500 ÷ 12 = 208.33. Your average is now 208, which means you've raised your average by 8 points. (*Note:* Bowling averages don't get rounded up or down, so just ignore anything that comes after the decimal point.)

Depending on how well you bowl each week, your average can fluctuate. You can also have different averages in different leagues. For example, you may have a 157 average in a Sunday morning league, when you're more relaxed, but you may have just a 142 average in a Wednesday night league after a long day at work. Don't beat yourself up if your averages are different in each league you're a part of. Instead, focus on whether your average is growing throughout the season.

Calculating your team's average

Teams have averages too. These are calculated by adding up each individual bowler's average and dividing it by the number of players on the team. So if on a four-person team, Baylee's average is 200, Tyler's average is 150, John's average is 175, and Steve's average is 190, the total of all four players' averages is 715. To find the team's average, you divide 715 by 4 to get 178.75, or just 178 (no need to count the decimal or round up).

If you have three members on your team and one absentee bowler, you add the averages up the same way. Just remember that the absentee bowler gets an average of 150 (depending on the league, of course). In the earlier example, if Tyler were the absentee bowler, the team's average would still be 178.

The league's secretary tabulates the teams' averages each week, but mistakes can be made. Keep your own score sheet and record your team's scores and averages each week. If you have your own record of the information, you have evidence to back up anything you're questioning.

Tapping into some extra fun with a beer frame

Ever hear the term *beer frame*, and wonder what it means? Typically, among bowlers of legal drinking age, a beer frame is called when a teammate doesn't mark with a strike or spare but everyone else on the team does. The person who didn't mark buys refreshments — beer, soda, bottled water, and so on — for the rest of the team. Another version of the beer frame is to have the bowler with the lowest pin count in the frame buy the refreshments. Either way, have fun and make sure you don't drink and drive.

Calculating handicaps

Handicap points help level the playing field when teams of differing skill levels play each other. How many handicap points your team receives depends on which formula your league uses. Some leagues use a formula of 80 percent of a 200 average, others use 80 percent of a 240 average, some use 90 percent of a 200 average, and still others use a 100 percent handicap. Ask your league which formula it uses.

At coauthor A.J.'s centers, some leagues use the formula that individual and team handicaps are based on 80 percent of a 200 average. So if Ed has a 150 average: 200 − 150 = 50 × 80% = 40 individual handicap points. A 150 average plus 40 handicap points equals a 190 handicap average. So Ed's handicapped average for the games in that league is 190.

To calculate a team handicap of 80 percent of a 200 average:

1. **Add up all four individual averages.**

   Say the total is 700 points.

2. **Subtract this total from 800.**

   Wondering where the 800 comes from? In this example, that figure comes from the league's formula that a team handicap is based on 80 percent of a 200 average for each team member (200 average × 4 players = 800). When you subtract 700 from 800, you get 100.

3. **Multiply this answer by 80%.**

   The team handicap is 80 points (100 × 80% = 80 points), and those 80 points get added to Ed's team's total game score that week.

The team handicap goes up or down each week based on how you and your teammates bowl. The team you're bowling against has no effect on your handicap.

Figure 18-1 shows what a league's score sheet looks like during the course of a season. The score sheet includes team and individual bowler standings, points won, and averages.

02/03/2010 Week 3 of 16   **SWEET 16**   Page1

Wednesday 6:30 pm   *HOLIDAY*   Lanes 27–36
USBC Certification:

Team Standings

Place	Team Name	Points Won	Points Lost	Team Ave	HDCP	Pins + HDCP	Place	Team Name	Points Won	Points Lost	Team Ave	HDCP	Pins + HDCP
1	SPLIT HAPPENS	16	5	630	151	7098	6	Team 10	10	11	640	145	7274
2	THERE'S NO CRYING	14	7	538	235	7011	7	Team 9	9	12	579	197	6926
3	Team 7	13	8	650	133	7204	8	THE WANNA BEES	8	13	550	223	7031
4	SPANKY'S	12	9	614	166	7198	9	Team 4	7	14	396	362	6724
5	ODD SQUAD	11	10	416	343	6957	10	Team 3	5	16	496	271	6877

Lane Assignments

		27-28	29-30	31-32	33-34	35-36
	Today	9-1	5-3	4-7	8-6	10-2
	Next Week	10-7	6-2	8-3	4-1	5-9

Season High Scores

	Scratch Game	761	Team 7	712 Team 10	684 SPLIT HAPPENS	
	Scratch Series	2045	Team 7	2013 Team 10	1964 SPLIT HAPPENS	
	Handicap Game	912	Team 7	894 Team 10	869 SPANKY'S	
	Handicap Series	2559	Team 10	2498 Team 7	2485 THE WANNA BEES	
Men	Scratch Game	266	ANDRE	265 PETER	216 SETH	
	Scratch Series	672	MARTY	622 PAT	564 TONY	
	Handicap Game	251	GARY	247 TIM M	242 STU	
	Handicap Series	684	MIKE	658 AL	647 BRUCE	
Women	Scratch Game	211	KELLY	176 FRAN	154 MARY	
	Scratch Series	433	TRACEY	430 EILEEN	356 KRISTEN	
	Handicap Game	232	SUE	225 ANNETTE	179 MEGAN	
	Handicap Series	620	MONICA	554 JACKIE		

Team Rosters

Name	Pins	Gms	Ave	HDCP	Name	Pins	Gms	Ave	HDCP
1 - SPLIT HAPPENS *Lane 28 HDCP=151 Ave=630*					**2 - THERE'S NO CRYING IN BOWLING** *Lane 36 HDCP=235 Ave=538*				
LEVI	1445	9	160	36	DAN	919	9	102	88
SEAN	1256	9	139	54	STU	1181	9	131	62
MIKE	1401	9	155	40	AL	1454	9	161	35
KELLY	1592	9	176	21	JOSH	1297	9	144	50
Name	**Pins**	**Gms**	**Ave**	**HDCP**	**Name**	**Pins**	**Gms**	**Ave**	**HDCP**
3 - Team 3 *Lane 30 HDCP=271 Ave=496*					**4 - Team 4** *Lane 31 HDCP=362 Ave=396*				
SEAN	1225	9	136	57	MEGAN	892	9	99	90
RICK	1163	9	129	63	KAITLIN	263	3	87	101
TIM M	1035	9	115	76	MARY	991	9	110	81
ANDY	1048	9	116	75	KRISTEN	907	9	100	90
Name	**Pins**	**Gms**	**Ave**	**HDCP**	**Name**	**Pins**	**Gms**	**Ave**	**HDCP**
5 - SPANKY'S *Lane 29 HDCP=166 Ave=614*					**6 - THE WANNA BEES** *Lane 34 HDCP=223 Ave=550*				
MONICA	1000	9	111	80	SUE	1052	9	116	75
JIM	1515	9	168	28	FRAN	1140	9	126	66
TRACEY	1270	9	141	53	RICHIE	1394	9	154	41
PAT	1754	9	194	5	GARY	1393	9	154	41
Name	**Pins**	**Gms**	**Ave**	**HDCP**	**Name**	**Pins**	**Gms**	**Ave**	**HDCP**
7 - Team 7 *Lane 32 HDCP=133 Ave=650*					**8 - ODD SQUAD** *Lane 33 HDCP=343 Ave=416*				
EILEEN	939	7	134	59	BRUCE	894	9	99	90
TIM S	914	6	152	43	JOAN	624	6	104	86
ANDRE	1602	9	178	19	AMY	532	6	88	100
SETH	1676	9	186	12	BILL	1125	9	125	67
Name	**Pins**	**Gms**	**Ave**	**HDCP**	**Name**	**Pins**	**Gms**	**Ave**	**HDCP**
9 - Team 9 *Lane 27 HDCP=197 Ave=579*					**10 - Team 10** *Lane 35 HDCP=145 Ave=640*				
ANNETTE	787	9	87	101	ERIC JR	1242	9	138	55
JACKIE	1130	9	125	67	ERIC SR	1434	9	159	36
TONY	1531	9	170	27	MATT	1262	9	140	54
MARTY	1777	9	197	2	PETER	1830	9	203	0

Temporary Substitutes

Name	Pins	Gms	Ave	Book Ave	Name	Pins	Gms	Ave	Book Ave
JILLIAN	359	3	119	—	TOM	338	3	112	—

Figure 18-1:
A sample of a league's score sheet.

Racking up USBC awards

If you bowl in a sanctioned league, you and your teammates may be eligible for awards from the USBC. These awards include plaques, magnets, and a ring (which is reserved for specific high-score games).

Your scores and averages determine the awards you're eligible for. You can also win awards for throwing 11 strikes in a row or for achieving a certain series. A *series* is the total of your scores for the three games that you bowl on a given night. If your average is 150 and you bowl a 150 in all three games, you have

a 450 series that night. If the next week you achieve a 600 series, you may be eligible for a 600 series magnet.

Your league may also give out cash prizes or trophies to those folks who achieve high series or who are the most improved bowlers. (Note that for some awards, you may need to have bowled a minimum amount of games to qualify.) Team prizes typically go to the three teams with the highest scores, but other team awards can include prizes for high team scratch series and high team handicapped series.

Competing in Tournament Play

If you want to bowl with others in a competitive environment but you don't want the weeks- or months-long commitment required of a league (or you want it in addition to the competition your league offers), consider entering a bowling tournament. Whether you want to challenge yourself and compete against bowlers who are more advanced than you or whether you want to compete against others who bowl at your skill level, we're positive that you can find a tournament for yourself.

Tournaments are much like a regular afternoon or evening of bowling, meaning you can take breaks to hit the snack stand or restroom when it's not your turn. The only real difference is the tension level, which varies based on the intensity of the competition. In the following sections, we explain what sorts of tournaments are offered and how to sign up for them.

Contrary to what some people may think, you don't always have to travel far for tournaments. Most centers hold their own, so check with your center's staff about any upcoming tournaments. Participating in a tournament at your home center is a great way to see whether competing is really something you want to do without the time and expense of traveling.

Tournaments are competitive, but they should be fun too. You may be competing against better bowlers from across your local area or maybe even the country, but so what? Just do your best. You gain more and more valuable experience with each tournament you enter.

Checking out the types of tournaments you can enter

Some tournaments are sanctioned by the USBC and follow all the USBC rules, including allowing a maximum number of USBC-registered bowlers. Other tournaments aren't sanctioned, which means they make their own rules and don't include USBC awards.

The USBC-sanctioned tournaments are local and national events that occur throughout the year. Often league bowlers on the same or even different teams travel together for the fun and excitement of participating in a USBC-sanctioned tournament. Here are just a few of the adult tournaments the USBC sponsors each year (we cover youth tournaments in Chapter 17). For more information on any of these tournaments, head to the USBC's Web site (bowl.com) and search for the tournament in question.

- **The USBC Master's Tournament:** The Master's Tournament is *the* major national tournament that pits the world's best pro and amateur bowlers against each other. You must meet certain eligibility requirements to be able to participate in this event.

- **The USBC Open Championships:** These tournaments, which are held in a different city every year and last six months, consist of team, doubles, singles, and optional all-events competitions.

- **The USBC Women's Championships:** For women only, this annual tournament is for all levels of bowlers and takes place at a different location each year.

Of course, not all tournaments are big-deal, high-pressure affairs. Some are just plain fun, but these for-fun-only kinds aren't sanctioned. Following are a few of them that are worth keeping an eye out for:

- **Low-score tournament:** This one is just like it sounds. The bowler with the lowest score wins.

- **Nine-pin tap tournament:** Do you often find yourself wishing that knocking down nine pins would count for a strike? Well, in a nine-pin tap tournament, every time you hit nine pins with your first ball, you get scored for a strike. Not too shabby, huh? (Of course, knocking down ten pins on the first ball still counts as a strike.)

- **Scotch doubles:** In this tournament, partners alternate taking shots in each frame. The only time a bowler completes a frame on her own is if she scores a strike.

- **3-6-9 tournament:** This score-boosting tournament gives every bowler a strike in the third, sixth, and ninth frames.

Signing up for your chance to play and win

Most tournaments require you to fill out an application prior to the day of competition in order to reserve your spot, although some allow walk-in entries on tournament day. The application may be for singles, doubles, or teams, so make sure you have all the necessary details, including contact information and averages for each participant, as well as sanction cards and any fees.

Tournament fees can range from $5 to hundreds of dollars depending on the tournament and the prizes involved. Before you enter a tournament, ask for a breakdown of the fee so you know what you're paying for. These items may include, but aren't limited to, *lineage* (the amount the house gets for the tournament), a banquet (if any), the prize fund, trophies, and administrative costs.

Some tournaments only accept cash, whereas others may only accept certified checks or money orders. Check with the tournament organizers so you're not disqualified for sending in the wrong type of payment.

When you sign up for a tournament, be sure to ask for a copy of the rules (they differ from tournament to tournament) and know your average. The tournament organizers need this information so they can establish a handicap if it's a handicapped tournament. In a sanctioned tournament, the average you use should be the average you have in your sanctioned league, if you're in one.

Part VI
The Part of Tens

The 5th Wave   By Rich Tennant

"I can understand collecting autographed bowling balls, and I can understand wanting to own a houseboat. But why in heaven's name you decided to combine the two, I'll never understand!"

In this part . . .

It's tips, tips, and tips galore in this part! Here's where you discover suggestions for adding more points to your score and throwing the best hook shot you can. And because bowling is all about fun, we throw in some terrific ideas for how to make bowling an even bigger part of your life.

This part also features a glossary you can flip to when you need to find out the meaning of a bowling term.

Chapter 19

Ten Ways to Add 10 Points (Or More) to Your Score

In This Chapter

▶ Putting in some practice time and making adjustments

▶ Having the right mental attitude

*W*hat bowler doesn't like to see his score go higher and higher? We certainly can't think of one, which is why we're sharing the ten tried-and-true tactics for increasing your score. Good luck and good scoring!

Note: If you're only bowling once a month, your score may not improve as quickly as someone who's bowling a few times a week. Like any new skill, bowling well takes dedication and persistence.

Give Your Ball a Tune-Up

If you want to boost your bowling score, you need to make sure your equipment is in good working order and that it's right for you. Get to know your local pro shop owner and visit every now and then to have your bowling ball checked out.

If you're in a league, you should have your equipment checked once before the start of the league and again midway through the season. If you're not in a league, get your ball checked at least once or twice a year, depending on how often you're bowling and whether or not your health has changed (for instance, have you injured your arm or wrist?). You should also have your ball checked whenever something about it just doesn't feel right. Most pro shops are willing to perform a courtesy check and give you an idea of the cost of repairs if any are necessary.

Here's a checklist of what the pro shop experts look at when you bring your ball in for a tune-up:

- ✔ **The fit:** A too-tight or too-loose grip will prevent you from bowling a better game. You may drop the ball if it's too loose, or you may have a hard time releasing it if your fingers get stuck. You may need to have the holes redrilled and made bigger or have inserts added to make the holes smaller. Or, if you have a touch of arthritis now and the span of your grip is too difficult for you, the holes may need to be plugged and redrilled.

- ✔ **The weight:** A bowling ball should weigh 10 percent of your body weight. Of course, this general guideline doesn't take into consideration whether you have any medical problems or whether a ball that's the appropriate weight just may not be comfortable for you. Work with the staffers at your local pro shop to verify that your ball is a comfortable weight for you.

- ✔ **The surface of the ball:** Dirt, oil, dings, and scratches can all affect how your ball reacts as it rolls down the lane and hits the pins. Cleaning the ball by hand is a good idea (see Chapter 4 for information on taking care of your equipment). For any dirt or oil that you can't remove yourself, consider having the ball professionally cleaned.

If the pro shop staff finds a significant problem with your ball, it may be time to buy a new one. On the other hand, if the ball is in good condition for hitting the pocket but you struggle making certain single-pin spares (such as the 7 or 10 pin), consider investing in a second ball that's meant only for converting certain spares. Many hook bowlers switch to a plastic ball that goes straight when they're converting single-pin spares. The plastic ball rolls straight toward the pin, makes hitting it much easier, and adds points to your score.

Practice, Practice, Practice

The best way to get better at something, including bowling, is to practice, practice, practice. In addition to any weekly fun or league play that you do, go to the bowling alley at least once a week for the sole purpose of brushing up on your skills. You can practice by yourself or with friends. Just remember to focus on things such as fine-tuning your form, improving your strike ball, or making certain spares.

If you're not into solo bowling practice, find a friend who wants to practice his bowling too so you can help each other remain committed to regular practice sessions and goals. Or consider joining a league. Bowling in a league can push you to do better because you know your team is counting on you to do well. For an additional challenge, ask your local bowling center for information about a league that's slightly above your skill level. Get involved with that league by asking to serve as a substitute when the league needs one. (Chapter 18 has additional details about league play.)

Be careful not to overdo the practice. Bowling too much in one week can tire out your body. By the time you're ready to bowl when it counts, your body may be too stressed to perform at its peak. If you're bowling in a league and practicing two or three times a week, cut back for a little while and see whether your game improves with a little rest.

Improve Your Approach

Every part of your approach, including your footwork, balance, timing, and release, needs to be perfect and in sync in order for your score to improve. If your balance is off even slightly or if your feet are too slow or too fast, your throw is going to be off, which of course affects how many pins you're able to knock down.

Working on your approach and consistently hitting the pocket immediately pay off in a higher score, so keep these pointers in mind to ensure a perfect approach (flip back to Chapter 6 for specifics):

- ✔ Keep your arm swing loose.
- ✔ Make sure you release the ball at the right time — down by your ankles as you near the foul line.
- ✔ If you're a hook bowler, make sure your hand comes up, following through in the handshake position.
- ✔ If you're a straight bowler, make sure your hand comes up, following through with your palm facing up toward the ceiling.

Analyze Your Hook

If you throw a hook and your score isn't improving, analyze what you may be doing wrong. By simply making some adjustments to your hook, you can hit the pocket more frequently and bump up your score. Check out Chapters 9 and 20 for the full scoop on hook shots and pointers for changing yours up.

You may find that throwing your ball from a different starting point and aiming at a different target arrow causes you to hit the pocket more often than you were before, boosting your score and giving you more control.

Move Around

In Chapter 6, we tell you about your starting point and how you should start there for the first throw of every frame. That's true. But occasionally the conditions of the lanes change, which means your usual starting point may not always work for any given lane. Practice throwing from different starting points so you can be better prepared to adjust your positioning when you need to during a real game.

Understand the Oil

Just because a lane is oiled one way at your local center doesn't mean the lanes at another center are going to be oiled the same way. Different patterns may be used, and the lane conditions at different centers can vary. Heck, lane conditions can even vary in the same center depending on the time of day you bowl. For example, if you head to the center right when it opens, the newly oiled lanes may be much slicker than if you bowl after a day's worth of bowlers have broken down all the oil. Good bowlers know how to read the lanes and adjust where they start and how they throw. See Chapter 13 for the skinny on how oil affects your game.

Ask the center's management about the lanes before you start to bowl so you can know what to expect and how to adjust. Try to find out when they were oiled, what oil pattern was used, and whether the lane is wood or synthetic.

Consistently Hit Your Target

Hit the target, get a strike! Sure, it sounds like something someone might shout out at a carnival game, but it's the truth. If you're hitting your target (the pocket) on your first throw, you should see a strike (Chapter 10 covers strikes). If you don't get a strike on the first throw, hitting the target with your second throw gives you a spare, which equals much-needed points.

Adjust for Spares

To improve your chances of picking up spares, you need to be able to adjust your approach depending on what you left behind. If you stand in the same spot that you did when you threw your first ball, you run the risk of missing your spare. (*Note:* You *can* stay in the same spot to pick up headpin spares, but these are exceptions.) Chapter 11 has pointers on how to make the adjustments necessary for picking up all kinds of spares.

Take Care of Your Body and Your Mind

Believe it or not, your mental and physical well-being contribute greatly to your bowling score. If your mind and body aren't into the game, your score is going to suffer.

Follow these tips to help you bring your A-game to the center each and every time:

- ✔ **Be well-rested.** When your body is tired, the ball feels heavier, which throws off your approach, so try to rest a little bit before bowling if you've had a long day. Even sitting and relaxing for five minutes before bowling can make a world of difference.

- ✔ **Stretch out.** When you're at the center, your body should be limber and ready to bowl so you can avoid injuries and bowl better. We provide instructions for several stretches you can try in Chapter 14.

- ✔ **Take breaks.** Get up and bowl. Sit down. Repeat. If you're not bowling with too many other bowlers, this rhythm can wear your body out quickly. Don't let it. Take frequent breaks and give your arms and legs time to rest, or just stay standing when it's not your turn to bowl. If your legs and arms are fatigued, you're not going to bowl very well. Taking breaks, even when you're practicing, is important if you want to improve your score.

- ✔ **Think positively.** Having a good mental attitude is perhaps the easiest thing you can do to improve your game. Thinking positively doesn't take much brainpower, and you reap the rewards from it almost immediately. Always remember that each frame is a new chance to get a score-boosting strike or spare.

Stay Calm, Relax, and Have Fun

For the vast majority of people, bowling is primarily a way of having fun. No one enjoys losing, but getting all tense about how your game is going isn't going to change your score for the better. Stay calm, relax, and have fun — if you do, your score will rise before you know it.

Chapter 20

Ten Tricks to Throwing a Great Hook

In This Chapter

▶ Bowling with a ball that's the perfect fit for you

▶ Figuring out what to do when you're at the center

▶ Staying in the zone and making time for practice

*A*nyone can march up to the foul line, fling a bowling ball, and make it hook and hit some pins, but that doesn't mean she threw the right type of hook shot. It takes skill and practice to throw a hook the right way — as in the way that gives you a better chance of scoring a strike. We cover hook shot how-tos in Chapter 9, but here we reveal the ten tricks to a great hook. Well, what are you waiting for? The secrets to a perfect hook await!

Have the Right Kind of Ball

Throwing a great hook starts with having the right bowling ball. A plastic ball is great to start with when you're just learning the basics of bowling, but if you want to throw a mean hook, a plastic ball simply isn't going to do the job the way a urethane or reactive resin ball will (we describe all three types of bowling balls in detail in Chapter 4). Why? Because a plastic bowling ball isn't meant to hook — it doesn't grip the oil on the lane well or cause a lot of friction. Without friction, you can't throw a hook.

The weight blocks inside urethane and reactive resin balls are one of the factors that help the ball hook. Talk to someone in your center's pro shop who can explain what effect different weight blocks will have on your hook.

Make Sure Your Ball Fits Right

Your bowling ball should be the right fit for you and only you, so get friendly with the staff members at your local pro shop. Not only can they help you figure out which bowling ball provides the type of hook you want but they can also drill the ball to fit your hand like a glove.

A comfortable fit makes all the difference in the world when you throw the ball. If your bowling ball feels too loose or too tight on your fingers, speak up and ask someone at the pro shop to take another look at it.

If your fingers have blisters or cuts, or if your hands are in pain, your bowling ball doesn't fit your hand properly. Revisit the pro shop as soon as possible for an adjustment and don't bowl with your ball again until you get it adjusted.

Get a (Fingertip) Grip

You need to get a grip — on your bowling ball, that is — if you want to nail a perfect hook. To do so, use the *fingertip grip,* where your thumb is inserted all the way in and your middle and ring fingers are only inserted up to your first knuckle (see Chapter 4 for more details on this grip). The fingertip grip gives you a greater ability to put spin on the ball, which is why many league and other experienced bowlers prefer it.

When you throw a hook ball with a fingertip grip, your thumb should come out of the hole first, leaving your fingers responsible for turning the ball and sending it down the lane.

Clean Up Your Stance and Approach

Your *approach* is everything you do from the moment you step onto the approach (the area between the seats and the foul line) until you release the ball and follow through; your *stance* is how you set yourself up for the approach. You can set yourself in a good stance by

✔ Staying balanced

✔ Planting your feet and pointing them toward the pins

✔ Setting your head straight

> ✔ Holding the ball comfortably
>
> ✔ Bending your knees slightly (if that's not uncomfortable for you)

As for your approach, we encourage you to use the traditional four-step version. During your first and second steps, swing the ball down and back. Bring the ball forward on your third step; while you're doing so, begin turning your wrist to create your hook shot. Follow through and release smoothly on your fourth step. (Head to Chapter 6 for more in-depth coverage of the four-step approach.)

Work on Your Timing

Good timing is vital for any shot, but it's even more important for a success-ful hook shot. Your footwork and arm swing should flow together, and your ball release should occur at the right moment so that the ball slides over your target (which should be one of the arrows on the lane, not the pins themselves).

To improve your timing, try walking through your approach, counting your steps out loud. Is your arm where it should be when you count each number? (See the preceding section for a breakdown of where your arm should be as you take each step.)

Spin That Ball

A perfectly released ball has come out of your backswing and is approach-ing your ankle before being let go. After it's released, it starts down the lane and continues to its *breakpoint,* which is where it begins turning toward the pocket. You need to have the right amount of spin on the ball in order for it to break at the right time.

You put spin on your ball by turning your wrist and hand toward your body as your arm and ball follow through from your backswing. If you're a righty, turn your hand and wrist in a counterclockwise position. If you're a lefty, turn your hand and wrist in a clockwise position. Either way, when you release the ball, your wrist and hand should wind up in the handshake position, with your thumb pointing skyward.

Keep your hand and wrist strong as you add spin to your ball. If you need to, wear a wrist brace for additional support.

Hit the Target

The right bowling ball and a good strong throw are necessary for a great hook shot, but if you don't hit your target, you're missing the key to your success. Your target is always one of the arrows on the lane (or two if you're rolling the ball between them), never the pins. If you hit your target just right, the next stop for the ball should be the pocket. And when you hit the pocket, be ready to yell, "Strike!"

Know How to Read the Lane

The condition of the lanes at a bowling center change throughout the day. They may have too much oil or too little oil depending on the time of day, and both scenarios can affect the way your ball hooks. Or maybe they were oiled earlier in the day, but since then many bowlers have used the lanes, and the lanes have dried up quite a bit. Dry lanes can also change how your ball hooks.

Typically, a heavily oiled lane calls for a ball that has maximum hooking potential, whereas a dry lane requires a ball with little hooking potential. No, this doesn't mean you have to purchase two bowling balls (although some bowlers do). You just need to know how to adjust your shot.

Use your practice session to figure out how your ball moves on a particular lane. Throw different spare shots in addition to your strike shot — for example, pretend you're trying to pick up the 7- or 10-pin spare. Depending on how your ball is moving on the lane, you may need to shift your starting point a little to the left or right in order to get your hook shot into the pocket.

Avoid Overthinking

Bowling requires some thinking, true. You need to think about how you're going to make your approach, how you're going to throw, and how you can change your shot when you need to pick up a certain spare or accommodate a lane condition. Just be careful that you're not overthinking any aspects of your game.

Thinking too much can ruin your shot. You may become too eager and release the ball too early or grow too hesitant and release the ball too late. Whenever you have to make an adjustment to change any part of your game, decide what the adjustment is going to be and just do it.

Commit to Practicing

No one throws a perfect hook shot on her first try. It takes time to figure out exactly how to throw a hook, and it takes practice — *lots* of practice — to do it perfectly every time.

During one of your practice sessions, ask the local pro shop owner, center manager, or an experienced bowler whose hook you admire to watch you throw a few and give you some pointers. A knowledgeable observer can help you tweak what you're doing just from watching you throw.

Chapter 21

Ten Ways to Make Bowling More Fun

* *

* *

*T*he bowling fun doesn't have to end just because you've completed the tenth frame, handed in your rental shoes, and paid for your games. Bowling can be a big part of your life both in and out of the center. You can join a league or create a league of your very own. You can make a difference by organizing a bowling fundraiser for a local charity or by using bowling to help build team spirit at your company. For every event and every occasion, there's a place for bowling, including virtual bowling, which is a great way to keep the bowling fun going in the comfort of your own home.

Whether you're bowling virtually or at the center, this chapter provides several fun and exciting ways to keep bowling a part of your life. Think of it as a jumping-off point for coming up with your own fun bowling-related ideas.

Coordinating Team Building through Bowling

In the past, bowling was seen solely as an after-work or after-school activity that you enjoyed with family, friends, or co-workers. Today, some companies are taking employees to the center as part of team-building exercises that pit department against department or combine employees from multiple departments on one team to get them interacting with folks they normally never work with. Bowling builds friendships, morale, communication, teamwork, and understanding. It's also a fun and affordable team-building activity. Plus, you never have to worry about bad weather, and everyone can participate.

The first, and probably easiest, team-building bowling activity is traditional team-style bowling. Each team consists of up to five players who work together to create a team name. The teams then bowl a designated number of games (typically three), and the players' individual scores get added up to produce a team total. Finally, the three team totals from each game are added up. The highest team score of all three games added together wins. (However, if you want to buck tradition, you can move the winners on to another week and have them compete until you have two final teams and one can be declared the winner.)

Create awards to be presented at the end of the event. Award individual and team prizes for highest score, lowest score, highest team score, most strikes, and so on. Make them fun (corny is okay too for the purposes of building camaraderie).

If you're the one organizing bowling as a team-building activity and you know that certain employees are really good bowlers, make sure they aren't allocated to just one team. Spread the wealth around to keep the game fun for everyone.

Starting a League

You can start a bowling league for just about any group of people. Case in point: We've created a teachers league for a specific school district, another one for motorcycle riders, and another for members of a law organization.

If you're interested in setting up a league, contact your local center and ask what days and times it has open. Ask about weekly rates and whether the league can be sanctioned by the United States Bowling Congress (USBC), which we recommend, especially for new leagues. If it can't be sanctioned, decide who needs to be responsible for the paperwork. Management at the center can help you through all the particulars to set up your league. (See Chapter 18 for the scoop on how leagues work.)

Organizing a Fundraiser

Bowling is a great way to keep the word *fun* in fundraiser. Bowl-a-thons and tournaments are popular one-day activities used to raise money for charities and organizations.

In a bowl-a-thon, participants solicit pledges from sponsors who donate based on an entrant's bowling score. For example, a bowler might ask a sponsor to donate 50 cents per pin knocked down. If that person has a final score of 100, the sponsor donates $50, which the bowler collects after the event. A portion of the money pays the bowling center for the use of the facility, and the rest goes to charity. Bowl-a-thon participants can also pay a higher fee for entering without raising pledges and then just bowl, knowing that the money is going toward charity.

Most centers are willing to negotiate a lower per-bowler rate for bowl-a-thons than the regular open bowling rates in the name of charity. Negotiate with your center's management to see whether it's willing to do this for your bowl-a-thon.

A charity bowling tournament is a one-day competition during which bowlers pay a fee to enter and try to win prizes by achieving the highest score. A portion of the entry fee pays the bowling center for the use of the facility, another portion goes toward a prize fund, and a third portion goes toward charity.

Following are some suggestions for holding a great bowl-a-thon or charity tournament:

- ✔ **Start planning early and choose the right date.** Bowl-a-thons and tournaments take months to organize, so start your planning at least three to six months out from your desired event date. Speaking of dates, bowling center managers are helpful in selecting the right dates for bowl-a-thons and tournaments because they arrange these events often and know what works for their individual centers. After you've decided to host a charity bowling fundraiser, talk to your local bowling center's manager right away to set a firm date.

- ✔ **Compare package deals.** If your area boasts more than one bowling center, compare their fundraiser packages. A good package includes the money the house will receive for use of the facility as well as the cost of rental shoes, food, and drinks. If the package doesn't include food, ask the center to offer discounts on food purchased during the event.

  Although some centers are willing to donate the use of their lanes for charity, not all are. Why? Because if they did it for your organization, they'd have to do it for every organization that asked, and many do. You can, however, always discuss a discounted per-bowler rate.

- ✔ **Have help.** Nobody should run a bowling fundraiser alone. It's always good to have another person onboard to help. Better yet, organize an entire volunteer team. Ask friends, family, and co-workers to help out; check with your local high schools, colleges, and churches for students who may want to volunteer or need volunteer hours for graduation or religious requirements; use Web sites such as Craigslist to request help;

and send a "volunteers needed" notice to your local newspaper and radio station. After you have volunteers, hold regular meetings so everyone can stay up to date on logistics and make sure to recruit volunteers for the day of the event.

✔ **Find corporate sponsors.** Want to raise more money at your event? Have a company sponsor a lane, raffle table, or snack stand. After all, having the company's name connected to a charity event is great publicity for it too.

✔ **Ask for prize donations.** Ask your local Chamber of Commerce or other business organizations to donate gift certificates and/or other prizes that you can give out to the highest fundraiser, the bowler with the best/worst score, the bowler with the most/least strikes, and so on. You can also call the businesses or go door-to-door.

Most businesses will require a letter from you explaining the purpose of your bowl-a-thon/tournament, dates, times, and other information. Some may even need to send your letter to their corporate headquarters to get approval first, so don't put off asking for prize donations until two days or weeks before your event.

✔ **Secure publicity.** Send a press release or e-mail to your local radio and television stations, newspapers, and magazines, and browse the outlets' Web sites for online community calendars that you can submit entries to. Include all the relevant event information, especially how to register. For additional publicity, design and print flyers and ask the bowling center's management for permission to pass them out during open bowling or league nights. Most managers will put up your flyers at the center too.

Take advantage of a totally free publicity outlet by creating a blog for your event at www.blogger.com. You can put all the information on your blog and refer people to it when they want to know more. Update it regularly and post photos of the event afterward so people can see how fun it was and plan to get involved next year.

✔ **Say thanks to all those involved.** After the event, send either an e-mail or a handwritten thank-you note to the participants as well as the businesses that provided prize donations or corporate sponsorship. Be sure to mention how much money was raised for the sponsored charity.

Participating in Charity Bowling Events

If organizing events isn't your thing but you like the idea of bowling for a cause, then you'll be glad to know there are plenty of bowl-a-thons and charity fundraisers you can participate in. Ask the staff members at your local bowling center about upcoming charity events. They can put you in touch with organizations that are holding fundraisers in their center and may even have sign-up materials right at the desk.

For a more direct route, contact your favorite local charity to see whether it's planning on hosting any bowling fundraisers in the future. Charity organizations are always in need of bowlers for their events.

One example of a popular charity event is Bowl for the Cure, a year-round fundraising and breast cancer awareness initiative sponsored by the USBC and The Bowling Foundation in partnership with Susan G. Komen for the Cure, a foundation that has raised more than $1 billion to fight breast cancer. According to the USBC, bowlers have raised close to $8 million for Susan G. Komen for the Cure and its affiliates since 2000. For more information on Bowl for the Cure, visit bowl.com/bftc.

Hosting Parties and Celebrations

When you don't want a special night to end or you want to celebrate notable events, why not head to the nearest bowling center? Some bowling centers hold after-prom or graduation parties for high school students. Yes, we've seen students bowl in prom dresses — and bowling shoes of course — and they've had a bunch of fun bowling, playing video games, and eating pizza and other snacks. Many centers are open late on weekends or will stay open even later to accommodate local high schools if asked ahead of time.

If you're a cast or crew member for your local theater, you can hold your cast party at the bowling center. Birthday parties are another option. Chapter 17 has tips on holding a child's party at a bowling center, but adults can have just as much fun as youngsters do celebrating birthdays. Heck, you can even head to the center to celebrate an anniversary or a promotion. What you celebrate is up to you, so get creative!

Getting Hitched at a Bowling Center

Couples get married while skydiving or while dressed as Elvis and Priscilla Presley in Las Vegas, so why not get married in a bowling center? If that's a little too far-fetched for you, consider renting out the center's private room or bar area and following up your ceremony with some bowling.

Your local bowling center can also be a great venue for a bridal shower, bachelor/bachelorette party, rehearsal gathering, or thank-you party for your bridesmaids and groomsmen.

Engaging in Virtual Bowling

Even we understand that you can't be at the bowling center all the time, but nothing's stopping you from enjoying bowling at home, on vacation, or on your phone thanks to the myriad of virtual bowling games available today. Here are just a few of them:

- **Brunswick Pro Bowling:** *Brunswick Pro Bowling* is a video game designed for avid bowlers and casual game players alike. Whether you want to master the oil patterns and lane conditions during a tournament or play a fast round in quick play, you'll have a ball. You can customize features to pick a character, choose a name and a ball, select music tracks, and more. *Brunswick Pro Bowling* is available for the Wii, PSP, and Playstation 2 game systems. Prefer to bowl on the go? If you have an iPhone or an iTouch, you can download the game for about $5.

- **AMF Bowling World Lanes:** This video game offers mini bowling games such as pin invaders, pocket pool, and soccer. It includes several playable characters — the Surfer, the Princess, the Drill Sergeant, the Punk Rock Girl, the Cowgirl, and the Jock — so you can have fun bowling as different people. Setting the game up for single-player, practice, and tournament modes is easy. *AMF Bowling World Lanes* is available for the Wii and Nintendo DS game systems.

- **Wii Sports Resort:** Anyone who has purchased a Wii is familiar with the system's own version of bowling, but *Wii Sports Resort* offers an updated version of this now-classic bowling video game. Of course, you aren't going to have perfect form when you're using a Wii remote, but that's okay because it keeps the bowling fun going when getting to the center is impossible. Wii bowling parties with friends and family are quite popular because everyone can bowl no matter what his skill level may be.

- **Bowling Buddies:** In this computer game, you move a mouse, click around, create your own three-dimensional character, and play in either single-player mode or the challenge mode (which allows you to compete head to head against your friends). You can find *Bowling Buddies* for free online at `playfish.com` or as a game on Facebook (`www.facebook.com`).

Changing Up the Routine

When you want to shake up the routine at the bowling center a bit, suggest one of these variations on the traditional bowling game:

✔ **Alternating:** Instead of a bowler taking his or her maximum of two turns in one frame, encourage your fellow bowlers to alternate with another player for each shot. For example, have Mary bowl the first ball and John bowl the second ball. Or have Mary bowl the first ball and have John bowl the second ball if Mary leaves a 10-pin spare because John has been designated the 10-pin spare bowler.

✔ **Switching hands:** Bowl one game with your regular bowling hand. Then bowl the next game with your opposite hand.

Watching a Tournament

Want to see the best of the best bowl? Watch amateur and pro bowlers battle it out for the top spot at a local or national tournament. You can watch a tournament at a center near you or you can travel to watch one of the USBC or Professional Bowlers Association tournaments. Visit the organizations' Web sites (bowl.com and www.pba.com, respectively) for a schedule of tournaments.

You can catch many of the major bowling tournaments on TV if you can't travel to watch them in person. ESPN carries many of the tournaments.

Visiting the International Bowling Museum

Consider planning a trip to the International Bowling Museum and Hall of Fame (IBMHF) in Arlington, Texas. The IBMHF collects, preserves, and displays a 5,000-year history of bowling that's fascinating to view for history buffs and fun for young and old alike. From computer databases and the bowling pin car to world-famous Mettlach steins and zany '50s team shirts, the IBMHF holds the entire story of bowling in its 50,000-square-foot, three-story building. For more information, visit www.bowlingmuseum.com.

Glossary

absentee bowler: An imaginary person, usually with a 150 average, used to fill in for an absent team member during league play.

anchor: The last, and typically best, bowler on a team.

approach: The part of the lane from the back of the ball-return area up to the foul line. Also the start of a bowler's motion to bowl — from her stance all the way to her release and follow-through.

arrows: The targets on the lane designed to help you aim your ball.

average: A number that measures your performance, based on your game scores, as a league's season goes on.

baby split: Pins left after your first throw that are considered an easy split because the ball can just roll between them to knock them both down.

backswing: The motion of a bowler's arm as it goes back and prepares for the throw and follow-through.

backup: A ball that rolls the opposite way of a bowler's natural motion. For example, a right-handed bowler throws a backup ball that goes out to the left, and a left-handed bowler throws a backup ball that goes out to the right.

ball return: The area where the ball is stored after being returned from the pit.

bedposts: A nickname for the 7-10 split.

beer frame: The bowler who doesn't strike (or in some cases just mark) in a particular frame must treat the other teammates to a refreshment.

blind: The score entered for an absentee bowler in league bowling, usually with a 5- or 10-point penalty.

board: An individual piece of the lane.

bowling: A game in which a heavy ball is rolled down a wooden lane in an attempt to knock down ten pins at the other end of the lane.

bowling ball: A ball containing a weight block and holes for your fingers and thumb that you throw down a lane to knock down pins.

bowling center: A facility in which you bowl that may also include arcade games and a restaurant or bar.

bowling glove: A device that helps keep your hand steady so you can throw the ball accurately and with more power.

bowling shoes: Special shoes designed solely for use on the bowling lane.

breakpoint: The spot on the lane where your hook ball starts to change direction after you throw it.

Brooklyn strike: Bowling toward the pocket opposite of what you're supposed to be aiming for (so when a left-handed bowler throws into the 1-3 pocket or a right-handed bowler throws into the 1-2 pocket).

bumper: A device placed over or in the gutter to prevent the ball from rolling into the gutter.

chop: Knocking down one pin of a spare while leaving the other pin standing.

closed league: A league that accepts only those individuals who belong to a particular organization, attend a particular school, work at a particular place, and so on.

clothesline: When the 1-2-4-7 or 1-3-6-10 pins are left standing.

conventional grip: A way of holding a bowling ball in which your thumb and your middle and ring fingers are inserted into the ball up to the second knuckle.

conversion: Knocking down all the pins on your second ball. Also known as "converting the spare."

core: Material that surrounds the weight block in a bowling ball.

coverstock: The outer part of the ball that makes contact with the lane.

cranker: When you turn your hand and wrist even more to generate more speed and hook action on your throw. Typically a move for a more advanced bowler.

deflection: How the ball hits the pins and how the ball and pins move to one side or the other.

dots: Sets of circles on the approach used to help bowlers get in the proper position for bowling.

double: Two strikes in a row.

double wood: When one of the two pins left standing after your first throw is directly behind the other one.

fence posts: A nickname for the 7-10 split.

field goal: When the ball rolls between two pins of a split without knocking anything down.

finger grips: Inserts that can be put into the finger and/or thumb holes to allow you to grip the ball better.

fingertip grip: A way of holding a bowling ball in which your middle and ring fingers are inserted into the ball only up to the first joint and your thumb is inserted all the way in. Typically for advanced hook bowlers.

five-bagger: Five strikes in a row.

follow-through: The motion you make after releasing the ball.

foul: When your foot or hand crosses the foul line during your throw. A buzzer may sound.

foul line: The line that determines the beginning of the lane.

four-bagger: Four strikes in a row.

four-step approach: When you take four steps while swinging the ball and releasing it onto the lane.

frame: One section of a game.

goal posts: A nickname for the 7-10 split.

Grandma's teeth: Pins left standing across the lane.

gutter: The channel on each side of the lane where the ball can fall if you don't throw it properly.

gutterball: A ball that goes into the gutter.

handicap: Extra points given to individuals or teams to make all bowlers even in competition.

headpin: The first or number one pin in a rack.

hook: A ball that breaks to the left for righties and to the right for lefties.

house: A bowling center.

house ball: A bowling ball that the center lets you borrow.

lane: The 60-feet-long (not including the approach) and 42-inch-wide (not including the gutters) playing surface in bowling.

league: A large group of bowlers divided into teams that compete against each other over the course of several weeks.

lofting: Lifting the ball into the air rather than rolling it onto the lane.

mark: When you make either a strike or a spare in a frame.

miss: When you fail to pick up a spare.

oil: A substance applied to the lane to keep it conditioned and allow for bowling.

open bowling: When the public is allowed to come into the center and bowl for fun or practice.

open frame: A frame that doesn't have a strike or spare.

open league: A league that lets anyone join as long as there's room on a team.

perfect game: Twelve strikes in a row resulting in a 300 score.

pin: Objects at the end of the bowling lane that you try to knock over with one throw of the bowling ball.

pin action: The reaction of the pins after the ball has hit them.

pin deck: The area where the pins stand at the end of the lane.

pinsetter: A machine that repositions pins on the pin deck, sends your ball back to you, and determines how many pins you knocked down.

pit: The area behind the pin deck where the pins may wind up after being hit by the ball.

pocket: The area of the pins that's best to hit for a strike (between the 1-3 pins for righties and the 1-2 pins for lefties).

position rounds: When teams or individuals compete against each other based on how they're doing in the standings (first place meets second place, second place meets third place, and so on). Applicable only in league or tournament play.

Professional Bowlers Association (PBA): An organization whose membership consists of professional bowlers. Also runs local and national PBA tournaments.

reading the lanes: Watching your ball to determine whether the lane is oily or dry, whether or not your ball hooks, and how you need to adjust your approach to compensate.

rebound: When your ball reenters the lane after going into the gutter or pit, at which point it knocks down some pins.

release: Letting the ball go as you roll it onto the lane.

reset: When the pinsetter repositions the pins on the pin deck (done only if the pins aren't sitting properly on their marks or the sweep hasn't come down to take the pins away).

rosin bag: A sealed pouch filled with powder that soaks up the moisture on your hands so the ball doesn't slip out.

sanctioned: A league or tournament that follows the rules of a national organization such as the United States Bowling Congress or the Professional Bowlers Association.

score sheet: A piece of paper or computer program where your score is recorded after each shot.

scratch: Your actual score without handicap points.

seesaw towel: A towel with handles that makes it easy (and fun) to clean your bowling ball.

series: The total of your scores for the three games that you bowl on a given night during league play.

six-pack: Six strikes in a row.

slide: The last step of your delivery.

span: How far your hand stretches between the thumb and finger holes.

spare: What you get when you knock down the remainder of the pins on your second throw.

split: When the pins left standing have a varying amount of distance between them.

straight: A ball that rolls in a straight line toward the pins.

strike: The result of knocking down all ten pins with your first throw.

strike out: What happens when you get all three strikes in the tenth frame.

sweep: The bar that comes down after you've hit the pins to pick up the remaining standing pins and sweep away the ones that have been knocked down.

team captain: Team member responsible for the team, its membership, lineup, and signing of the bowling sheets. Applicable only in league play.

300 game: A perfect game consisting of 12 strikes in a row.

topping the ball: When your hand comes over the top of the ball during your release.

tournament: A one-day or multiweekend event in which bowlers compete for various prizes and awards.

track area: The part of the ball that rolls on the lane and picks up oil.

turkey: Three strikes in a row.

United States Bowling Congress (USBC): A governing body with an extensive set of league rules that all leagues under the auspices of the organization must follow.

washout: When you leave the 1-2-10, 1-2-4-10, 1-3-7, or 1-3-6-7 split.

weight block: The weighted interior portion of a bowling ball.

Index

• M •

• *R* •

Business/Accounting & Bookkeeping

Bookkeeping For Dummies
978-0-7645-9848-7

eBay Business
All-in-One For Dummies,
2nd Edition
978-0-470-38536-4

Job Interviews
For Dummies,
3rd Edition
978-0-470-17748-8

Resumes For Dummies,
5th Edition
978-0-470-08037-5

Stock Investing
For Dummies,
3rd Edition
978-0-470-40114-9

Successful Time
Management
For Dummies
978-0-470-29034-7

Computer Hardware

BlackBerry For Dummies,
3rd Edition
978-0-470-45762-7

Computers For Seniors
For Dummies
978-0-470-24055-7

iPhone For Dummies,
2nd Edition
978-0-470-42342-4

Laptops For Dummies,
3rd Edition
978-0-470-27759-1

Macs For Dummies,
10th Edition
978-0-470-27817-8

Cooking & Entertaining

Cooking Basics
For Dummies,
3rd Edition
978-0-7645-7206-7

Wine For Dummies,
4th Edition
978-0-470-04579-4

Diet & Nutrition

Dieting For Dummies,
2nd Edition
978-0-7645-4149-0

Nutrition For Dummies,
4th Edition
978-0-471-79868-2

Weight Training
For Dummies,
3rd Edition
978-0-471-76845-6

Digital Photography

Digital Photography
For Dummies,
6th Edition
978-0-470-25074-7

Photoshop Elements 7
For Dummies
978-0-470-39700-8

Gardening

Gardening Basics
For Dummies
978-0-470-03749-2

Organic Gardening
For Dummies,
2nd Edition
978-0-470-43067-5

Green/Sustainable

Green Building
& Remodeling
For Dummies
978-0-470-17559-0

Green Cleaning
For Dummies
978-0-470-39106-8

Green IT For Dummies
978-0-470-38688-0

Health

Diabetes For Dummies,
3rd Edition
978-0-470-27086-8

Food Allergies
For Dummies
978-0-470-09584-3

Living Gluten-Free
For Dummies
978-0-471-77383-2

Hobbies/General

Chess For Dummies,
2nd Edition
978-0-7645-8404-6

Drawing For Dummies
978-0-7645-5476-6

Knitting For Dummies,
2nd Edition
978-0-470-28747-7

Organizing For Dummies
978-0-7645-5300-4

SuDoku For Dummies
978-0-470-01892-7

Home Improvement

Energy Efficient Homes
For Dummies
978-0-470-37602-7

Home Theater
For Dummies,
3rd Edition
978-0-470-41189-6

Living the Country Lifestyle
All-in-One For Dummies
978-0-470-43061-3

Solar Power Your Home
For Dummies
978-0-470-17569-9

Internet

Blogging For Dummies,
2nd Edition
978-0-470-23017-6

eBay For Dummies,
6th Edition
978-0-470-49741-8

Facebook For Dummies
978-0-470-26273-3

Google Blogger
For Dummies
978-0-470-40742-4

Web Marketing
For Dummies,
2nd Edition
978-0-470-37181-7

WordPress For Dummies,
2nd Edition
978-0-470-40296-2

Language & Foreign Language

French For Dummies
978-0-7645-5193-2

Italian Phrases
For Dummies
978-0-7645-7203-6

Spanish For Dummies
978-0-7645-5194-9

Spanish For Dummies,
Audio Set
978-0-470-09585-0

Macintosh

Mac OS X Snow Leopard
For Dummies
978-0-470-43543-4

Math & Science

Algebra I For Dummies,
2nd Edition
978-0-470-55964-2

Biology For Dummies
978-0-7645-5326-4

Calculus For Dummies
978-0-7645-2498-1

Chemistry For Dummies
978-0-7645-5430-8

Microsoft Office

Excel 2007 For Dummies
978-0-470-03737-9

Office 2007 All-in-One
Desk Reference
For Dummies
978-0-471-78279-7

Music

Guitar For Dummies,
2nd Edition
978-0-7645-9904-0

iPod & iTunes
For Dummies,
6th Edition
978-0-470-39062-7

Piano Exercises
For Dummies
978-0-470-38765-8

Parenting & Education

Parenting For Dummies,
2nd Edition
978-0-7645-5418-6

Type 1 Diabetes
For Dummies
978-0-470-17811-9

Pets

Cats For Dummies,
2nd Edition
978-0-7645-5275-5

Dog Training For Dummies,
2nd Edition
978-0-7645-8418-3

Puppies For Dummies,
2nd Edition
978-0-470-03717-1

Religion & Inspiration

The Bible For Dummies
978-0-7645-5296-0

Catholicism For Dummies
978-0-7645-5391-2

Women in the Bible
For Dummies
978-0-7645-8475-6

Self-Help & Relationship

Anger Management
For Dummies
978-0-470-03715-7

Overcoming Anxiety
For Dummies
978-0-7645-5447-6

Sports

Baseball For Dummies,
3rd Edition
978-0-7645-7537-2

Basketball For Dummies,
2nd Edition
978-0-7645-5248-9

Golf For Dummies,
3rd Edition
978-0-471-76871-5

Web Development

Web Design All-in-One
For Dummies
978-0-470-41796-6

Windows Vista

Windows Vista
For Dummies
978-0-471-75421-3

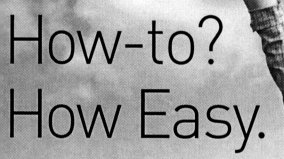

How-to?
How Easy.

From hooking up a modem to cooking up a
casserole, knitting a scarf to navigating an iPod,
you can trust Dummies.com to show you how
to get things done the easy way.

Visit us at Dummies.com

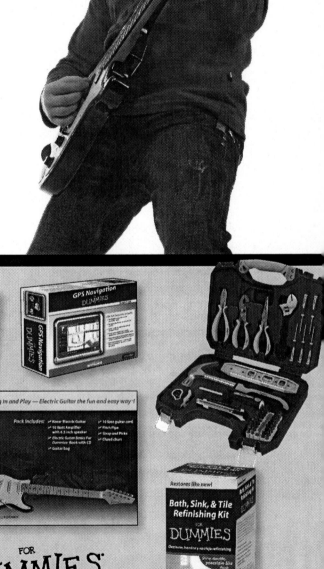

DISCARD

Printed in the United States of America
ED-12-13-12